ESSENTIAL GUIDE *to* BOATING

BOAT MAINTENANCE

THE COMPLETE GUIDE TO KEEPING YOUR BOAT SHIPSHAPE

ESSENTIAL GUIDE *to* BOATING

BOAT MAINTENANCE

THE COMPLETE GUIDE TO KEEPING YOUR BOAT SHIPSHAPE

© 2011 by Skills Institute Press LLC
"Essential Guide to Boating" series trademark of Skills Institute Press
Published and distributed in North America by Fox Chapel Publishing Company, Inc., East Petersburg, PA.

Boat Maintenance is an original work, first published in 2011.

Portions of text and art previously published by and reproduced under license with Direct Holdings Americas Inc.

ISBN 978-1-56523-549-6

Library of Congress Cataloging-in-Publication Data

Boat maintenance.
p. cm. -- (Essential guide to boating)
Includes index.
ISBN 978-1-56523-549-6
1. Boats and boating--Maintenance and repair--Handbooks, manuals, etc.
VM322.B625 2011
623.820028'8--dc22
2010050565

To learn more about the other great books from Fox Chapel Publishing,
or to find a retailer near you, call toll-free 800-457-9112 or visit us at
www.FoxChapelPublishing.com.

Note to Authors: We are always looking for talented authors to write new books.
Please send a brief letter describing your idea to
Acquisition Editor, 1970 Broad Street, East Petersburg, PA 17520.

Printed in China
First printing: June 2011

Because boating and working with boats inherently include the risk of injury and damage, this book cannot guarantee that creating the projects in this book is safe for everyone. For this reason, this book is sold without warranties or guarantees of any kind, expressed or implied, and the publisher and the author disclaim any liability for any injuries, losses, or damages caused in any way by the content of this book or the reader's use of the tools needed to complete the projects presented here. The publisher and the author urge all readers to thoroughly review each project and to understand the use of all tools before beginning any project.

Table of Contents

What You Can Learn

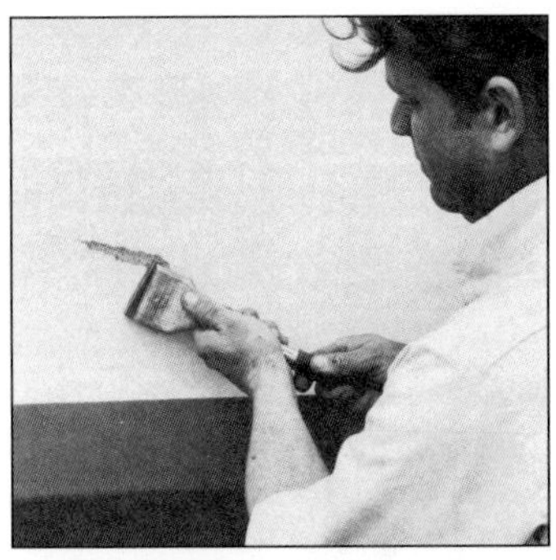

Hull Care, page 14

No hull materials are truly free of the need for upkeep, but they are generally tougher than one would expect.

Painting, page 54

Paint shields a boat against wind, salt spray, and sunlight and must be replenished at regular intervals.

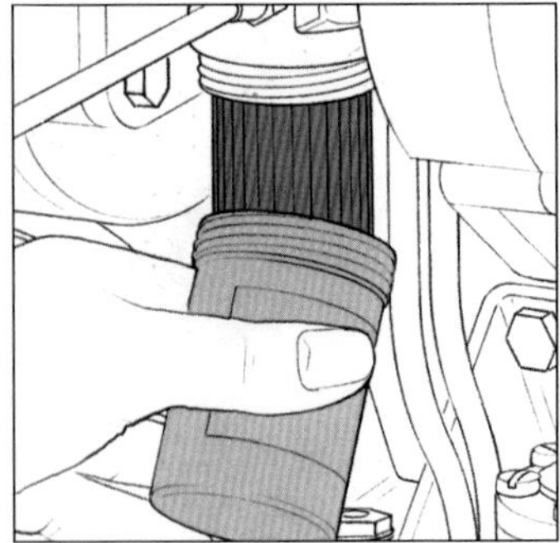

Engine Upkeep, page 74

The additional weight and strain to a boat's engine makes it far more dependent on regular upkeep than a car's engine.

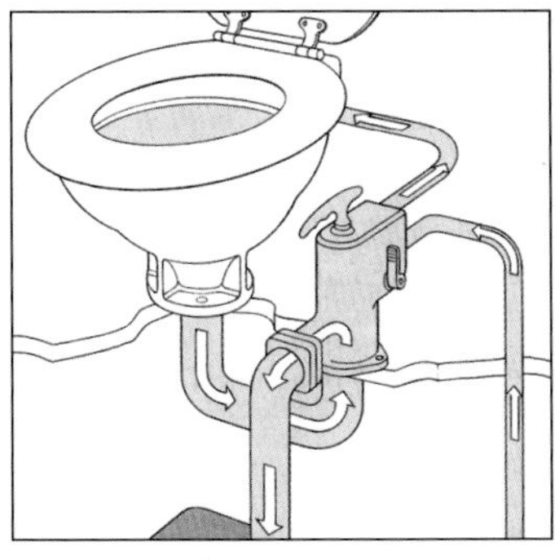

Belowdecks, page 106

Belowdecks equipment, including machinery that supplies electricity, air, water, and waste removal, must stay watertight to avoid taking on water.

Fittings, page 124

A jammed winch or block can transform a beautiful day on the water to an embarrassing bungle, or worse.

Winterizing, page 146

Every boater should learn how to store his or her boat for extended periods, be it winter or repair.

The Creative Task of Maintenance

There is no such thing as a no-maintenance boat. A man who loves his boat usually enjoys making it handsomer and safer through proper maintenance; at the same time, he saves money by catching trouble before it starts.

I have learned a lot about maintenance by operating an old wooden boat in a harsh environment. I grew up in and around boats, and in 1956, after college, military service, and a year of wandering through Europe, I headed for the Caribbean to try out its blend of warm climate and good sailing. I have been in the Lesser Antilles ever since, supporting a wife and three children by working as a boat rigger, insurance broker, surveyor, and writer, and by chartering my 45-foot yawl, *Iolaire*. She was built in the Harris Brothers yard, in England, of oak, teak, and pine, and was launched in 1905. She has had 11 different owners and seven changes of rig, has crossed the Atlantic five times since World War II, and, from the time I bought her in 1957, has been raced, cruised, and chartered almost continuously.

Some say that wooden boats do not last, especially in the tropics. The truth is that, with proper care, any boat anywhere can last almost indefinitely, and a stout, well-maintained boat will often survive drastic misadventure. Once when an anchor shackle gave way in a heavy ground swell, *Iolaire* ended up in three feet of water with her port side stove in and was declared a total loss by the underwriters. I bought her back from the insurance company for $100, and in 13 weeks of intensive effort I was able to get her refloated, extensively rebuilt, and back on charter.

Maintaining *Iolaire* is a continuous job for me, my wife, Trich, and a West Indian crewman. Wear and tear on a boat in the tropics is about three times as great as up north. The combination of heat and rain causes everything to deteriorate faster—paint, fiberglass, wood, steel, plastic. Dacron rots away. Stainless-steel rigging corrodes. Spars mended with casein glue tend to fall apart more rapidly. I know of a carpenter in Grenada who has spent the last nine years—eight hours a day, five days a week—repairing casein-glued spars, and I've also had a firsthand lesson in why his business is so good. A previous owner of *Iolaire* used casein glue in replacing a rotted section of the mast; after I bought the boat, the glue got damp, lost its adhesion, and, one day, the top six feet of the spar came down. We made it back to our home port of St. George's, Grenada, under jury-rig and installed an aluminum mast.

Iolaire has had some maintenance handicaps from the very beginning. When I scraped her deck down to bare wood I discovered that it was beautifully laid with New Zealand kauri pine, brilliantly white when scrubbed. But thereafter, years of scrubbing thinned the deck until the heads of iron nails began to appear; by using iron instead of bronze, her thrifty builders had saved a little money. I spent a lot more, as rot developed in holes around the rusting nails, removing pieces of deck planking and putting in so many of the patches called dutchmen that *Iolaire* is now perhaps the only boat in the world with a parquet deck.

Maintenance has always been a dominant feature of maritime life, if not the most glamorous one. The crews of seafarers like Columbus, Magellan, and Drake, perforce, included skilled carpenters, metalworkers,

MS 7480 G

coopers, caulkers, and painters; these specialists were kept so busy that most of their ships returned from long voyages in seaworthy condition despite sustaining heavy damages. In this age of miracle polymers and corrosion-resistant alloys, maintenance is easier, but no less vital. All too often even the best-intentioned boatman will concentrate on the ministrations he likes best and neglect the kinds he likes least. Many a family weekend of Sunfish sailing has ended on Saturday noon when a rudder split at a point where a crack had long been evident—and just as long disregarded. Or consider the plight of the powerboat-man who has worked all week in the office anticipating the joys of towing his wife, children, and in-laws on water skis. Come Saturday, the weather is perfect—lake like glass, sun blazing down—but after half an hour of skiing, the bolts holding the towing bitt shear off where corrosion cracks have been developing for several months.

A poorly maintained boat will constantly inconvenience its owner and may very well injure or kill him. For example, gas galley stoves, properly installed and maintained, are as safe as any; but poor connections, faulty burners, and tiny leaks in gas lines hidden behind bulkheads can cause explosions that singe the cook bald or possibly sink the boat. A competent young couple I know took over an apparently sound 65-foot powerboat without realizing that the line from the on-deck gas bottle to the stove had never been replaced and had developed pinhole corrosion leaks—not in the galley where the cook would have smelled the escaping gas, but in the engine room. The boat was diesel powered and it had no bilge blower, so the gas accumulating in the bilges was ignited by a spark from the starter motor. Because the crew was on deck, all hands aboard, though battered and bruised, survived the explosion. But the boat was a total wreck.

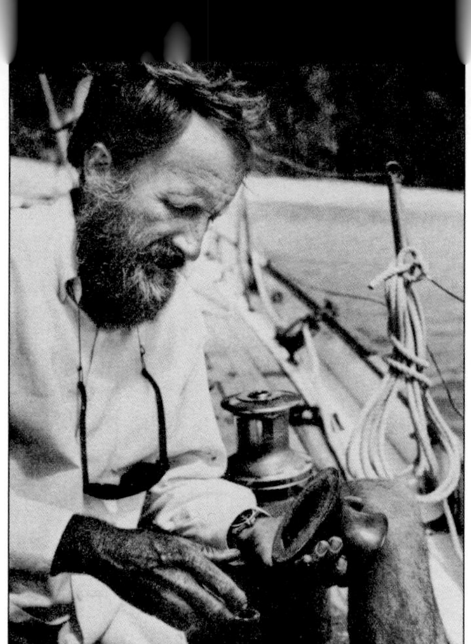

In his home port on the Caribbean island of Grenada, author Donald Street inspects a winch aboard his yawl in preparation for a 1975 voyage 12,000 miles across the Atlantic and back. Street has written five books and dozens of articles, many of them on the techniques of upkeep he has mastered while maintaining his 70-year-old wood boat against the ravages of a tropical climate.

A prospective boat buyer should first consider the hull material and then decide how much time, money, and inclination he is prepared to invest in maintenance. Wood hulls need more care than others, but people like myself find wood esthetically pleasing and enjoy working with it. Steel, especially in larger vessels, makes an extremely strong hull and, for a mechanic who can cut, bend, and weld steel, one that is relatively easy to maintain. Light, strong, aluminum hulls are becoming increasingly popular and competitive in price with wood, steel, and fiberglass as more and more yards—and laymen—learn to handle the material. Ferro-cement hulls offer the advantage of being perhaps the easiest of any to patch. And a properly constructed fiberglass hull requires the least maintenance of any: a fiberglass boat can be brought back into condition after being left locked up in a shed for two or three years, whereas a wood or even a metal hull subjected to such treatment may deteriorate beyond hope of practical repair.

Having selected a hull, a boatman should consider the maintenance aspects of propulsion. I favor sail. I installed an engine in *Iolaire* in 1959, but over the next 12 years, sailing in an area where one is seldom becalmed, I rarely needed it—and when I did, it usually failed. Engines baffle me; I dislike working on them. I eventually replaced *Iolaire's* engine with a chart table and have never regretted it. Boating friends of mine who do understand engines are just as happy grinding valves, with a can of beer handy and a ball game on the radio, as I am whipping and splicing lines—and their engines usually work perfectly. The boatman who regards sails as I do engines will enjoy more peace of mind on a straight powerboat than he would on a sailboat or even a motor sailer.

The amount and kind of other equipment a boatman installs will raise further maintenance problems. An old seagoing axiom holds that if you can't fix it yourself, it doesn't belong on the boat—but this is obviously not as applicable as it once was. Depth and direction finders, for instance, are vital aids to boatmen cruising in fogbound waters, although well beyond the abilities of most people to repair. However, another axiom—that aboard a boat anything that can break down, *will* break down—still possesses a good measure of truth. And the upshot is clear: the more equipment you carry on your boat, the more time and energy you will have to devote to maintenance. Even a relatively small boat can be overloaded with conveniences that are expensive both to install and to maintain. I often see powerboats—and sailboats, too—laden with everything from deep freezers to water heaters, from TV to air conditioning. But they are not at sea. They are usually tied to a dock, while one or another piece of their equipment is being repaired.

However, some boatmen find that this is an ideal situation. A few years ago my friend Dave Saville bought *Golden West,* a sadly rundown 60-foot trawler-type yacht, and he has been happily rebuilding her ever since. "What, go to sea?" says Dave. "Hell, no! Boat rocks, people get seasick, it's hard to move around, hard to work on the engine, things fall overboard, hard to cook on the stove. No, I have much more fun working on the boat alongside the dock. Never go to sea in a boat."

Another friend, Frank Casper, prefers sailing to maintenance. Now over 70, Frank has commuted back and forth across the Atlantic singlehanded with astonishing regularity; in 1970 he won a Blue Water Medal, awarded by the Cruising Club of America, for distinguished small-boat seamanship. He has cut his maintenance time and expense to a minimum by limiting extra equipment aboard his 30-foot Bermuda-rigged cutter, *Elsie,* to only two items—a steering vane and a small engine.

Most boatowners steer a course somewhere between Dave and Frank, and enjoy doing some of their own maintenance once they get started. Gone are the days when boatmen learned maintenance as small boys by being allowed aboard a beautiful cruising boat every sunny day to remove the sail covers, air the sails, open the hatches for ventilation, wash down decks to keep them tight, polish the brass and chamois the varnish work. But one can still learn much by asking questions of builders, riggers, electricians, electronics men, and mechanics; by watching professionals work; by reading; by experimenting—and by making mistakes.

Do simple maintenance jobs first, then work up to more complicated projects. When in doubt about whether your skills are equal to a particular job, get competent advice. You can stop a leak around a deck fitting on your fiberglass boat yourself, but a leak where the deck joins the hull may demand a boatyard's expertise. Most boatmen quickly learn to make eye splices in line; some master the art of splicing line to wire; but after a lifetime of sailing, maintaining, and rigging boats, I still prefer to leave to professionals the ferocious complications of splicing 19-strand wire rope.

Keep a maintenance log that is divided into such categories as hull, engine, propeller, rig, sails, electrical system, plumbing, and safety equipment. If you sail regularly with the same people, make each crewman responsible for one or more of these categories. Anyone who spots a deficiency in his department enters it in the log. From the log, compile a list of items to be checked annually, quarterly, or weekly. The log will indicate when the standing rigging was last replaced and how long the engine has run since its last overhaul. To my intense regret, I did not start a really comprehensive maintenance log until about four years ago. While the crew of *Iolaire* can remember when the bottom was last recaulked, nobody is quite sure when the keel bolts were last replaced.

Break down long jobs into a number of convenient components. To avoid the rigors of eight hours or more of painting in a bosun's chair, paint or varnish a 60-foot mast in three steps—say from the masthead to the upper spreaders, then from the upper to the lower spreaders, and finally from the lower spreaders to the deck.

Do all the maintenance you can on the boat while it is laid up for winter. After removing the boat from the water, you should—if weather conditions permit—scrub, sand, and touch up the bottom, topsides, and deck paint work in preparation for a final coat in the spring. In cold weather, much interior work can be done in the comforting glow of a portable electric heater. Paint topsides and bottom during the first warm days of spring; then you can do the rest of the work with the boat in the water—which is usually a more congenial locale than the middle of a crowded shipyard, especially if the boat's crew includes a wife and children.

Set intelligent priorities. Mounting a fancy nameplate or fine-tuning the engine may be fun, but neglecting dry rot in the underbody may sink the boat. On *Iolaire* we spend most of our time, energy, and money on sails, rigging, and spars. We paint and varnish, which for us is essential, but we never polish the brass. Polish, of course, has its place. The distinguished yachtsman Cornelius Shields, known as the Gray Fox of Long Island Sound, has asserted that for him maintaining his boat was half the pleasure of sailing. Even as a boy, he could never bear to take his boat out until he had spent an hour or so polishing cleats and winches. Just to see his boat sparkling in the sun was reward enough for Shields, though he knew that salt spray would dull the brass again after half an hour's sailing. Bob Hardy, a highly professional British yacht captain, makes a more practical point about polish. He points out that anyone who regularly polishes a boat's fittings will spot flaws in them before they fail, and that leaks are more easily detected in belowdecks piping that is polished rather than painted.

Buy tools and materials conservatively, starting small and working up as your skills and needs increase. Boating is a comradely sport, and tools are always borrowed back and forth. Inevitably some disappear, so I buy good-quality, medium-priced tools that work well but whose loss I can bear.

Modern materials and power tools have greatly simplified maintenance: one man with an electric sander can accomplish in half a day what used to take four men two days to do. But technology has its price. While bottom paints now last 10 months to a year and thus eliminate midseason hull painting, some of these new products seem to require a boatman to be a chemist. One could thin oil-based paints or clean brushes with anything handy—thinners, turpentine, methylated spirits, kerosene, or petroleum. Epoxy paints are different. On one occasion when I was using epoxy paint, I ran out of the prescribed thinner, and none was available on Grenada; so I bought a thinner recommended by the manufacturer of another epoxy finish. When I tried to thin my paint with it, I got a chemical reaction one step less than an explosion and ended up with a quart of what looked like very poor sour cream. Similarly, I have dumped brushes into a thinner for cleaning, only to have them instantly turn as hard as so many pieces of teak.

Even a boatman who is reasonably skilled at maintenance ought to have his boat surveyed regularly, the intervals depending on environment and amount of usage. Lloyd's underwriters recommend surveys every three years. The surveyor's trained eye will catch deficiencies the boatman himself might never notice, and will discriminate between those that really need attention and those that are merely cosmetic and do not affect the boat's basic seaworthiness. Investigate the surveyor's credentials. A yachtsman I know bought a large twin-screw motor sailer on the strength of a survey performed at bargain rates by an apparently well-qualified surveyor. Unfortunately the man's experience had been largely in cargo surveying, and he missed not only major dry rot in the bilge but also defects that later caused the insurers to condemn the mainmast and the electrical system. Hiring a surveyor at $25 or so per hour may not be practical for a small-boat owner; but at least he should ask an experienced friend to go over his boat with a fine-tooth comb.

The rewards of maintenance will grow as the boatman's skills increase. Under his hands the boat becomes not only a thing of beauty and of pride but a craft in which he can put to sea with a confidence shared by his insurance company. He enjoys the thrill of the creative artist as well as the satisfaction of a seamanlike job well done.

-Donald M. Street Jr.

CHAPTER 1: Hull Care

The hull of a boat is generally far tougher than any landsman might dream. A well-engineered hull will last for decades if given proper care. But that care must be conscientiously given: despite some overzealous advertising claims, no hull material comes close to being truly free of the need for upkeep. However, impressive and fairly regular strides in that direction have been made since seafaring began.

The earliest true boats were constructed of naturally buoyant bundles of reeds or of hand-hewn planks. They were almost impossible to maintain, since they tended to become unfastened or waterlogged even before they had a chance to rot. Shipwrights later learned to age and oil wood planks as a protection against rot, to fasten them with stout pegs, and to seal up seams with hemp or flax, and pitch. These measures allowed wood to be used for such durable vessels as Viking longships, oaken men-of-war, and commercial windjammers whose working life might be as long as 50 years or more. Many tradition-minded boatmen still prefer wood although, being organic, it remains vulnerable to fungi and other organisms that feed on its cellulose.

Iron boats appeared in the 18th Century, followed by steel and aluminum in the late 19th; they proved stronger, pound for pound, than wood, and indifferent to parasites. But iron and steel rusted, required incessant painting, and were heavy and hard to work with; it was nearly impossible for an amateur to replace a structural piece—and very hard to install a new fitting.

When fiberglass appeared in the early 1950s, it was hailed as the beginning of a carefree era in boating. Not only was the new substance proof against rust, it was also impervious to rot, tough for its weight, and could be inexpensively molded into seaworthy shapes. And indeed fiberglass may be fairly described as the closest thing yet to the ultimate hull material. Nevertheless, as many an owner has ruefully discovered, even fiberglass will crack, discolor, or peel apart if not properly maintained.

Proper maintenance does not mean waiting to treat serious hull ailments such as massive dry rot, structural damage, or extensive rusting. In fact, rectifying such disasters is usually beyond the skills of the average boatman, and often beyond his pocketbook as well. Prudent hull maintenance, then, should be an incessant search for small failings before they *become* disasters. It is the habitual process of cleaning, painting, patching, and tightening.

Even the faintest hint of trouble should receive prompt attention. Bear in mind that a small surface blemish may hide a deep inner flaw. A dented transom from a dockside collision could be the outward sign of a split sternpost or a disaligned propeller shaft.

Forklifted onto a boat rack for nightly storage, these fiberglass runabouts are free from barnacles, driftwood dents, and other maintenance-producing hazards of regular mooring.

FL 5248 AY
FL 5248 AY
FL 7641 AY
FL 3449 BF
FL 2754

Fiberglass Anatomy

Fiberglass, the most popular of pleasure-boat materials, is also one of the easiest to maintain. Normally, it requires little more than waxing twice a year on topside surfaces and an annual coat of antifouling paint on the bottom. Moreover, the average boatman should be able to repair the kind of everyday damage that a fiberglass hull is likely to sustain, from scuffs to holes as large as a foot across. But before undertaking repairs, especially if the damage is serious, he should know how the hull was constructed. For repairs must replicate—in approximate form, at least—the original anatomy of the material.

Synthetic resins and hairlike fibers of glass are the principal materials used in creating a fiberglass hull. The boat is built from the outside in. First, a mold is sprayed with wax and then with a thin coat of colored resin that forms the hull's outer armor—and color. Inside this hard, smooth, waterproof finish—known as the gel coat—are laid layer upon layer of differing forms of fiberglass *(opposite, middle).* Each layer is saturated with resin as it goes on, binding together the layers—and the glass fibers—to produce a laminated substance with a strength-to-weight ratio even greater than that of steel.

Parts of some fiberglass hulls are given extra rigidity and additional buoyancy by means of "core construction" *(opposite, bottom)*, in which layers of fiberglass are wrapped around foamed plastic, balsa wood, or plywood. This method can be more costly than solid fiberglass construction, and it usually costs more to repair, since core material often has to be dug out and replaced—a job that is better left to the experts.

A completed fiberglass hull *(above)* rises from its mold, with colored boot top and sheer strake incorporated in its gleaming gel coat. The hull on a boat of this size is composed of six to 12 layers of fiberglass material—with additional layers at stress points.

At least two, and sometimes three, resins are used in fiberglass hulls. Before application, each one must be mixed with hardener, which comes in a tube or a separate can atop the container. The outer surface is composed of gel coat, a resin that can be tinted by mixing pigment as well as hardener into it. Either polyester or epoxy resin can serve for the interior layers of the laminate. Polyester is cheaper and easier to apply; epoxy is stronger and suited for repair work in areas subjected to unusual stress.

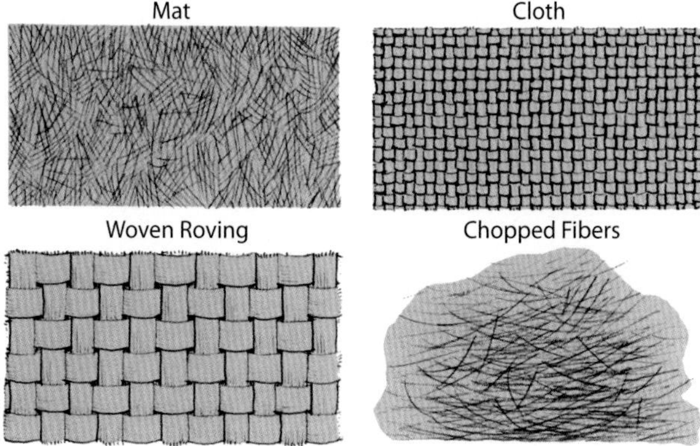

Fiberglass hulls utilize a variety of fabrics in the laminate, each with special virtues of its own. Mat, composed of fibers randomly pressed together as in felt, offers bulk and, because it also absorbs resin easily, provides rigidity and good adhesion between layers. Woven roving—loosely loomed fiberglass strands—combines bulk and flexibility. Cloth—tightly woven strands—is thin, flexible, and very strong. Loose chopped fibers are often used in place of matting by spraying them into a hull mold along with resin.

A blend of bulk, flexibility, and strength is built into a fiberglass hull by creating a sandwich of alternating fabrics—usually arrayed in the sequence shown at left. Six to nine layers are enough for most parts of the hull, but up to 18 are advisable for corners, joints, and other stress points. A final layer of fine cloth is sometimes added to provide a smooth finish on the inside of the hull.

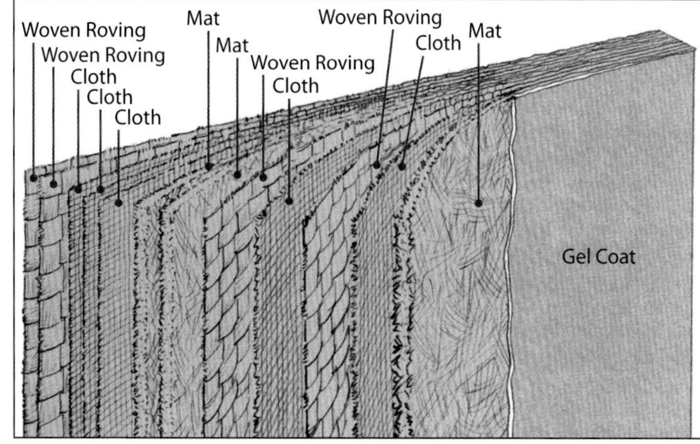

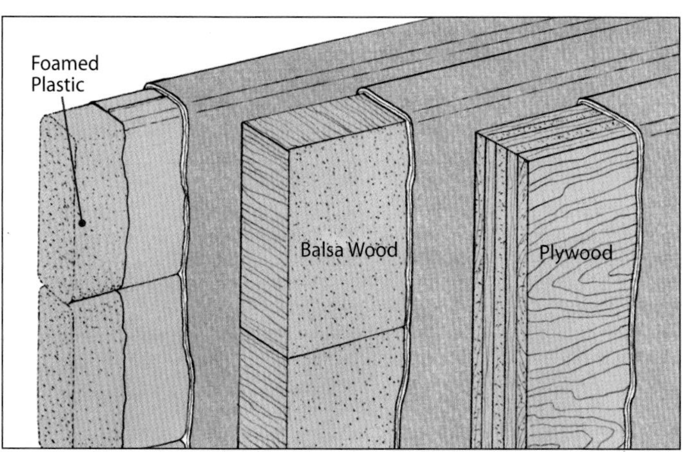

Core construction lends further rigidity to fiberglass structures and saves weight compared to solid laminate. A few layers of fiberglass are placed around a core of foamed plastic, balsa, or plywood, and finished with a film of gel coat. Of the three core materials, plywood is the heaviest and most rigid. Balsa is less rigid but lighter than plywood and, pound for pound, the strongest of the three. Foam is lightest (and weakest) of all, but it is a good insulator against heat and noise.

Cracks and Holes

Fiberglass hulls sometimes come from the manufacturer with an endowment of invisible flaws. If the gel coat is mixed in the wrong proportions, applied unevenly or too thickly, or not allowed to cure completely before launching, the chances are that small blisters or hairline cracks will appear within two years. Fractures may result from heat, impact, overly tight fastenings, or "oilcanning," the mariner's term for excessive bending of the sides of poorly supported hull panels as the boat moves through the waves.

The worst structural failures—a fiberglass hull that splits down the middle or parts company with its deck—may be salvageable; but the job should be given to professionals. However, the boatman himself can solve many problems that occur with fiberglass. He can buff away surface blemishes, plug shallow cracks, add braces to eliminate oilcanning, and build up new laminations where a hull has been deeply gouged or punctured.

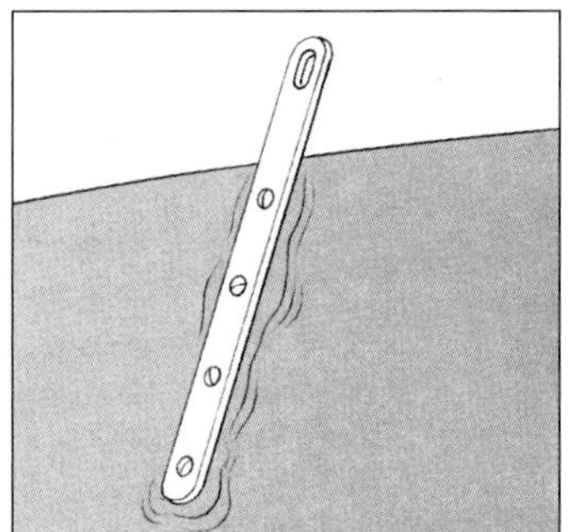

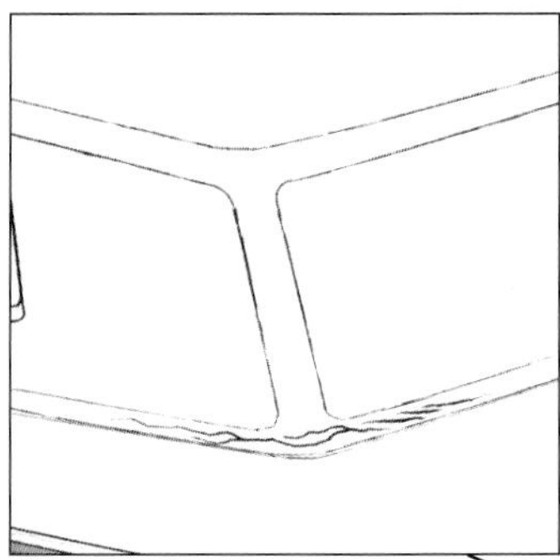

Stress cracks Pressure from overtight fastenings can cause cracks like those above at left in the gel coat—the result of screwing a chain plate too tightly to the transom. Cracks may also result from hull strains in normal operation; for example, whenever a boat heels, the deckhouse exerts stress at its right-angle juncture with the deck, perhaps causing breaks like those above at right.

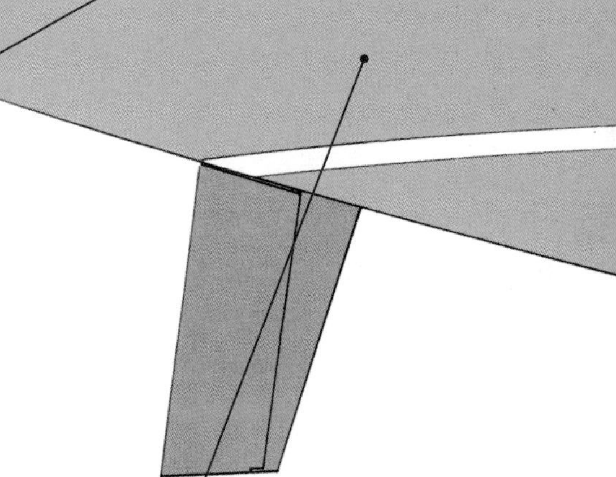

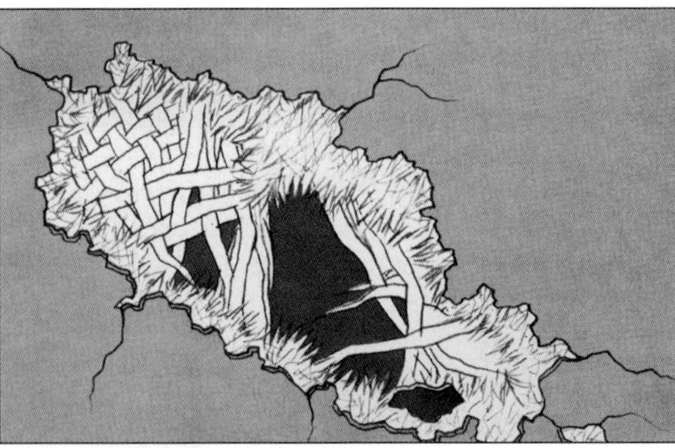

Holes A collision can result in a hole like this one in a fiberglass hull. At impact, the fiberglass will stretch only slightly before rupturing: its flexibility is about one eighth that of steel, one fifth that of aluminum. Happily, such a hole is considerably easier to repair in fiberglass than in metal.

Oilcanning Constant flexing of unsupported fiberglass panels will crack the gel coat and may fracture the laminate itself. A potential buyer of a fiberglass boat need not take the boat on a trial run to spot trouble of this kind: suspect areas can be tested by pressing against the hull with a knee or hands.

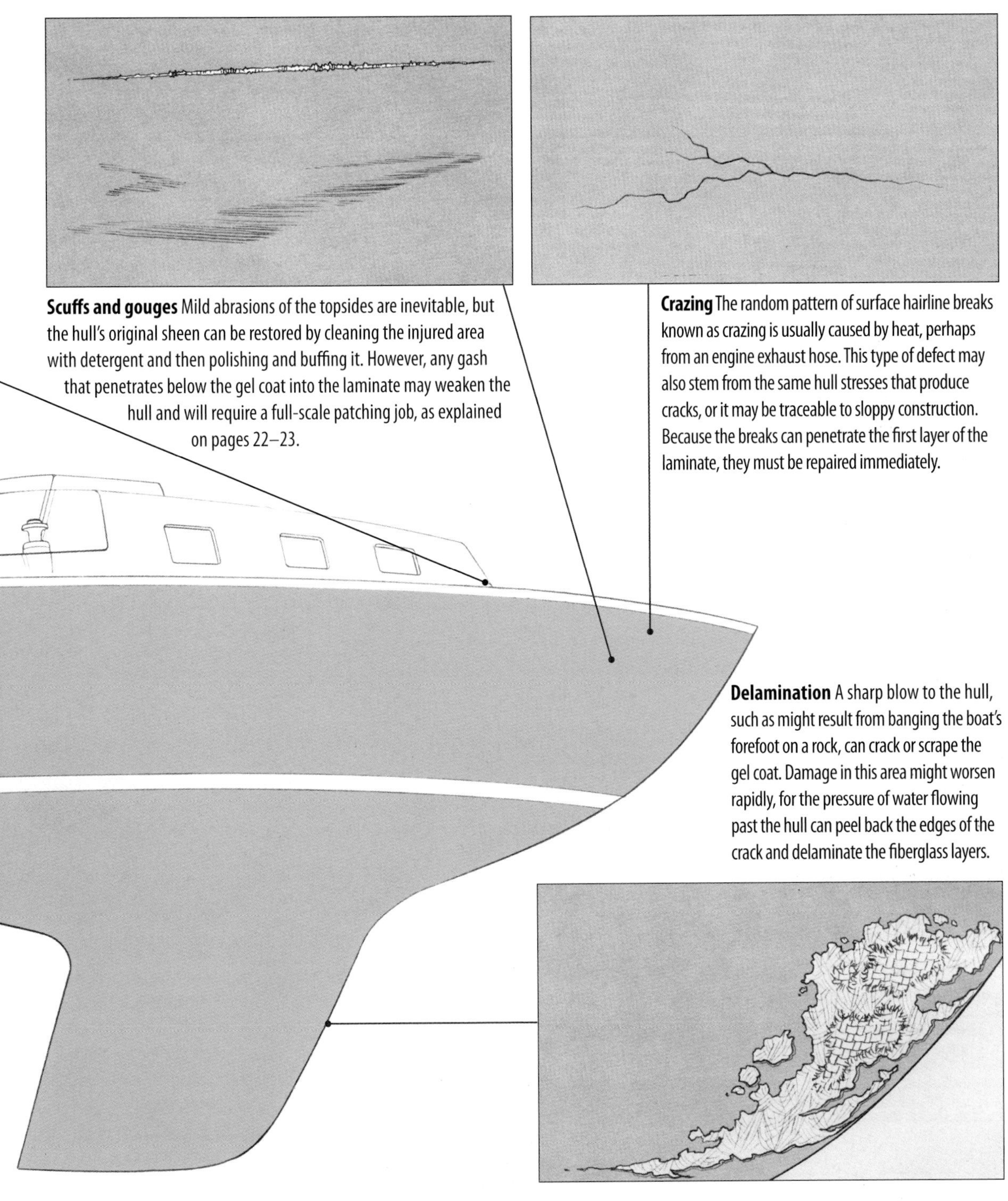

Scuffs and gouges Mild abrasions of the topsides are inevitable, but the hull's original sheen can be restored by cleaning the injured area with detergent and then polishing and buffing it. However, any gash that penetrates below the gel coat into the laminate may weaken the hull and will require a full-scale patching job, as explained on pages 22–23.

Crazing The random pattern of surface hairline breaks known as crazing is usually caused by heat, perhaps from an engine exhaust hose. This type of defect may also stem from the same hull stresses that produce cracks, or it may be traceable to sloppy construction. Because the breaks can penetrate the first layer of the laminate, they must be repaired immediately.

Delamination A sharp blow to the hull, such as might result from banging the boat's forefoot on a rock, can crack or scrape the gel coat. Damage in this area might worsen rapidly, for the pressure of water flowing past the hull can peel back the edges of the crack and delaminate the fiberglass layers.

Fixing Surface Flaws

The same resins or fabrics used to make a fiberglass hull are also employed in repairs—from the simple filling of a crack in the hull's outer surface, as shown here, to the more ambitious projects described on the following pages. In the case of a small scrape in the hull, no new fabric is needed. The restorative material is a putty made by mixing resin with chopped glass fibers or a thickening agent. The consistency of the putty is controlled by the amount of fibers and catalyst added, and this in turn should be determined by the extent of damage: the putty ought to be of a creamy consistency for application in narrow cracks, somewhat thicker for broader gouges.

The type of resin used as the base of the putty may also vary. Either epoxy or polyester resins may be used as a putty base in filling cracks that will later be painted over. Epoxy is the more likely of the two to adhere to any surface. A putty incorporating gel-coat resin is best for the hull's outer layer of gel coat.

Although many fiberglass repairs can be done with hand tools, a few power tools—notably an electric drill with a router bit, and sanding and buffing attachments—will speed the work and do a neater job. Wear rubber gloves to protect hands against glass fibers and splashes of resin, both of which can cause skin irritations. Don goggles and a respirator mask when sanding fiberglass, to keep fibers out of the eyes and lungs. And be sure the work area is well ventilated; resin fumes can cause nausea and faintness.

The rate at which the resin putty cures depends on the temperature. If the working area's temperature is between 60° and 80°, the filler will set in an hour or two and will be thoroughly cured in three days. At 50°, curing might take forever, and the boatman would be well advised to speed up the process by applying heat for a few minutes from a lamp placed nearby. The heat is needed only as a starter; once resin has begun to cure, the process itself generates enough heat to finish the job. Gel coat's curing traits are particularly tricky: unlike polyester or epoxy, it will never harden completely unless it is sealed off from air, as shown opposite.

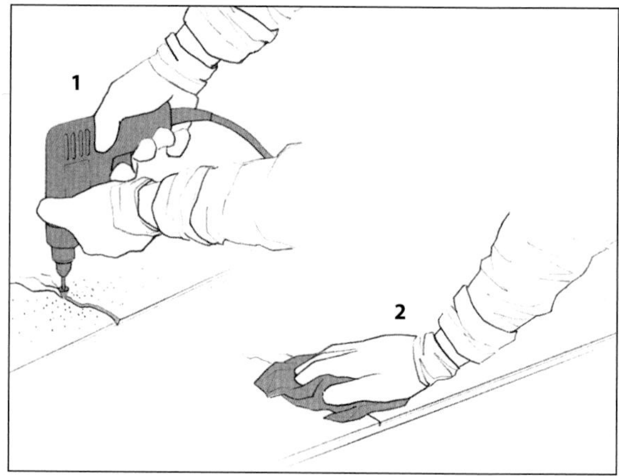

When repairing a crack in the gel coal of a fiberglass hull, first widen the crack enough so that it will hold putty, and extend the cut a quarter inch or so beyond the crack to relieve any stress. The best tool for the job is an electric drill equipped with a V-shaped grinding bit or a router (1). Brush all dust out of the crack and wipe away any surface dirt or wax that might keep putty from adhering (2). Do not use a solvent or sandpaper on the surface of the hull around the crack; either one will remove gel coal and only aggravate the problem. Avoid touching the crack with an ungloved hand, since even a film of skin oil can keep putty from adhering securely.

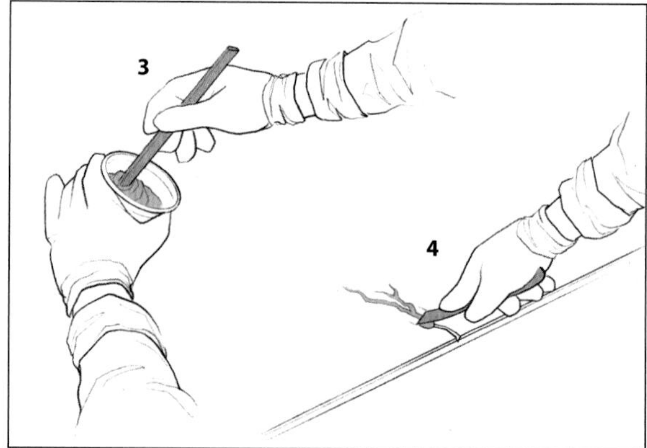

Mix together more than enough gel-coat resin, hardener, and loose fibers or thickener—in that order—for the job, stirring the putty to a smooth, homogeneous blend (3). Work the mixture firmly into the crack with a putty knife (4), so that no air bubbles remain to weaken the repair. Because the putty shrinks slightly as it cures, leave an excess of about one sixteenth of an inch above the filled-in crack.

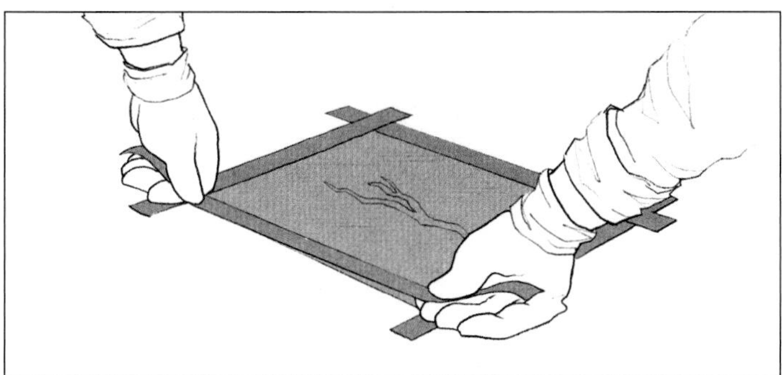

The crack must be sealed after filling, since gel coat, unlike epoxy or polyester, will not cure completely while exposed to air. Cover the puttied area with a sheet of cellophane or plastic food wrap and tape down the edges to make the covering airtight.

If the work is being done in temperatures below 60°, place a heat lamp or a 300-watt bulb 8 to 10 inches away from the repair. Apply the heat for a quarter of an hour or less; the label on a can of resin usually includes recommendations on applying heat. Then the curing process should continue at its own rate, since too much heat will cause the resin to run, sag, discolor, or even burn.

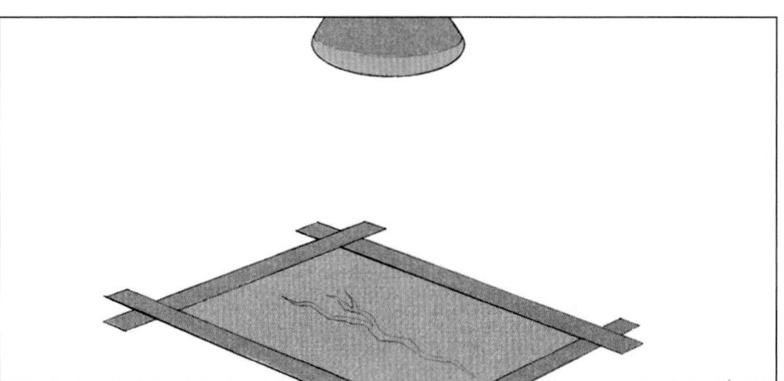

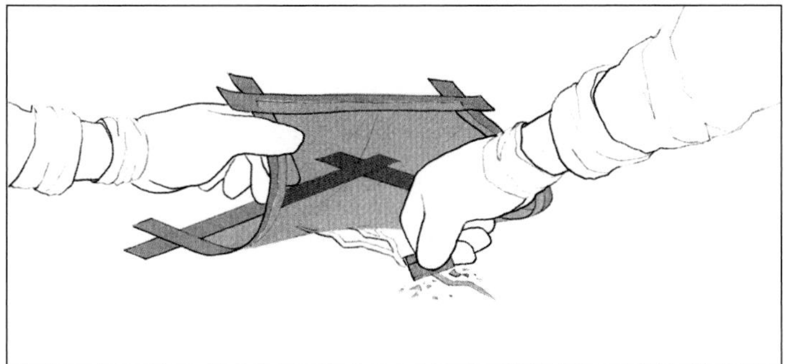

When the resin putty has cured to a tacky consistency, peel back the seal and, using a razor blade, carefully slice away any filler that protrudes above the surface of the crack, along with any inadvertent deposits of resin.

After the putty has hardened, remove the seal and burnish the filled crack with a power-driven buffing pad coated with a fine rubbing compound. Be sure to avoid overpolishing, lest the thin gel coat be worn away.

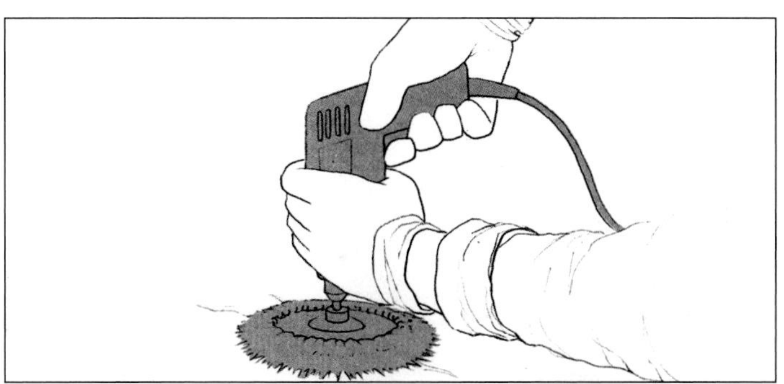

Patching a Puncture

Patching a punctured or stove-in fiberglass hull involves rebuilding the damaged area from the outside in with gel coat and fabric, as shown in these drawings and side views of the damaged hull portion. First, mark on the outer surface of the hull a circle or an oval enclosing all the damage. Cut out the damaged section with a saber saw, first drilling a hole to admit the saw blade.

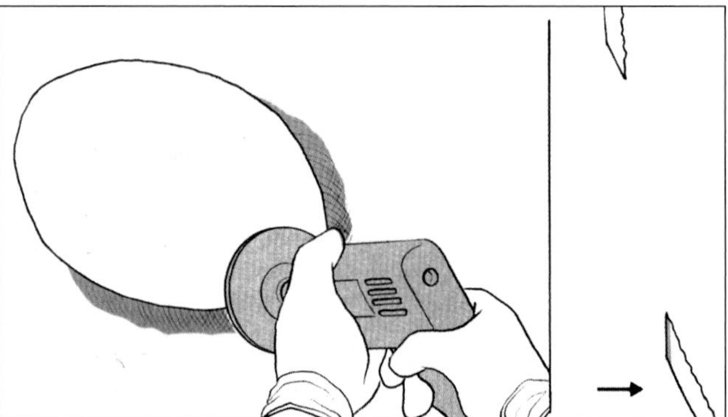

Still working outside the hull, attach a sanding disc and coarse paper to an electric drill and bevel the edge of the hole back on a shallow angle, creating a profile like that shown in the hull cross section at left. The bevel will make for a stronger mend by increasing the area where hull and patch join. Trim enough pieces of fiberglass to make a patch as thick as the hull and made of the same materials arranged in the same order. The first piece should be large enough to fill the entire beveled area, and each successive piece should be of a slightly smaller size to conform to the angle of the bevel.

Now, working inside the hull, sand down the nubbly interior surface with coarse sandpaper for a distance of six to eight inches all around the hole; this promotes adhesion of the fiberglass layers that will seal and reinforce the inside of the patch. Cut three more pieces of fiberglass fabric, making the first slightly larger than the hole, the next somewhat bigger, and the last one big enough to fill the sanded area almost to its perimeter.

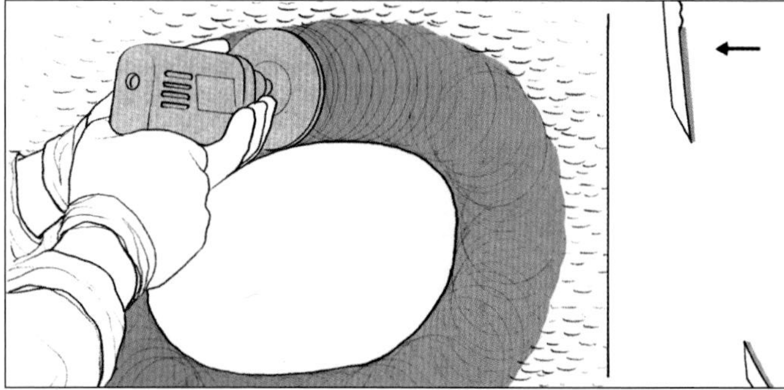

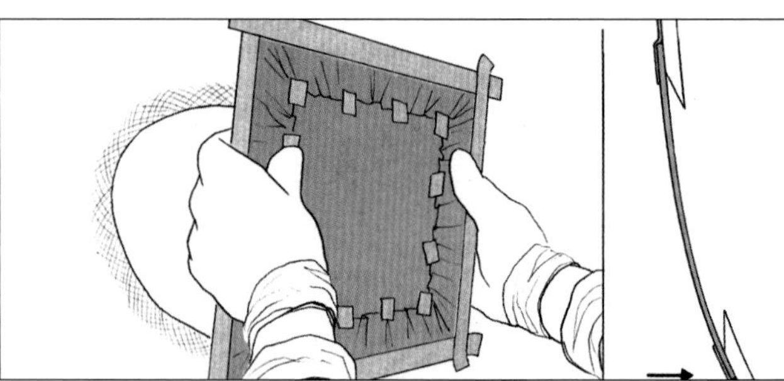

Prepare a backing plate of thin flexible metal or linoleum that will make the patch materials conform to the shape of the hull. Cover it with cellophane or plastic food wrap so the outer layer of the patch will not stick to the backing plate. In attaching the plate over the hole, affix tape all around the edges; the covering must be airtight to enable the gel coat to harden thoroughly.

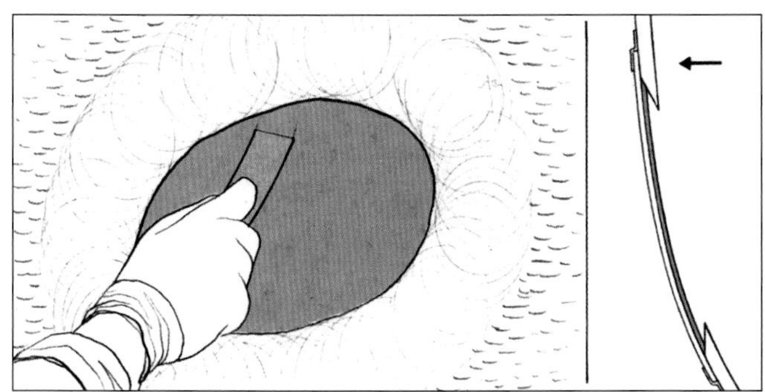

Mix a small amount of gel-coat resin with its hardener and the desired pigment. Then, with a putty knife, spread an even layer of the resin—about one-thirty-second of an inch thick—on the cellophane-wrapped inner side of the backing plate. Be sure to work the gel coat well into the crevice formed by the juncture of the plate and the outer edge of the hole. Leave the gel coat open to the air inside the hull until it is no longer tacky. The patch *(below)* will seal off the air from the gel coat and allow it to cure completely.

Mix polyester or epoxy resin with its hardener, and brush the resin into the first—and largest—of the fiberglass pieces cut for the patch. Insert this initial layer into the opening, pressing it gently against the gel coat; be sure the resin evenly saturates the material. Use a brush to tuck the edges under the beveled lip of the hole.

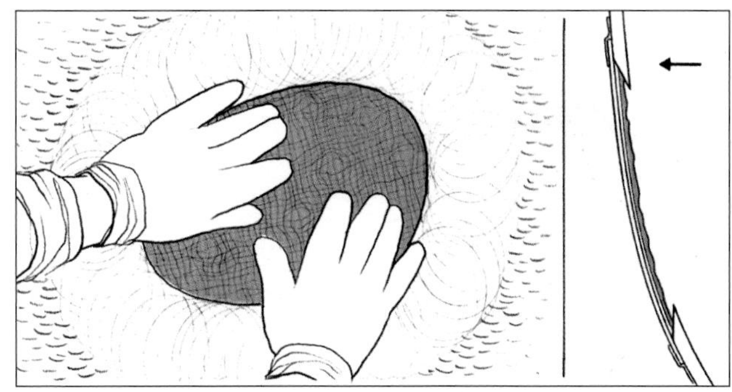

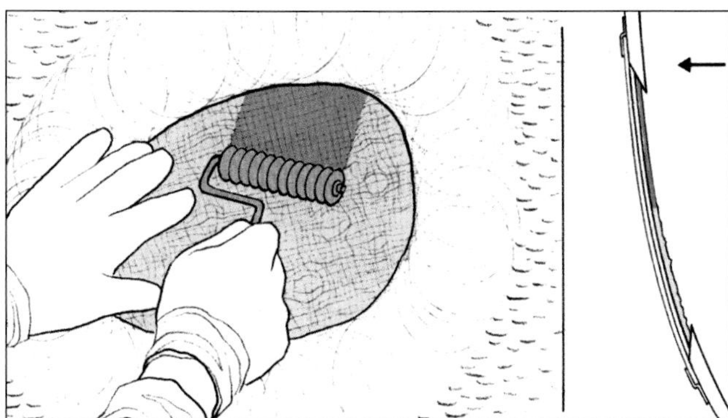

With a small aluminum roller, press out any air bubbles trapped under the layer of fiberglass. (Bubbles will show through as spots of lighter color and, unless removed, will weaken the patch.) One after another, fit the other pieces of resin-soaked fiberglass cloth into the hole, in the proper sequence, and work out all air bubbles with the roller. If the finished patch is to be more than three-sixteenths of an inch thick, apply only half of the fiberglass layers required for the patch. Let them harden for an hour or so until the surface feels leathery and forms a sound base for the rest; then finish the patch.

When the patch has hardened, gently detach the backing plate from the outside of the hull. If pits or other imperfections appear in the gel coat after drying, touch them up with gel coat; seal the repairs airtight until the resin cures, and then wet-sand and buff the surface of the patch area to a shiny finish.

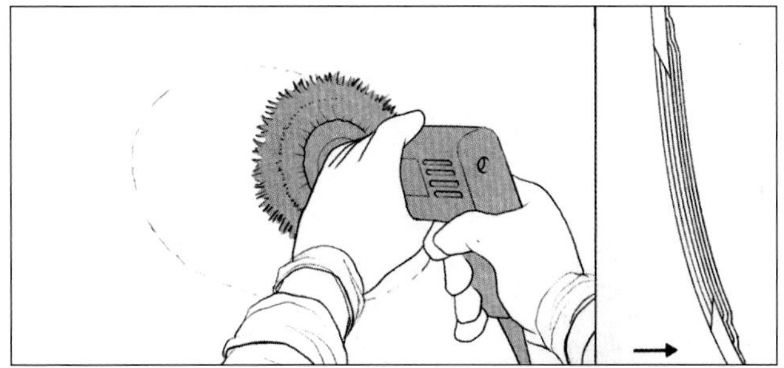

Repairing Delamination

A fiberglass hull that has begun to peel apart—delaminate—at a damage-prone point such as the forefoot, shown here, must be fixed at once. Replacing the abraded fabric keeps water from penetrating the damaged area and spreading the damage as the boat moves. Begin the repair by carefully removing all damaged fiberglass and resin with a sharp wood chisel and a carpenter's mallet, working down to completely sound laminate.

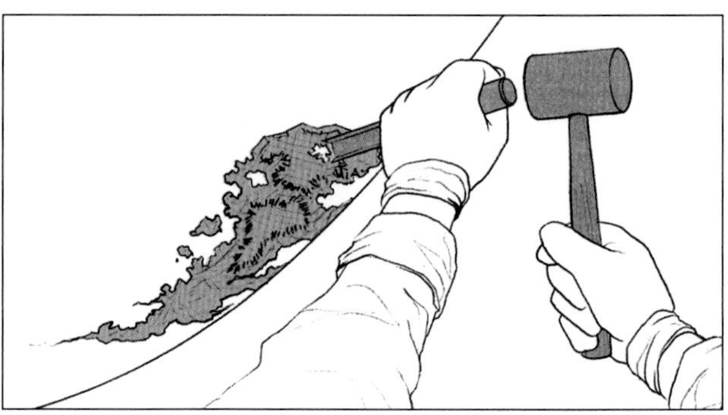

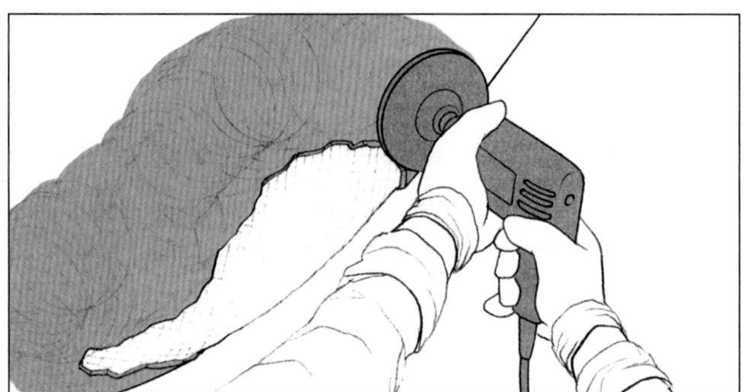

Next, sand all around the damaged area to a distance of about eight inches, using an electric drill fitted with a sanding disc and coarse-grained paper; this will help the new fabric to adhere firmly. Wipe away all dust and wash the sanded area with detergent.

Fit a piece of fiberglass mat into the area that is damaged, soak it with resin and work out the air bubbles with an aluminum roller. Repeat the operation with additional pieces of material until the shallow depression has been filled almost flush with the hull's surface. Mat—rather than a combination of materials—makes the best basis for such shallow repairs because it absorbs more resin than other fabrics and thus creates the strongest bond with the original fiberglass.

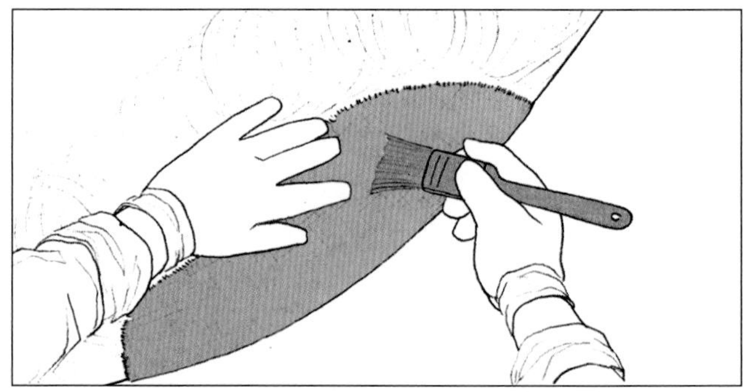

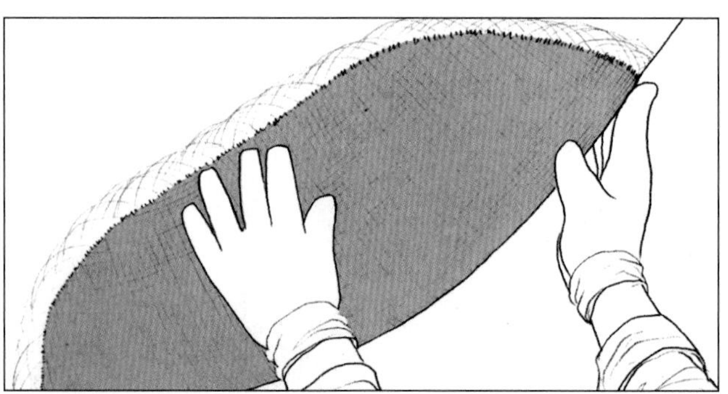

For a smooth, strong surface finish, cover the mat with three or four pieces of fiberglass cloth; each piece should be larger than its predecessor, and the top layer should extend almost to the perimeter of the sanded area. (Slits cut in the edges of each piece will help fit it to the boat's contours.) After the new laminate has hardened, feather the edges of the outer layer with the sander to keep water from getting under it. Then prime and paint.

Fashioning a Brace

Oilcanning in a curved hull section can be remedied with an easily installed brace that uses an ordinary cardboard mailing tube as its core. Slit the tube in half, lengthwise, and notch it so it will bend to conform to the hull's shape. Sand an area six inches on either side of its intended position, wipe the surface clean, then with epoxy, glue the tube in place (1). Drape two layers of resin-soaked matting over the tube, followed by a layer of woven roving (2); the layers should be of successively larger sizes and they should cover both ends of the tube so that water cannot seep in and rot the cardboard.

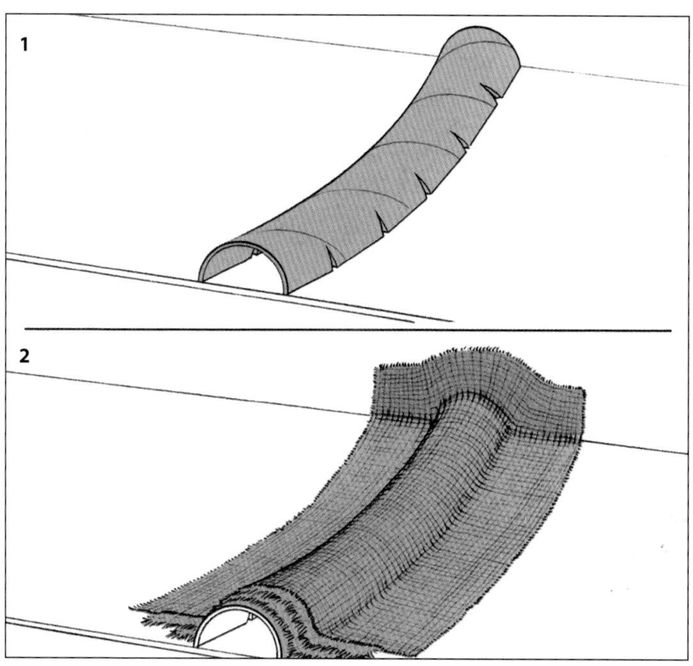

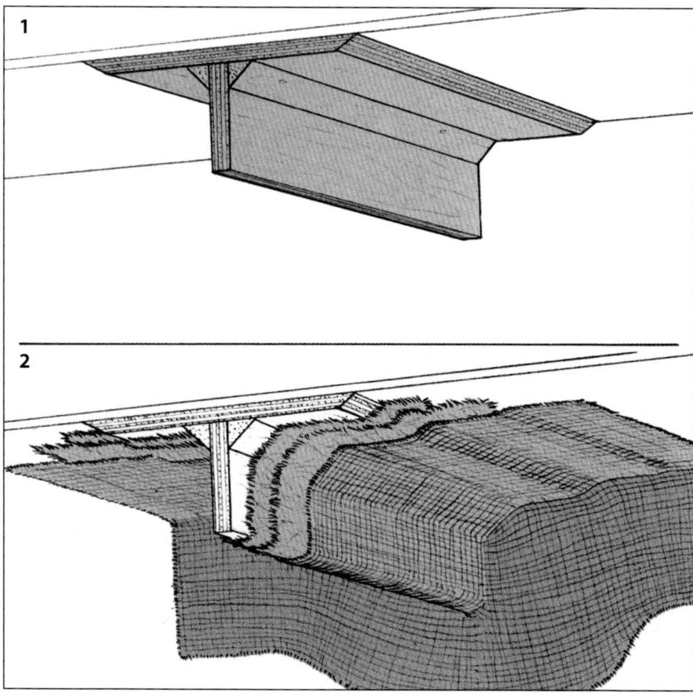

A deck can be stiffened with a fiberglass-covered wooden support. For the core (1), cut a piece of half-inch plywood six to eight inches wide and also long enough to fit between two bulkheads; bevel the edges so that the covering cloth will take a fair curve. This board, called a doubler, will help spread the bracing effect. Cut a second section of plywood and, with epoxy, glue it perpendicular to the doubler. Glue triangular pieces called fillets—shown here—along the joint, then glue the whole assemblage in place. Cover it with successively larger layers of resin-soaked fabric, two of matting and one of roving (2).

Damage to Ferro-Cement

Ferro-cement has gained a well-deserved reputation for toughness since it made its debut during the early '40s as a structural material for pleasure boats. A cement hull—typically about three quarters of an inch thick and reinforced with steel rods and wire mesh—is almost impossible to puncture. Moreover, any damage caused by a powerful blow will probably be confined to the point of impact; the same blow might produce a large dent in metal or widespread cracking in fiberglass.

However, injuries from impact should not be taken lightly: any cracks must be promptly patched up with a filler consisting of epoxy, sand, and water to prevent water from seeping into the wire mesh and corroding it. But such ministrations are quick and easy, and even major damage like a smashed gunwale *(opposite, bottom)* can be repaired in a matter of hours.

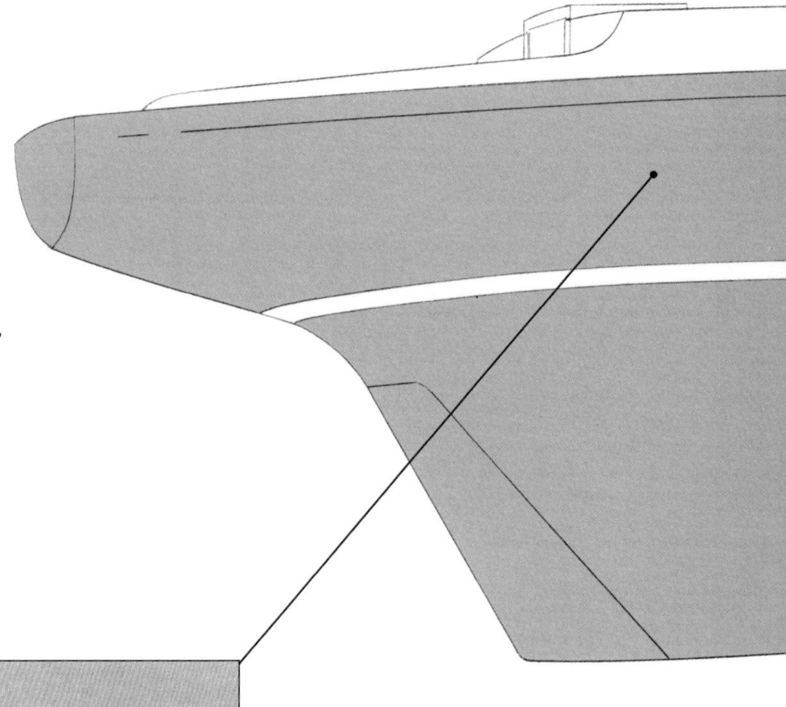

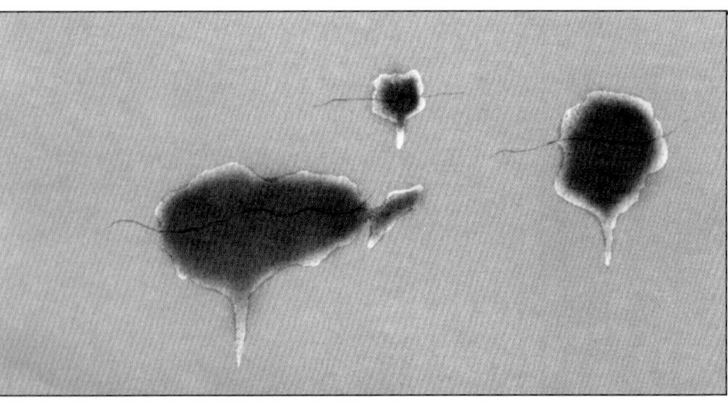

Cracks Any hull fracture that penetrates to the mesh must be fixed as quickly as possible to prevent corrosion. If rust stains have already appeared *(left)* before repairs are started, the cement should be scraped back to the mesh and the extent of corrosion examined. When the rusting is minor, it can be removed with a wire brush and the crack refilled. But serious corrosion may weaken the hull, and the area that is afflicted should be rebuilt, as explained on pages 29–31.

Gouges The most frequent damage to ferro-cement is a superficial gouge or scrape that removes topside's paint. Such abrasions may be unsightly, but they cause no serious harm. The temporarily paintless area of cement may absorb a little moisture, but the wire mesh will not corrode unless the gash is deep enough to expose the metal to air.

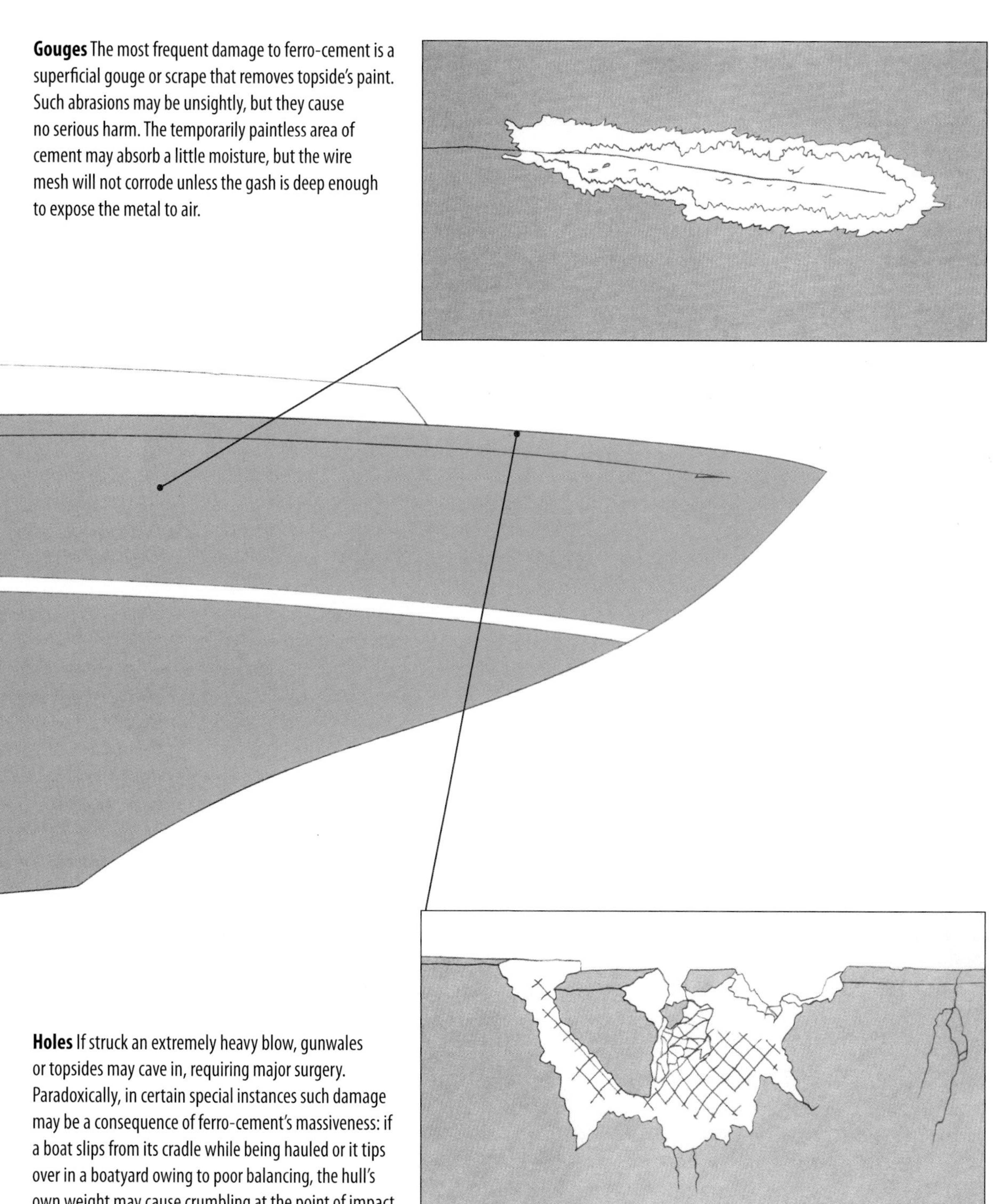

Holes If struck an extremely heavy blow, gunwales or topsides may cave in, requiring major surgery. Paradoxically, in certain special instances such damage may be a consequence of ferro-cement's massiveness: if a boat slips from its cradle while being hauled or it tips over in a boatyard owing to poor balancing, the hull's own weight may cause crumbling at the point of impact.

Minor Wounds

The first step in the repair of a superficial scratch or gouge in a ferro-cement hull is to rake over the damaged area with an ordinary paint scraper, dislodging any loose cement and creating a sound bed for the epoxy filler that will be used to patch the wound.

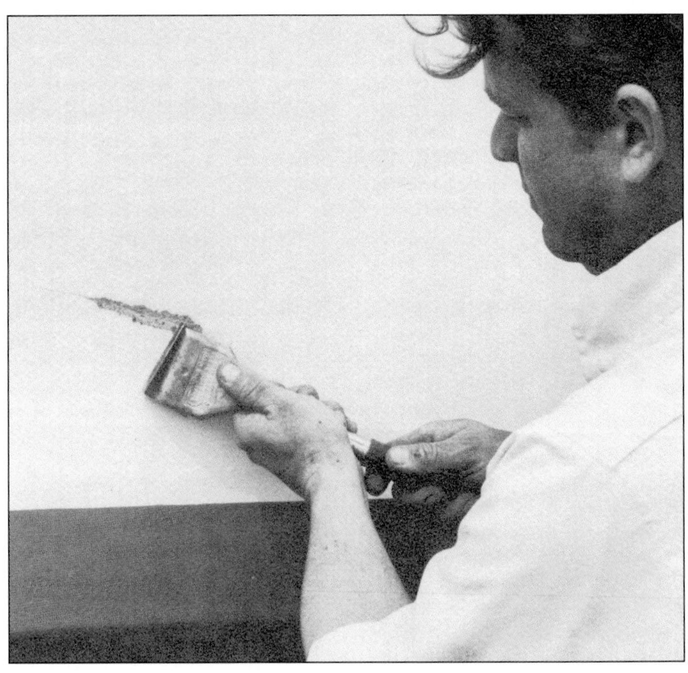

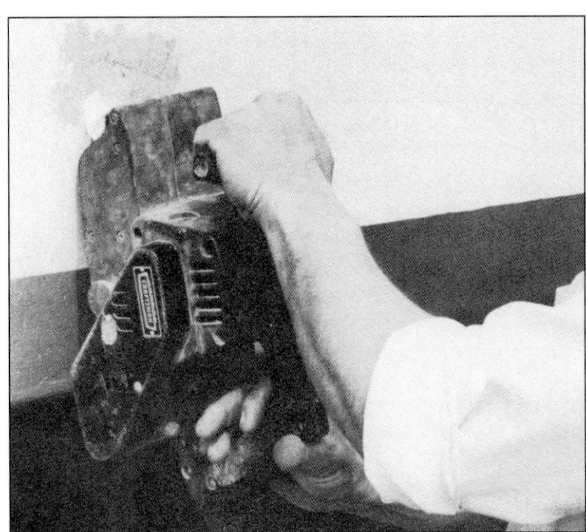

Next, sand the scar and a sizable area around it with a belt sander and a medium grade of aluminum oxide paper. Sanding of a broad area will ensure good adhesion of the epoxy and will also permit the filler to be faired off so that no bulge is left.

Spread epoxy compound on the sanded area with a squeegee—a flat ribbon tool available at marine-supply stores. The squeegee's flexibility permits the filler to be pressed into the opening and smoothed in a single motion. When the epoxy dries—with some epoxy the drying may take only 20 minutes or so—sand the area with a fine paper; then paint.

Major Breaks

When a hole is smashed through the hull, the damaged area must be completely reconstructed, beginning with removal of all the broken cement from the exposed mesh—which may be in two layers, as in this picture, or more. This job will probably require two workers, one to chip at the mesh with a hammer, the other to back up the blows with a maul or some other heavy object. Without the backup, the hammer's impact would simply bend the mesh without knocking off the concrete fragments.

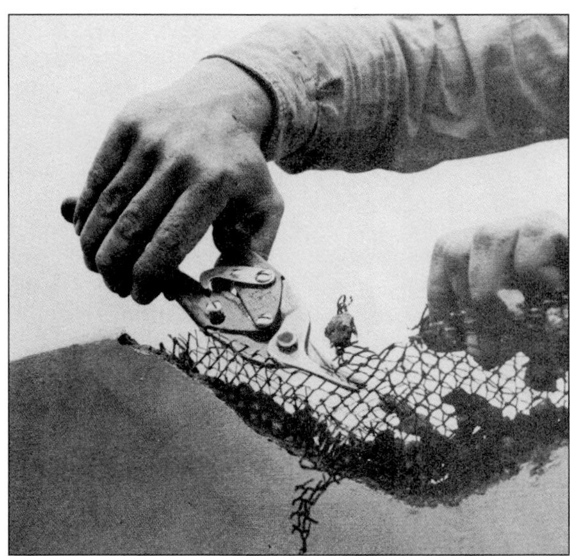

Once all the cement has been chipped away, the bent or broken layers of wire mesh must be excised with wire cutters. Leave a two-inch-wide strip of mesh around the edge of the hole as a base for attaching new mesh.

With a wire brush, remove any remaining loose cement from the mesh around the edges of the hole. All surfaces must be clean, too, for proper adhesion of the cement that will be used to rebuild the hull.

With the damaged area brushed clean and its wire mesh trimmed back, hold a fresh piece of mesh over the damaged area and trace the outline of the hole on it with chalk. Then cut a replacement piece to fit. Using this new section as a template, cut several more pieces—as many as were originally used in the hull. The type of mesh should also match the original as closely as possible.

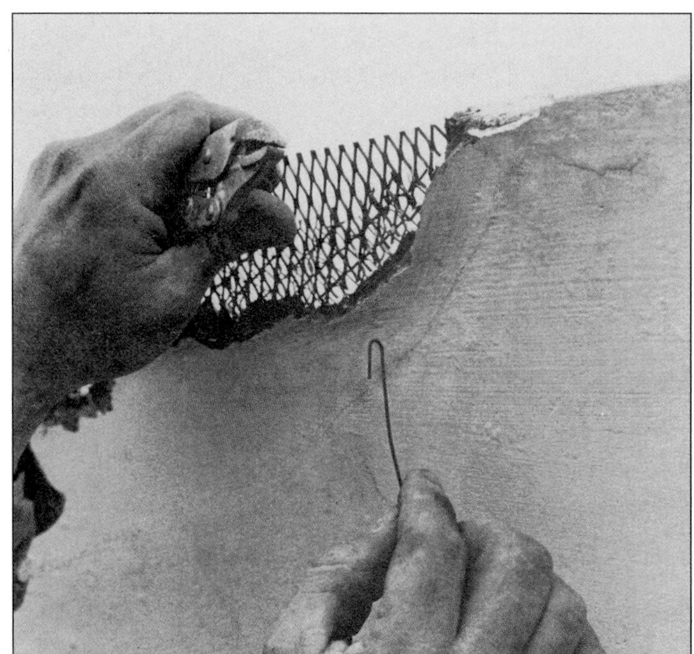

Position the new mesh over the old wire so the holes overlap rather than align; this will strengthen the patch by distributing the steel reinforcement evenly through the new cement. Cut several short pieces of flexible wire, bend a hook into the end of each, then hook these fastening wires around both the new and old mesh about every four inches.

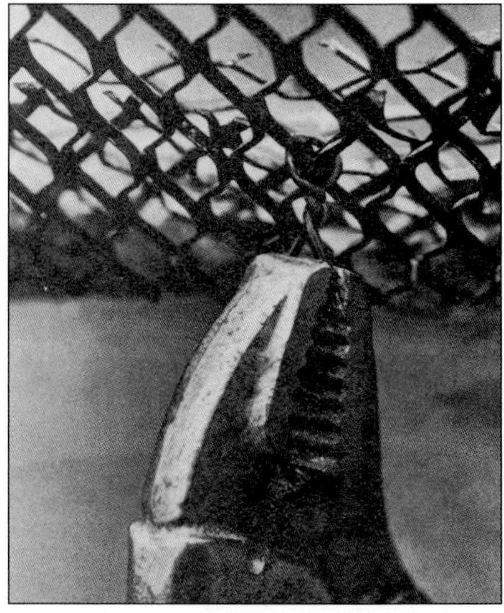

Using vise-grip pliers, twist the hooked end of each fastening wire to secure the mesh, and then snip off the protruding ends—which serve only for ease of handling during attachment. Add any other layers of replacement mesh, one at a time, and tie them with hooked wires; fastenings should be spaced evenly and twisted around all the mesh layers at each stage. Brush the mesh repair with a cement bonding agent available at hardware stores; this compound will help the cement to bond to the wire.

As a mold for the new cement that will be applied over the mesh, fasten a backup board to the outside of the hull. A piece of three-sixteenths-inch plywood as shown here, or even better, one-eighth-inch masonite, is sufficiently pliable to conform to the hull curvature when held down with clamps.

Now prepare to apply the fresh cement, which should consist of the same ingredients used in the boat's construction: typically one part silica sand, one part vinyl or epoxy bonding agent, and one part Portland cement, grade #5. Apply a generous amount of the mixture to the wire mesh with a trowel and press it firmly against the backup board to be sure it squeezes between all the wires. Smooth the inner surface with the trowel.

Although the cement starts to firm up in two to four hours, the backup board should be left in place for two days to allow the mixture to cure completely. During that time, keep the cement moist by laying damp towels over it. If allowed to dry out during curing, it will flake and crack. When the cement is properly cured, remove the board and smooth both sides of the patch with a belt sander, using a coarse grade of aluminum oxide paper at first, then a slightly finer grade. Eliminate the last imperfections by hand sanding; and finally, paint over the fresh patch.

Assaults on Aluminum

In some respects, aluminum is the most reassuring of all hull materials. It will not rot, it repels marine borers, it builds up its own protective coat of oxidation and it is highly resistant to fracturing. If an aluminum boat like the powerboat shown here hit a floating log, the hull would be considerably less likely to rupture than if it were made of fiberglass or wood. (Steel hulls offer the same strength at a lower price, but the much greater weight of structural steel limits it mainly to boats of 45 feet and more.) When an aluminum hull does tear, crack, break a weld, or lose rivets along a seam, repairs can normally be made by the layman. Dents—one form of damage to which aluminum boats are particularly susceptible—can usually be dealt with in short order.

Most such troubles are the results of accidents, and are quickly and easily detected. However, aluminum's worst enemy works more subtly. This is galvanic corrosion—the result of the juxtaposition of dissimilar metals in the presence of electrically conductive salt water. In extreme cases, galvanic corrosion can cause an iron fitting such as a shaft bearing to corrode in only a week or two. But if a boatman understands the problem and takes advantage of the proper preventive procedures *(page 38)*, he can eliminate the one real foe of a material that, pound for pound, is stronger than any other.

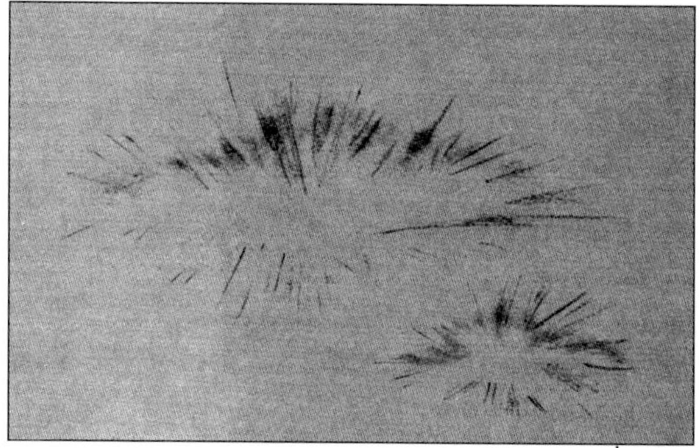

Dents Frequently found on the topsides as a result of docking accidents, dents are the commonest affliction of aluminum hulls. Because they usually do not affect safety, some boatmen simply ignore them; but if paint has been chipped, the spot should be touched up with primer and painted—especially below the waterline, where exposed metal may invite galvanic corrosion.

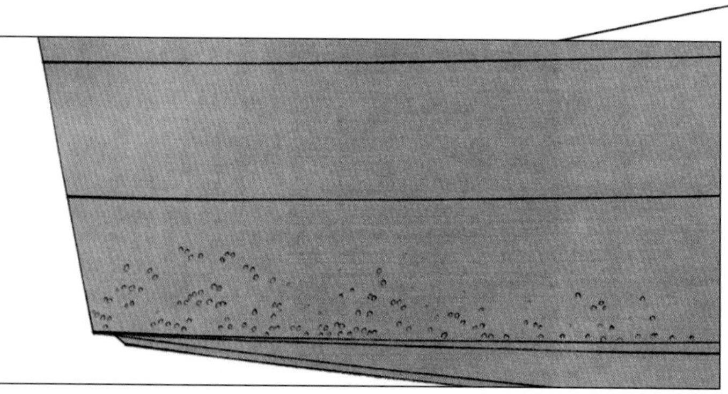

Corrosion The pernicious effects of galvanic corrosion often show up at the after end of the bottom, where a bronze propeller or a steel shaft may interact with the aluminum hull. However, corrosion can affect the entire hull if the boat's electrical systems are not properly grounded *(page 112)*.

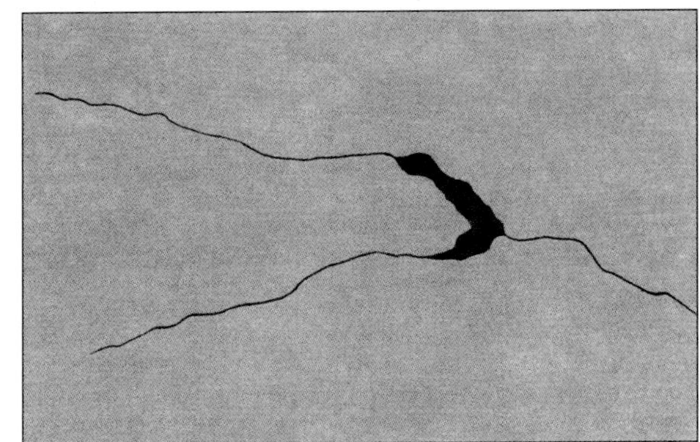

Tears Like dents, through-hull fractures are most often caused by a collision with a dock. The hole may be small (it may even be an imperceptible fracture at the edge of a dent), but the boat should be repaired immediately.

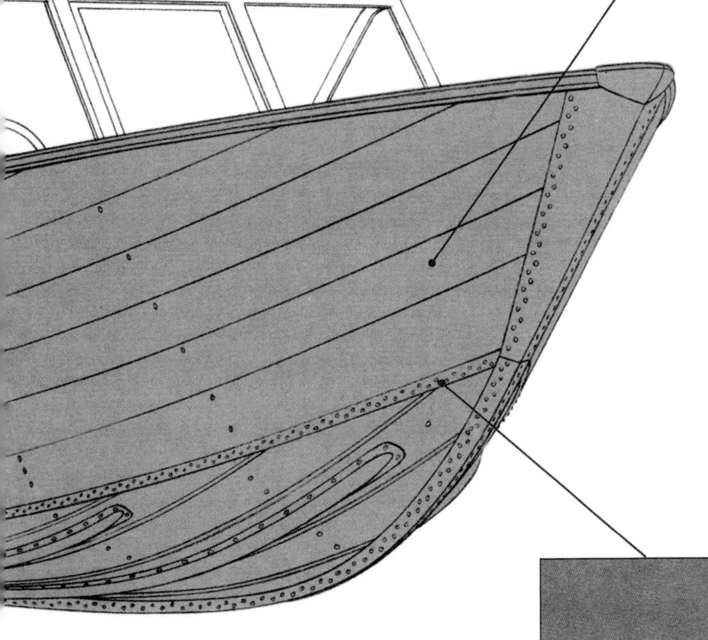

Loosened fastenings Impact, vibration, or abrasion, when the boat goes aground or is hauled up on a beach, can damage a weld or work loose rivets that fasten the seams—especially along the waterline or in the bottom. Loose rivets should be tightened immediately, before they become distorted and have to be removed and replaced.

Dents and Popped Rivets

Repairing a small shallow dent in a light aluminum hull is not a difficult task. Often a dent will spring back into place if given a firm push directly in the center; in some cases the boatowner, with his back braced against some solid object, can straighten out a dent by pressing against it with his feet. If neither of these tactics works, the dent can be hammered out with a rubber mallet.

Deep dents, those that have stretched the metal, are more of a problem. A hole may have to be drilled in the metal and the dent hammered flat *(bottom right).* In such instances a patch must be riveted into place to cover the hole and strengthen the area *(right and pages 36–37).*

Denting sometimes causes rivets along the hull seams to loosen or tear out. A loose rivet can often be tightened, but it may take two pairs of hands. The head must be hammered while another hammer or a piece of iron is held against the inboard end of the rivet. Naturally, a damaged rivet or one that has pulled out must be replaced; this is easy to do with an inexpensive pop-rivet gun, also called a riveting plier, whose workings are explained at right. Such guns are available at most hardware stores.

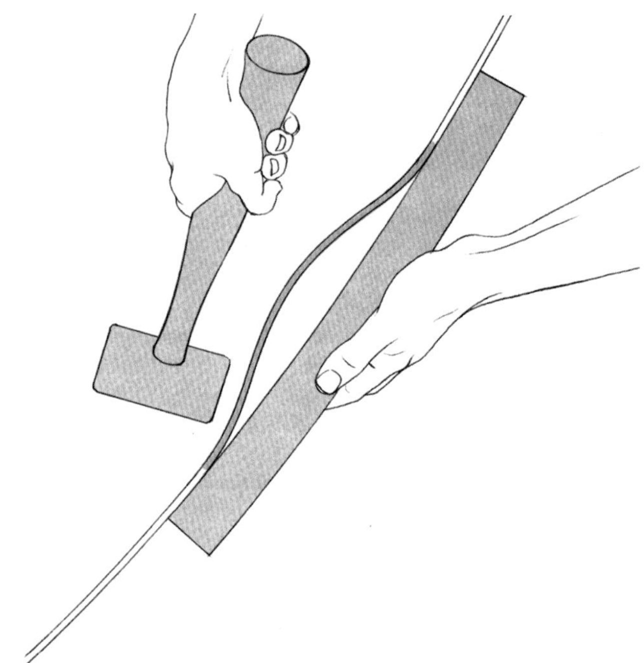

If a large shallow dent does not spring back into place under slight pressure, it can be hammered out by means of a series of light blows delivered with a rubber mallet. A hard wood or metal block should be held against the concave side of the dent while the damaged area is being hammered back into shape. The mallet blows should be struck close to one another and in concentric circles, beginning at the dent's perimeter.

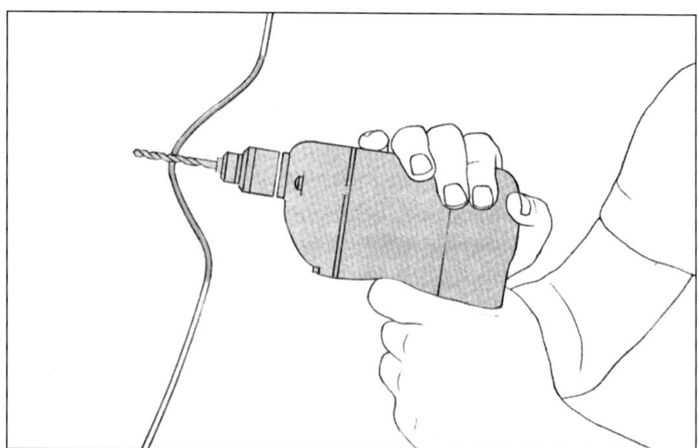

To repair a severe dent that has stretched the aluminum, drill a small hole into the center of the affected area. This will make room for the distended metal when it is hammered back into shape. The procedure for the hammering is the same as for shallow dents.

A Handy Rivet Gun

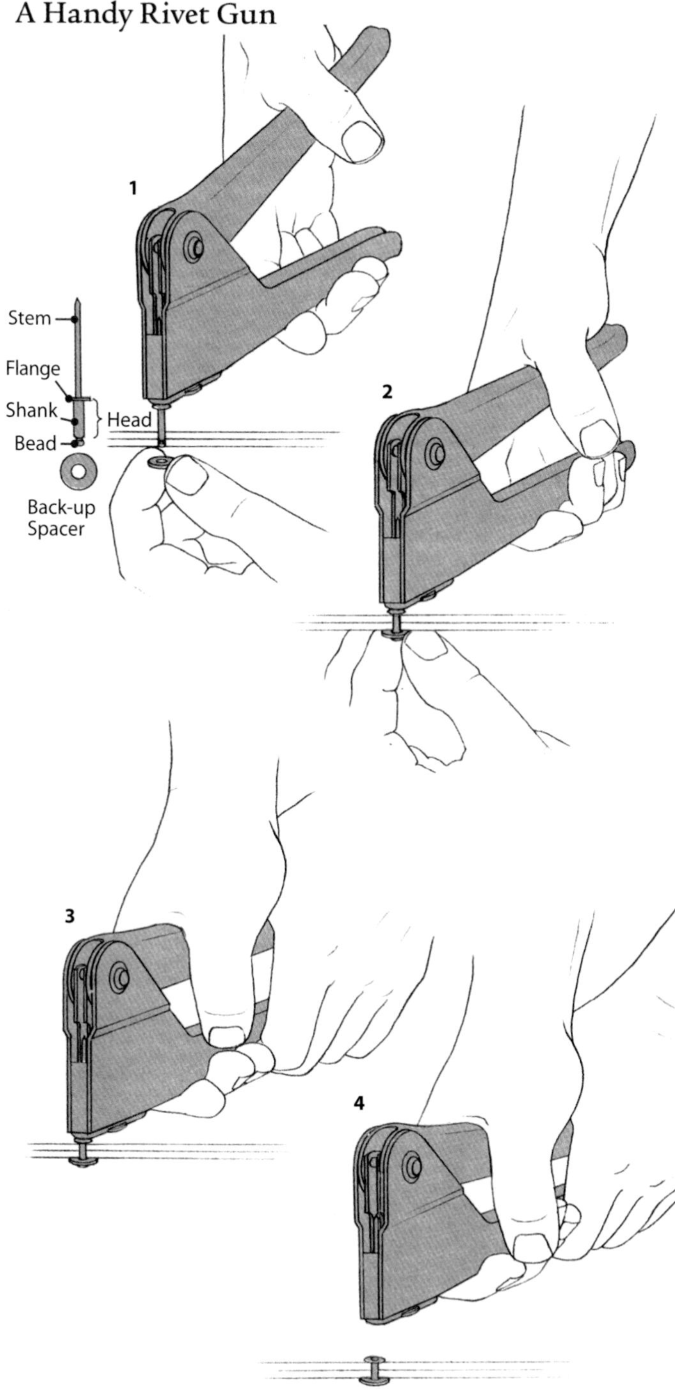

1 To put in a new rivet, first measure the combined thickness of the hull and the patch that is to be placed over it, using a micrometer or a pair of calipers. Load the rivet gun with an aluminum rivet slightly longer than the thickness of the patched hull and with a diameter of at least three sixteenths of an inch for strength. Insert the rivet shank through holes predrilled in the patch and the hull. For extra strength on the other side, place an aluminum washer—known as a backup spacer—over the bead, that is, the knob at the end of the rivet stem.

2 Pressing the gun firmly against the metal in a perpendicular position to ensure that the rivet will be driven straight, slowly squeeze the handles together. This causes the gun's internal mechanism to pull at the stem, drawing the bead up against the rivet's head. Since the bead is too large to be pulled through the head, the pulling pressure will make the head mushroom outward.

3 The rivet head usually broadens considerably during the first squeeze, but sometimes not quite enough to make a firm bond, in which case the action must be repeated. Open the handles wide and slowly squeeze them together again with both hands, making certain that the rivet gun is held firmly against the patch material.

4 When the head of the rivet has fully expanded, stress will cause the upper part of the stem to sheer off at the flange with a popping sound, leaving the top part inside the gun and a tight rivet on the hull, holding the two pieces of metal together. The upper stem piece is removed from the gun by opening the handles as far as possible and then shaking or tapping the gun.

Mending a Tear

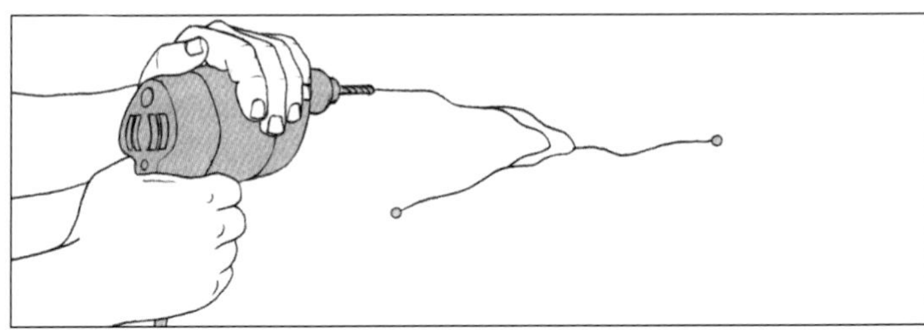

Before patching a tear in the hull, drill a three-sixteenths-inch hole at the end of any accompanying crack. The holes relieve stresses caused by separation of the metal and prevent the cracks from spreading.

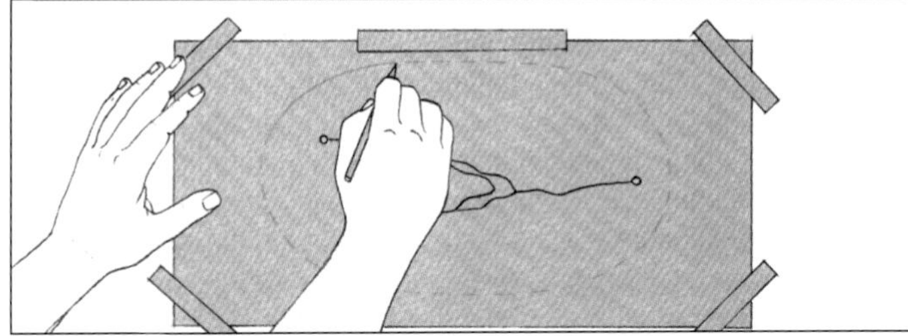

Outline the damaged area with a soft pencil or felt-tipped pen to determine the size and shape of the patch. The outline, basically oval, should extend at least three quarters of an inch beyond any denting or cracking. Tape a piece of heavy tracing paper over the damaged area and trace the oval.

Remove the paper, cut out the oval pattern and tape it to the sheet of aluminum that will be used for the patch; then transfer its outline to the metal. Since pencil marks could be rubbed off during the cutting of the patch, use a sharp awl for incising the aluminum. When you buy the patching material, determine that it is of the same alloy as your hull plating and of at least the same thickness—or slightly greater.

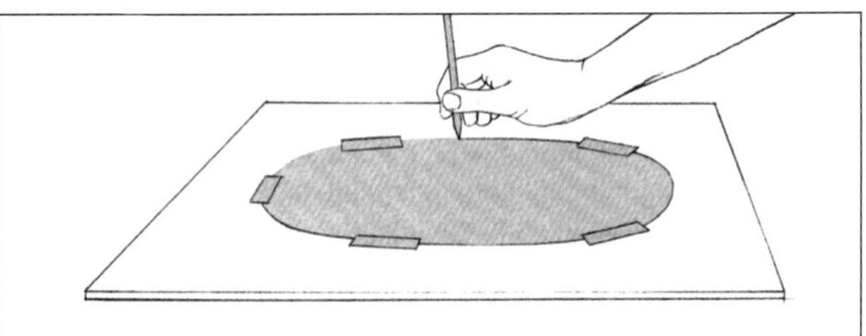

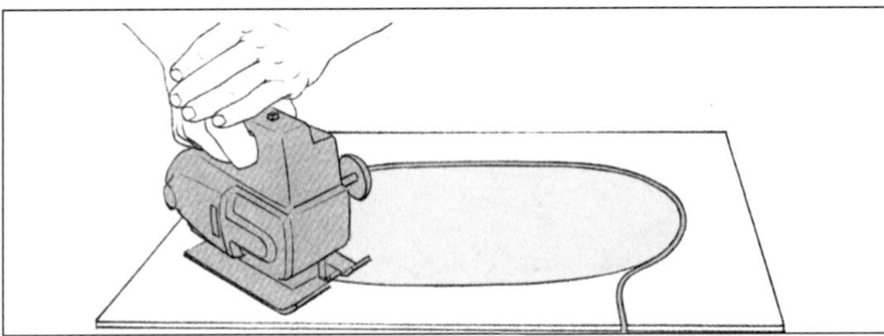

The best tool to cut out the patch is a saber saw equipped with a metal-cutting blade. Start at the edge of the sheet and move to the incised pattern line. Let the saw work at its own speed; if the blade is forced through the material, it will quickly become dull.

Shape the patch to fit the contour of the hull by pounding it with a rubber mallet on an appropriately shaped backing iron—available at auto-body shops. Work slowly, checking the patch's curvature against the hull's at frequent intervals until the fit is close, with gaps of no more than a sixteenth of an inch.

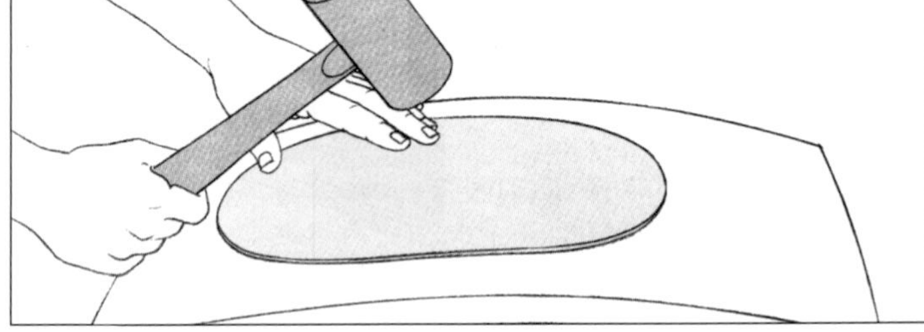

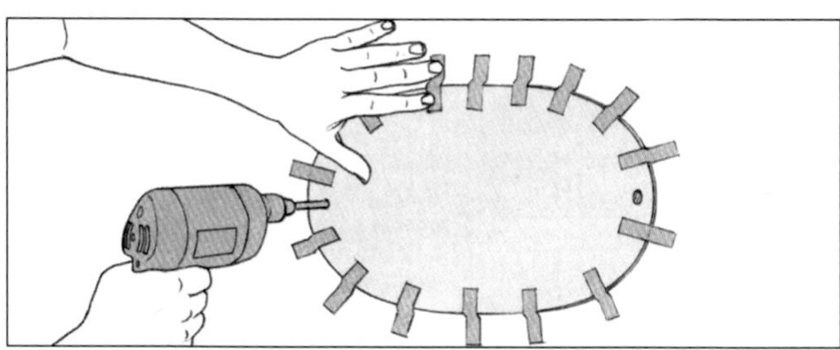

Position the patch against the original outline drawn on the hull and tape it firmly in place. At one end, three-eighths of an inch to half of an inch in from the edge, drill a three-sixteenth of an inch hole through the patch and the hull beneath it; be sure to hold the drill straight, so as to align the two holes. Temporarily fasten the patch to the hull with a nut and a bolt; then drill a second hole diagonally opposite the first one.

Turn the nut free and remove the bolt. Peel off the tape and remove the patch. Liberally coat the underside with a polysulphide or silicone caulking compound to ensure that the repair will be watertight. Replace the patch and bolt it tightly through both holes.

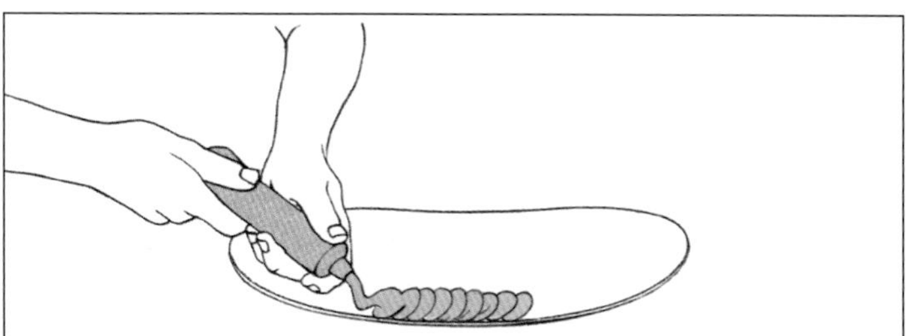

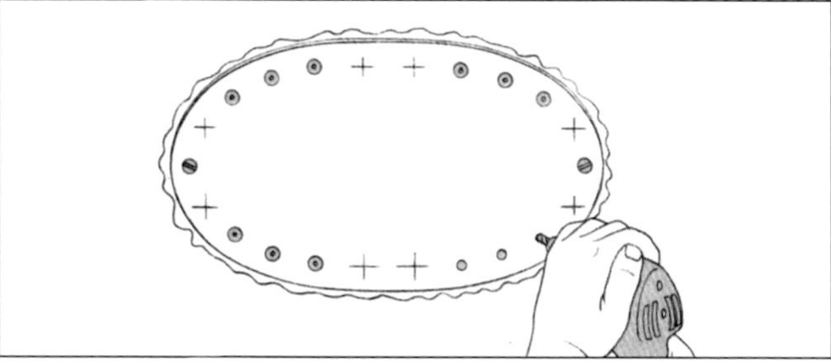

Beginning near one of the bolts, drill three three-sixteenth of an inch holes at one inch intervals about three-eighths of an inch to half of an inch from the edge. Rivet these with a pop-rivet gun *(page 35)*; then add similar three-rivet groups at widely spaced points around the patch. This will prevent any buckling or rippling of the metal. The caulking compound will squeeze out around the edges, but it is best to leave the wiping up until all riveting is completed.

Continue riveting around the edges until the patch is securely attached and all of the gaps between the hull and the patch have been eliminated. Then remove the two temporary nuts and bolts and insert rivets in their place.

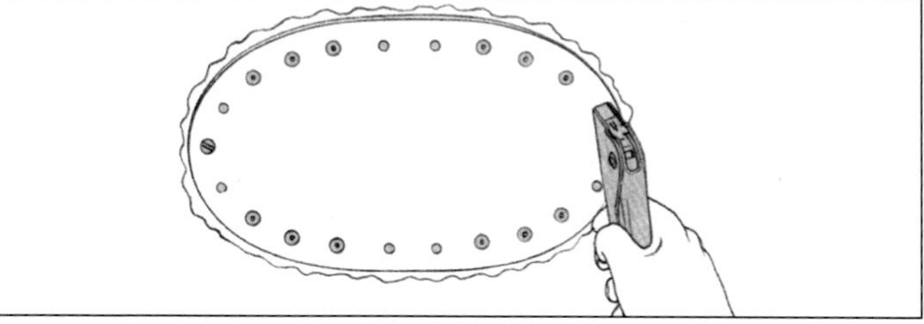

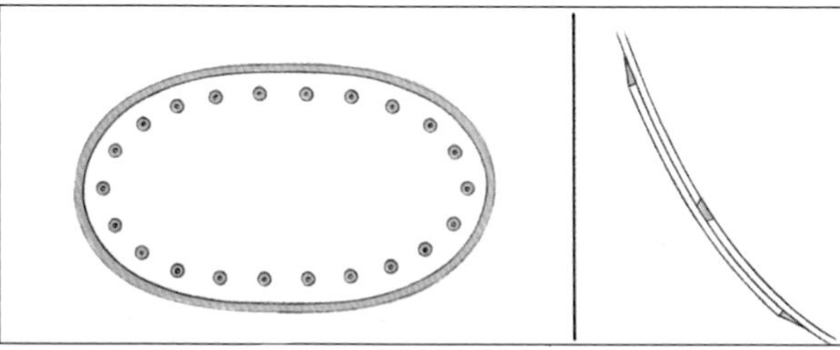

Wipe off excess caulking, using the remover recommended on the manufacturer's label. If the patch is to be painted, bevel the edges with caulking compound and a putty knife. Fill the original tear with compound and smooth the surface *(cross section, near left)*.

An Invisible Menace

Galvanic action is an electrochemical process with Jekyll-and-Hyde traits. When put to work in a battery, it creates the DC current that helps run a boat *(page 113)*. But under other circumstances, it may produce currents that mercilessly corrode crucial metal parts—or even the hull itself, if the boat is made of a volatile metal such as aluminum.

Galvanic action of this second type performs its destructive work if two uninsulated metals of different kinds are present under water. At launching, current will spontaneously begin to flow between them *(right)*. Of the two metals, only the one that reacts most strongly to the salts in the water will suffer corrosion.

Galvanic corrosion proceeds most rapidly when the two metals are close together on the boat, and especially when the immersing water is warm and salty. Sometimes the results are truly devastating. For example, a bronze rudder and propeller can swiftly turn a surrounding aluminum hull surface into a miniature moonscape if the bronze fittings are not properly insulated by inert substances, as shown opposite. For added insurance, a third, highly reactive metal—zinc, for example—should be introduced as a kind of decoy in the corrosive process *(opposite, right)*. The decoy will become the preferred partner in galvanic circuits, leaving the slightly less reactive aluminum safe until the decoy is completely gone—whereupon it can be replaced.

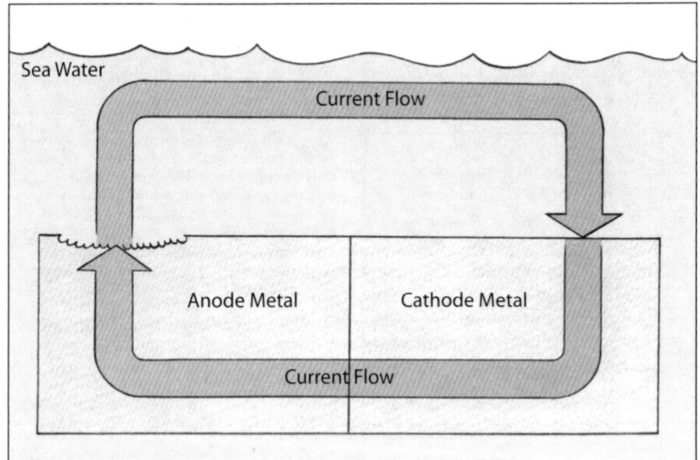

This schematic drawing shows the process of galvanic action that occurs when two dissimilar metals are immersed in a conductive solution like sea water. Electric current flows into the sea water from the anode—the scientific term applied to the metal that reacts most strongly to the salts in the water. The current then travels to the less reactive metal, called the cathode, and continues around in a circuit. The anode metal corrodes because ionized particles are electrochemically removed and carried into the water by the current.

Galvanic Pecking Order

Magnesium
Zinc
Aluminum
Cadmium
Mild steel
Wrought iron
Cast iron
Low-chromium stainless steel
Lead-tin solder
Lead
Tin
Brass
Copper
Bronze
Copper-nickel alloy
Nickel-copper alloy
High-chromium stainless steel (includes molybdenum)

This table ranks common marine metals according to their tendency to serve as the anode—and hence the victim of corrosion—in a galvanic circuit. A metal at the bottom of this list is known as passive—meaning that it contains elements, such as chromium or molybdenum, that render it less likely to corrode. The greater the difference between two metals, the more volatile is their partnership in galvanic action. Thus, a strong current will be set up between high-ranking aluminum and low-ranking bronze—and aluminum will be the victim.

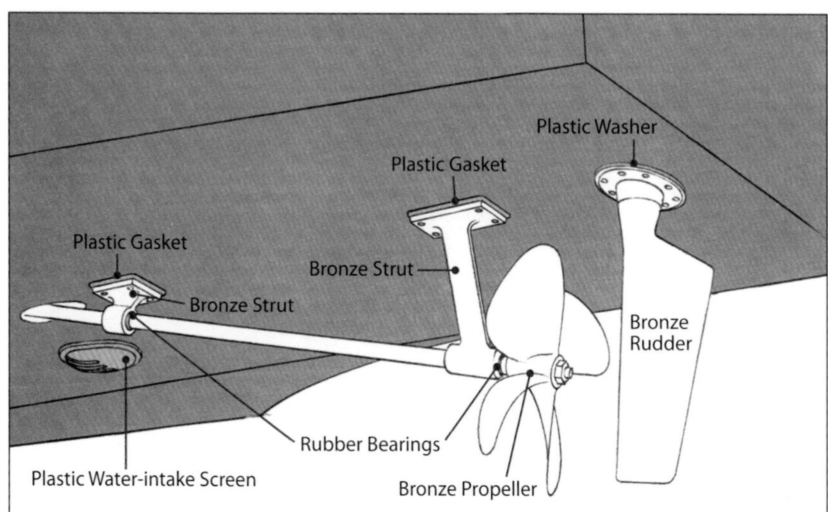

On an aluminum hull, the rudder, the propeller, its shaft and struts, and such fittings as the water-intake screen are commonly made of bronze, a strong and durable metal. Severe galvanic corrosion will occur unless these parts are insulated from the hull. Plastic gaskets or washers must be placed between the fittings and the aluminum; all fastenings must have plastic sleeves and washers; and rubber bearings must seal off the propeller shaft. Some metal fittings, such as the water-intake screen, can be exchanged for plastic versions.

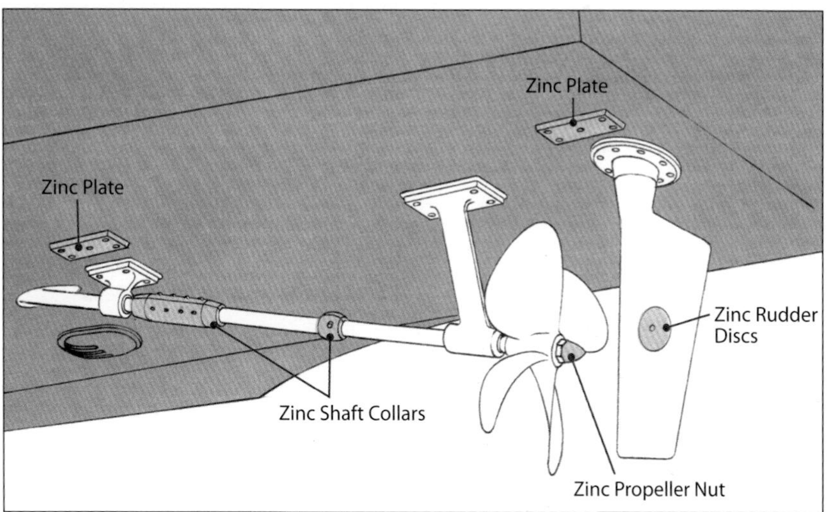

Special decoys, formally known as sacrificial anodes, should be installed at strategic points as double protection against galvanic corrosion. These sacrificial anodes include two-piece collars that can be bolted around the propeller shaft, plates bolted or welded to the hull close by bronze parts, a special terminal nut for the propeller and flat zinc discs through-bolted to each side of the rudder. As soon as a sacrificial anode has been eaten away, it should be replaced.

The Demands of Wood

Even in a world of tough plastics and versatile metal alloys, the virtues of wooden craft continue to attract many boatmen. Sturdy and resilient, they are also pleasing to the eye, and have a certain feel and smell and resonance that tradition-loving sailors find irresistible. But wood demands more vigilant maintenance than do many other boat-building materials. Frequent painting or varnishing is essential, for bare wood will absorb moisture and, under certain conditions, will fall prey to the fungus that causes dry rot.

Seams between planks must be caulked to make the hull watertight. And the screws that secure planks to frames must be inspected periodically for possible corrosion, which will not only weaken the screw but also create chemical reactions that break down the cellulose fibers in the surrounding wood. In time—possibly a most inopportune time—a plank may pull away from the boat's internal framework.

The first rule of wood-boat maintenance is to take care of all problems promptly. Check for screw corrosion or crumbling caulking before the yearly coat of paint goes on the hull. The cost of repairs will be far higher if defects are left unattended. Replacement of a plank is one repair task that demands more time and carpentry skill than the average boatman can muster.

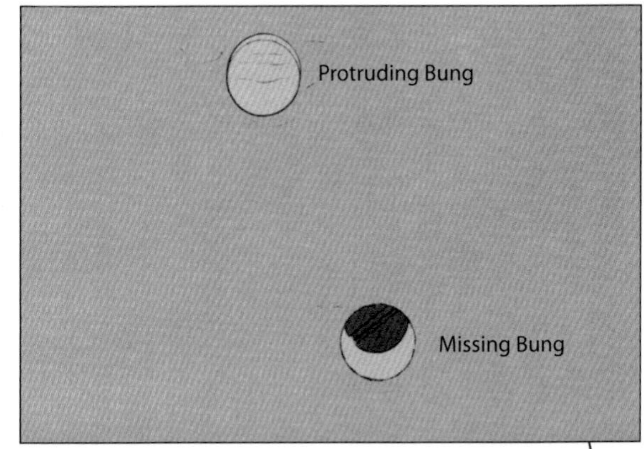

Faulty screws Protruding or missing bungs—the wood plugs inserted atop screwheads to protect the screws from water and damage—indicate possible fastening troubles. Corrosion of the screw can build up and force the bung out of its hole, or hull stresses may loosen the screw and force the bung free.

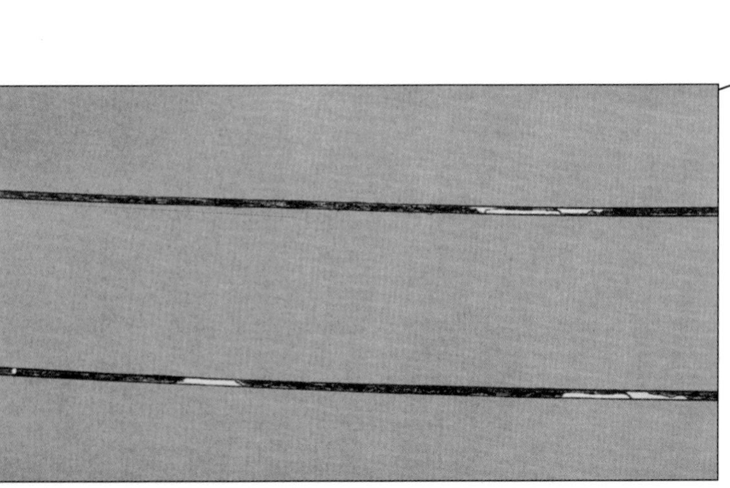

Leaky hull The seams between hull planks are filled with caulking—a packing of tough cotton fibers covered by a waterproofing compound—that can fail for a number of reasons. It may fall out when planks shrink during winter lay-up; it may work free because the planks themselves are loose; or it may simply shrivel away from old age. Leakage is not the only upshot; bottom paint will be lost at improperly caulked seams.

Leaky deck Loss of deck caulking will invite seepage of water into the cabin and also encourage rot in the deck planks and in their supporting beams. The compound is reasonably easy to replace; patching a rotted deck plank is a more demanding job but not so formidable as replacing a hull plank.

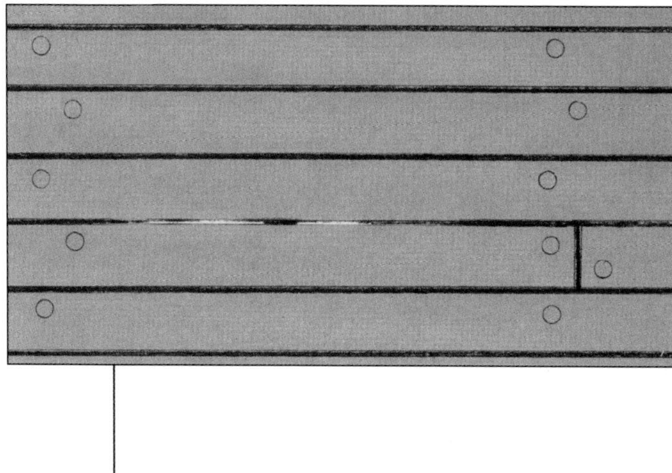

Dry rot The fungus responsible for rot develops at temperatures of 40° to 100° in wood with a moisture content of at least 20 percent that is not constantly immersed in water. The affliction can consume a plank and spread to the adjacent structure. The hull should be periodically checked by tapping with a hammer or carefully probing with a knife; any area that does not sound resonant or feels spongy must be promptly repaired.

To remove a protruding bung (1) in order to examine a screw suspected of being corroded, drill through the bung's center with a one-eighth-inch bit (2). Pry out the pieces of the bung with an awl (3), taking care not to mar the surface of the surrounding planking or the sides of the bung hole.

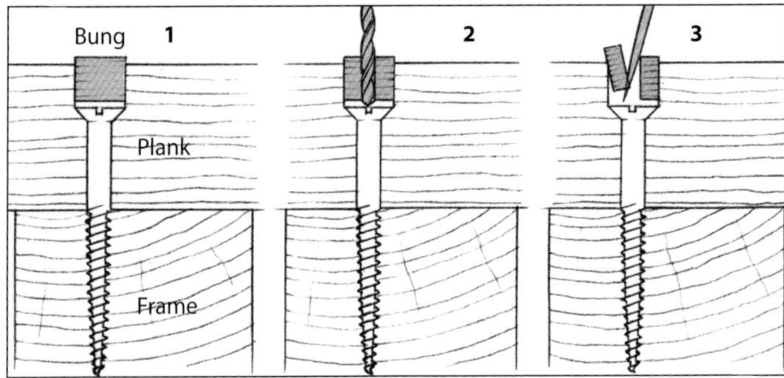

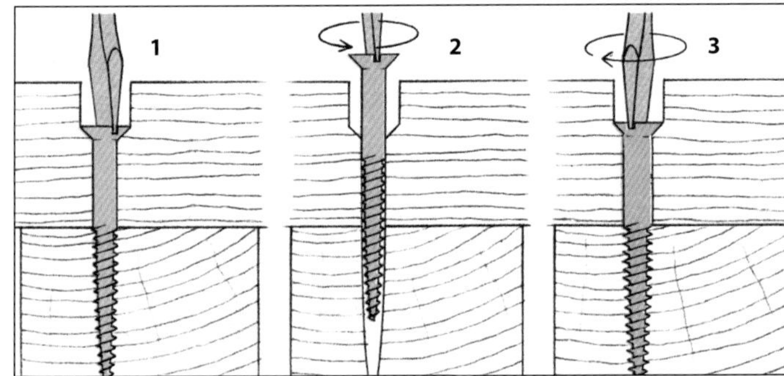

Insert a screwdriver that closely fits the screwhead, and tap the handle sharply with a hammer (1) in order to help loosen the grip of the screw threads. Withdraw the screw carefully (2) and examine its condition. If a replacement is necessary, coat the new screw with soap to lubricate it for driving into the wood (3). The new screw must be slightly larger and possibly longer than the old one so that it will hold securely in the fresh wood.

A replacement bung should be first coated with either glue, varnish, white lead, or thick paint to provide adhesion and a watertight fit. Insert the bung in the hole (1) and gently tap it in place. Let the adhesive harden for a day or two; then remove the excess bung by first cutting it near the top with a chisel (2) to determine the grain and to avoid chipping or splitting the bung off below the surface of the plank. Continue by reversing the chisel and working against the grain at a point slightly above the plank (3). Sand the bung flush with the plank, prime, and paint.

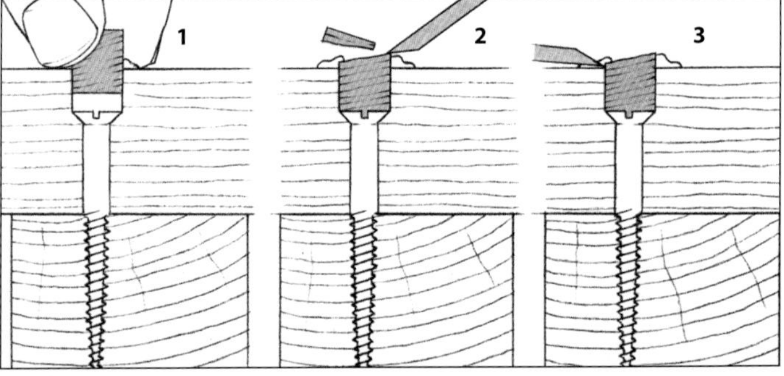

The Bygone Treenail

Until the turn of the century, wooden ships of 100 feet or more were fastened with pegs called treenails (pronounced—and sometimes spelled—"trunnels"). These hardwood dowels, ranging up to an inch across, were hammered into holes slightly smaller than their own diameters. Wooden wedges were driven into the split ends, and swelling of both plank and peg in water tightened the bond. Metal nails, easier to drive, eventually replaced treenails in boatbuilding, but their holding strength has never matched that of their predecessors.

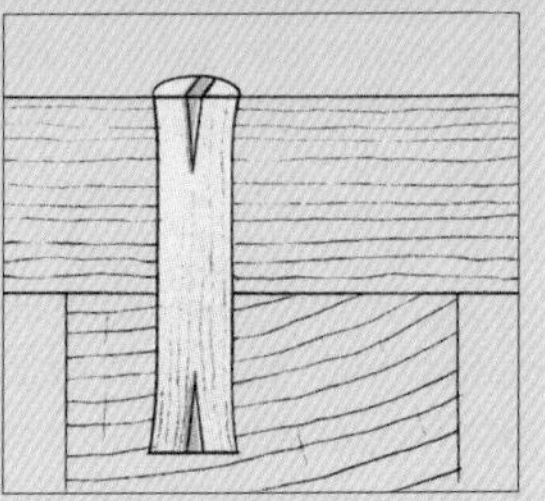

A Twist in Time

A thorough inspection of the screws that secure planking to hull frames is an important part of the annual fitting out. Corroded screws that the boatman fails to observe may loosen and let water into the hull; at the very least, they may create softness and eventual rot.

Any effective preventive-maintenance plan calls for inspection of each plank and the condition of the wooden bungs often used to cover and protect the fastenings.

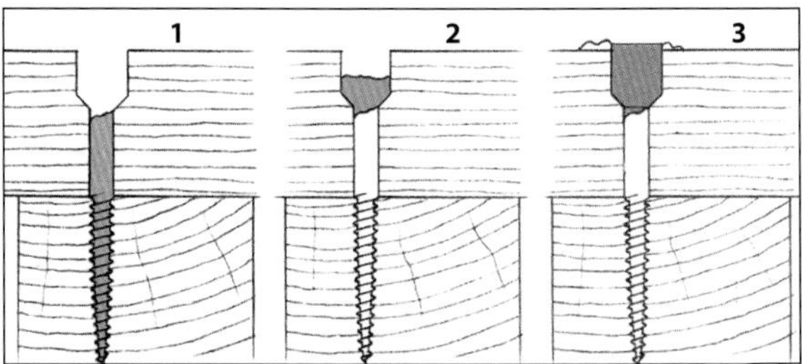

If a screw cannot be removed because its head has broken off or corroded away (1), pack the void with a wood plastic putty (2). Whittle the end of a new bung to fit the sloping sides where the screwhead existed; coat it with an adhesive; tap it into place (3); then shave and sand the bung smooth.

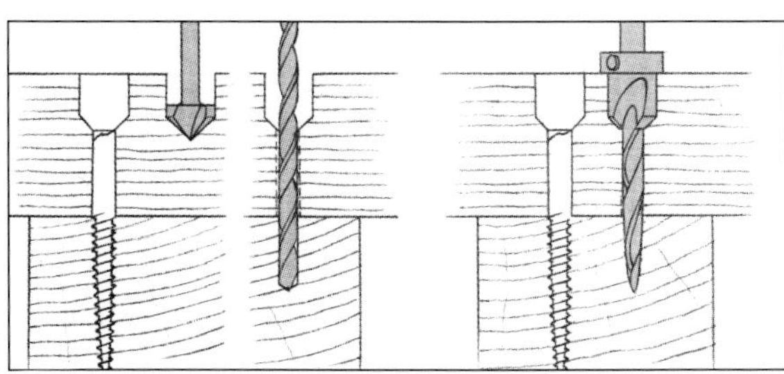

As close as possible to the old screw, drill a new hole by one of the methods diagramed above. In the traditional technique *(right)*, a countersink is used to drill the bung hole and to make a recess for the screwhead; then a "pilot" hole is drilled to half the depth of the screw's threaded portion. In hardwood, it may be necessary to widen the pilot hole with a second drill in order to accommodate the shank. A simpler method involves a combination drill that performs all the steps in one operation; an adjustable collar determines the depth of the hole.

A Guide to Proper-sized Screws

This chart gives recommended screw lengths and gauges (a measure of diameter), as well as diameters of pilot and countersink holes, to ensure adequate fastenings for various plank thicknesses. For decking, the screws can be a gauge smaller than the ones that are given here.

Plank thickness	⅝"	¾"	⅞"	1"	1⅛"	1¼"	1½"
Screw length	1¼"	1½"	1¾"	2"	2¼"	2½"	3"
Screw gauge	#9	#10	#12	#14	#16	#18	#20
Pilot-hole diameter	7/64"	7/64"	⅛"	9/64"	5/32	3/16"	13/64"
Countersink and bung diameter	⅜"	½"	½"	½"	⅝"	⅝"	¾"

A bung that appears to be the source of rust stains or that is projecting slightly from a plank is often an indication of a defective screw. As each such bung is found, it should be encircled with chalk for easy spotting and removal later. Since the presence of a bad screw is not always indicated by a popped or projecting bung, remove a few sound ones at widely scattered locations, as an additional check on the condition of the screws. Every bung that has been removed must be replaced.

If a screw is so badly corroded that it cannot be withdrawn and replaced, it should be sealed off with wood or epoxy putty and a new bung should be driven in place. Then a new screw hole should be drilled and a new screw installed as near as possible to the old one, but well in from the edge of the frame to which the plank is being refastened. New screws should be of the same material as the old, since dissimilar metals can corrode by electro-chemical reaction, even though they are separated by wood.

Recaulking Seams

Even the soundest planking, securely fastened, will fail to keep out water if the filler called caulking, which seals up the seams between the planks, begins to work loose or dry out. Replacing this caulking is an exacting art, nearly as old as boatbuilding itself; but any adroit boatman, by carefully observing a professional hand like the one whose work is shown on these pages, can learn to do the job.

Today's materials, available at most marine-supply stores, are synthetic-rubber sealant in lieu of the tar and cotton of days past. (Sealant alone will suffice for the shallow deck seams of some boats, as shown on pages 46–47.)

Old caulking is "raked" out, as at right. The new caulking, when it is firmly driven, should fill the raked seams to about one half of their depth, thus leaving room for the covering layer of sealant that will keep out water.

However, if too much cotton is wedged between the planks with a caulking iron, when the planks absorb moisture and swell up, the cotton may create pressures that will loosen the fastenings, force the planks from the hull frames, or even fracture the frames themselves. But if the job is done correctly, the boat should stay watertight for 15 years or more before it again needs recaulking.

Readying a vessel for spring launching, a professional pulls old caulking out of a hull seam—an operation known as raking. Recaulking is most often necessary when the sealant covering the cotton dries out or simply falls out from between open seams.

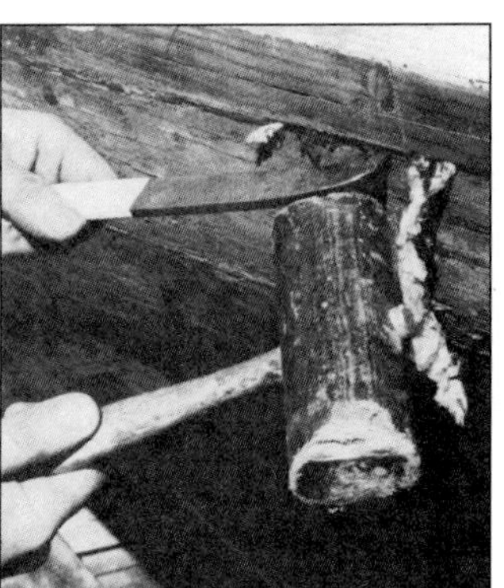

Raking is done with a wooden mallet and a raking tool, like those below, made from an old file. When raking, tap the point of the tool into the seam to hook the cotton; then drive the raker along the seam with the mallet, removing the old strips of caulking a few inches at a time. Next, clean out the seam with a stiff wire brush.

Tailor-made Scrapers

A curious facet of the caulker's art is the commercial unavailability of seam scraping tools, also known as clearing or reefing irons. Most professionals fashion their own from worn-out files, and a skillful amateur can do likewise. At right are three such tools, one *(top)* for shallow deck seams and two for the hull. Each was made by grinding one end of a file to a sharp point of precisely the right shape to fit a particular seam width, then heating that end cherry-red and bending it to the correct angle. Since no ordinary home stove or fire can come close to delivering the necessary heat, most boatowners will seek out the owner of a boatyard—or blacksmith—who, for a few dollars, will grind, heat and bend a file to the proper shape.

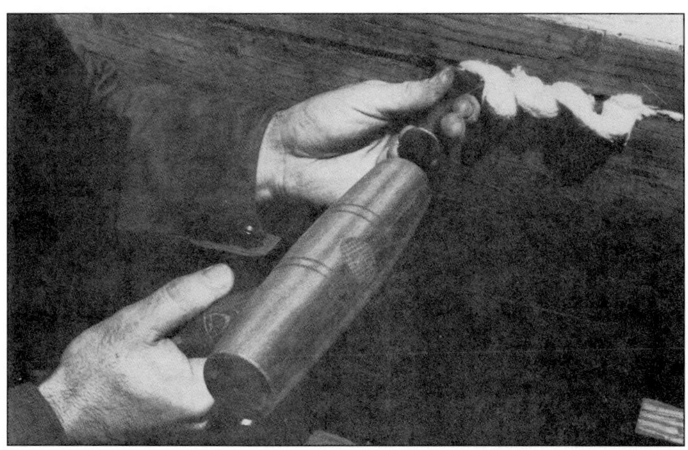

Caulking is forced between the planks with a chisel-like iron available from marine-supply stores. The iron should be lightly oiled and filed free of burrs to prevent its snagging on the cotton. With light taps of the mallet, force a length of cotton into a seam at six-inch intervals, being sure there is enough cotton to be bunched at wide places. Then go back and drive it home. With a little experience, the snugness of the cotton in a seam can be gauged both by its resistance to mallet blows and by the metallic ring of the caulking iron as the cotton is driven home.

Using a narrow seam brush, paint the cotton and wood inside the seam with the primer specified by the manufacturer of the sealant that will be used. The primer is absorbed by the cotton and helps to keep it watertight. Some experts paint the seam before driving in the cotton, to protect any bare wood.

After the primer is dry, insert elastic sealant in the seam, using a putty knife to force it firmly in place and to expel any air bubbles. Fill the seam to a level just below the surface; the sealant will be squeezed up flush when the planks swell after launching. Wipe away any excess from the surrounding planking.

Sealing a Deck

Deck seams are usually recaulked in the same manner as hull seams. But on about one boat in five, the deck seams are too shallow to accommodate cotton; in such cases they are waterproofed by the technique demonstrated on these pages—an easier job, since no hammering is required in either raking or filling them. When raking *(right)*, pull the hand-tooled scraper along the seam to remove the old sealant. Then sweep the seam free of any residue with a wire brush.

After a seam has been raked clean, lay wide strips of masking tape along both sides and both ends of it to keep the new sealant off the deck. Press the tape down firmly so that the filler will not creep under. Be sure the planks on either side are well covered, since the sealant will spread during the job.

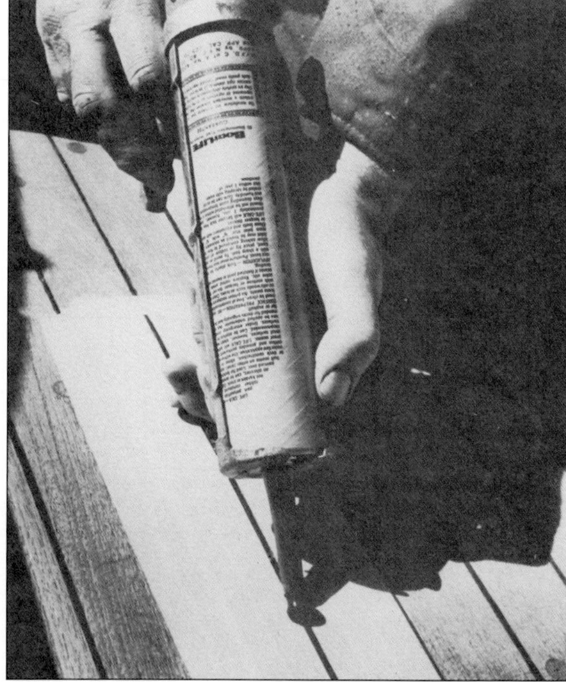

An inexpensive caulking gun, available at marine-supply stores, will speed up the job of refilling seams. Load the gun with a cartridge of synthetic-rubber deck sealant (it resembles hull sealant but is more heat resistant, since it will be baked by the sun). Insert the nozzle well into the seam, then squeeze the trigger slowly and steadily while moving the nozzle along. Overfill the seam slightly.

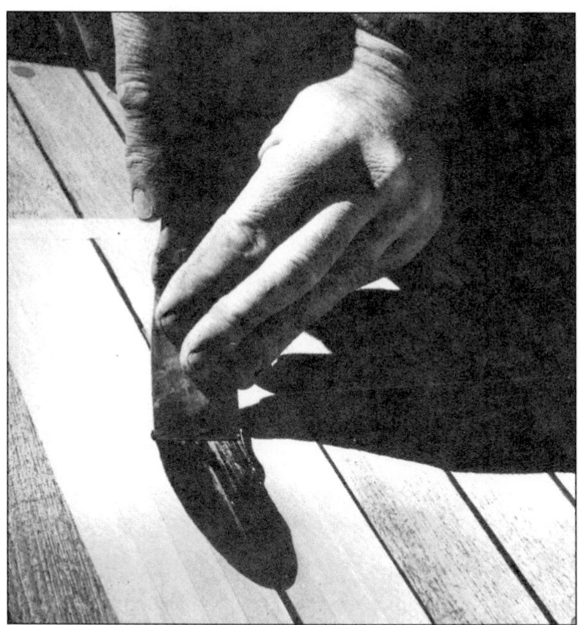

With a putty knife, force the sealant firmly into the seam to expel any air bubbles and fill all voids. At this point, the seam should be filled flush with the deck, because the filler will later shrink a bit as it dries.

After the sealant has dried to a tacky consistency, remove the masking tape with a slow, steady pull. If the compound is still soft, it may pull out of the seam along with the tape; if it has hardened completely, it may tear unevenly along the edges as the tape is removed. Since the time required for drying will vary with weather conditions, consult the directions on the cartridge.

The Devil to Pay

Mariners of past centuries called the process of slathering hot pitch into a seam "paying," and often they had to pay in a hurry. To expose seams below the waterline for recaulking, they moored their vessels in shallows where the receding tide would leave them high and dry *(right)*. The returning tide limited working time to 12 hours or so, and less than that for recaulking the seam next to the keel—the last seam uncovered by the ebbing tide and the first to go under when the waters returned. Sailors called the seam the "devil" because it had to be payed quickly, or the ship might well fill up and stay on the bottom. The phrase for their predicament—"the devil to pay"—passed into popular usage as a succinct description of any desperate situation.

Crouching under his broad-beamed ketch—built 53 years earlier in the Canary Islands—Hans Schneider measures the space left by the removal of a rotted plank to determine the width of its replacement. All the bottom planks except those being considered for removal have been given a coat of primer as a protection during the lay-up.

A Masterly Repair

Replacing a rotten plank in a wood hull appears relatively simple when the job is being carried out by an accomplished shipwright like the Florida craftsman shown on these pages. And although a talented weekend amateur could succeed at the job, he should think twice before tackling it. Replanking demands excellence in woodworking—especially if the repairs are to be done below the waterline, where mistakes could destroy a boat. Still, for a boatman with the appropriate skills, few undertakings are more satisfying.

The successful restoration of the deteriorating hull shown here is the work of Hans Schneider, a Swiss-bom skipper who bought a hefty but hard-used ketch and rebuilt it. As replacement lumber for several rotted planks near the bow, Schneider chose pine—the same as the hull's original wood and thus possessing the same degree of flexibility.

The new planks were subjected to three different shaping operations. Their inboard face required a special curvature to fit the hull's supporting frames; their edges had to be beveled to receive caulking compound; and the planks had to be bent lengthwise to conform to the hull.

Professionals ordinarily bend a plank by steaming it; however, the Florida boatyard where Schneider did his work lacked steaming equipment, and he had to resort to a laborious method—pulling a new plank against a frame with lines, securing it with screws and repeating the operation on the next frame. Between these and other exacting chores, Schneider toiled for three full weeks before the hull was ready for the sea.

With a carpenter's rule, Schneider measures the thickness of an adjoining plank in order to supply a matching mate. The inboard surface of the plank will be given a concave shape for a snug fit against the bend of the frames. This shaping is done manually with a hollow plane, a tool with a curved blade rather than the conventional straight one.

The rotted plank is fitted over a new pine board and secured in place with C-clamps to serve as a template. After its outline is traced, the new version will be cut with a circular power saw, then shaped with a plane.

With the new plank cut to shape, Schneider searches for raised spots along the plank by sliding a tool called a combination square along its surface. The square has in its handle a transparent tube of liquid with one bubble at its center. Any bump or bulge causes the bubble to move off center; pencil marks are then made at each irregularity, to indicate where the plank should be planed.

Schneider fairs off his spots on the plank with an old-fashioned but efficient tool called a spokeshave. Its handle grips, fixed on either side of a blade, enable the carpenter to pull the tool toward him, planing off the wood.

With the plank temporarily secured by lines, rows of screw holes are drilled with a brace and bit at each point where the new board crosses a frame. To bend the plank to the hull's shape for fastening at the next frame, Schneider will lean against it, then take up slack on the horizontal line, whose other end is tied to the base of the mast inside the hull.

Using a screwdriver bit set in the brace, Schneider now fastens the plank to the boat's stem, the principal structural member at its bow. A wood block has been bolted over the forward end of the bent plank to absorb the pressure until all the screws are in place.

Before painting, Schneider smooths the new planking with a disc sander. Earlier, he planed the edges of the adjoining boards to create an outgauge—a V-shaped space between planks that makes the application of caulking easier. The red on the new lumber is paint picked up by the sander from primed areas.

A coat of red-lead primer is brushed onto the freshly sanded area—and well into the seams. Since the wood is raw and highly absorptive, Schneider will lay on several coats of primer instead of the standard two called for on previously primed surfaces where the paint has been removed.

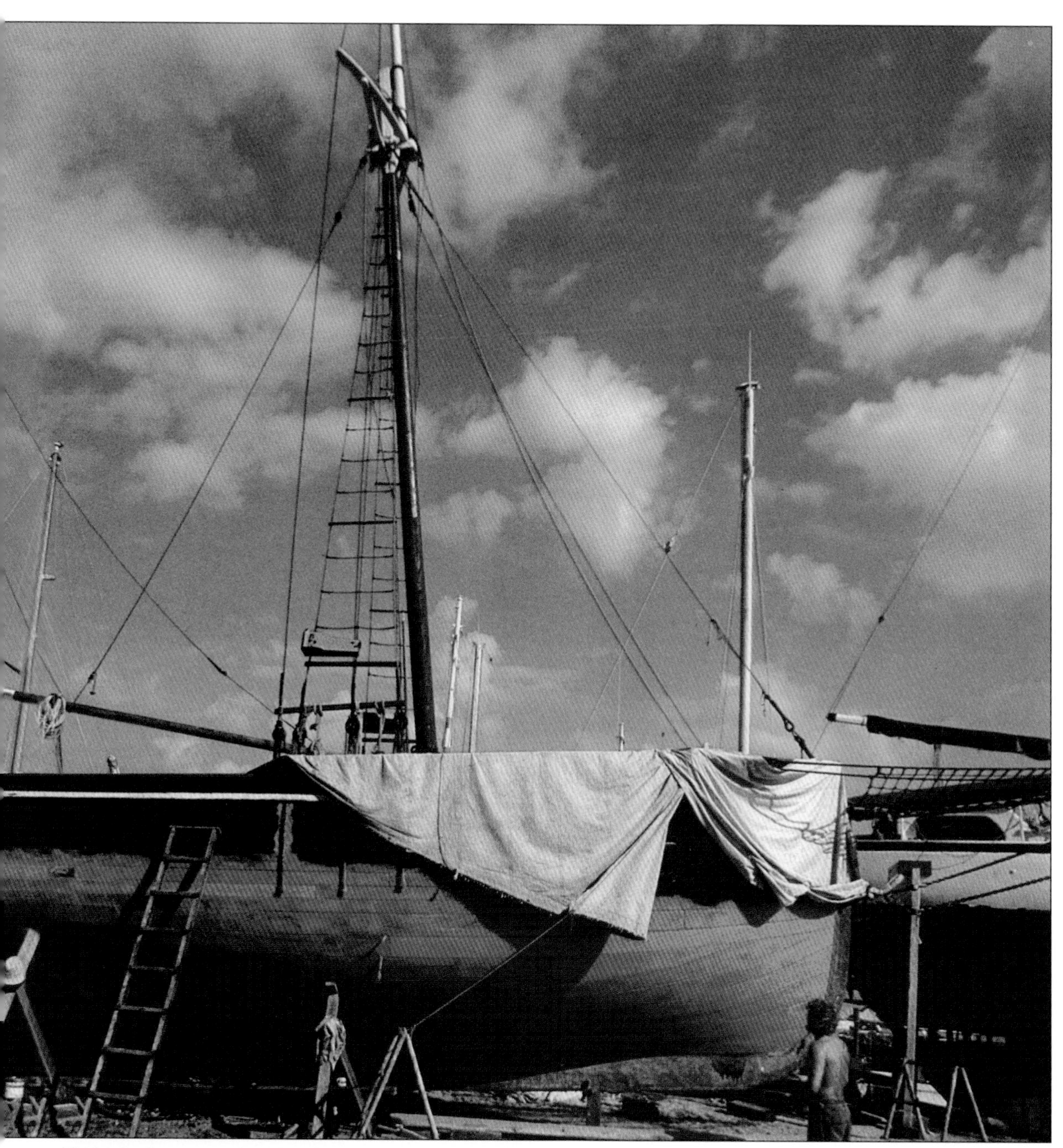

Waiting for the primer to dry, Schneider steps back to admire his work. He will give the topsides a fresh coat of paint, then apply antifouling paint to the bottom. After that, the hull will be ready to be tested in the sea.

CHAPTER 2: Painting

Wind, salt spray, and sunlight are an extraordinarily destructive combination, yet most boats are protected from them—and from underwater growths that could encumber or even destroy a hull—by nothing more than a layer of paint or varnish two or three millimeters thick. Replenishing this shield at regular intervals is perhaps the most critical of all maintenance tasks, since even the heaviest steel and timber, without adequate protection, can be quickly reduced to so much rust or rot.

A couple of centuries ago, seamen guarded decks and topsides against rot by brushing on linseed oil twice a year; overlapping sheets of copper were tacked on hull bottoms to ward off barnacles. Today, copper sheathing is still used by some yachtsmen in the tropics, where marine pests can be devastating, but copper-based antifouling paint serves for most boatmen elsewhere. Linseed oil, meanwhile, has given way to an almost inexhaustible variety of topsides finishes that are vastly superior in durability, completeness of protection, and esthetic value. Yet for all these technological advances, painting or varnishing a boat remains a demanding job—one that calls for forethought and scrupulously careful execution.

The first rule in painting is to read and follow the directions on the container. Then, before committing himself to a new shade or type of paint, a boatman would be wise to apply it first to a small area. This will provide a clearer look at the color than any paint chart could offer. It will also warn of such problems as improper adhesion due to a chemically incompatible surface beneath; for example, a vinyl or epoxy paint may soften an oil-based paint beneath, causing both coats to lift off the hull. Before painting, a surface should be dust-free and dry.

Fiberglass hulls present special problems. The topsides gel coat will stand up for many years without painting, provided it is waxed, buffed, and polished each spring and fall, and given an adequate winter cover. If this treatment is omitted, the gel coat will grow dull and dingy, and painting will eventually become necessary, if only to improve the boat's looks. However, the job should be relegated to professionals, since a dust-free, humidity-controlled environment is required to make the paint adhere properly and to achieve anything like the luster of the original gel coat. The bottom of a fiberglass hull is another story. As on other types of boats, it needs a yearly coat of antifouling paint. This can be applied outdoors by any amateur.

Though some sort of annual bout with a paintbrush is—or should be—inescapable, it need not be a tiresome chore. Since painting and varnishing are best done on bright, beautiful days, the weather alone can be a tonic. And if the work is performed in a boatyard, the novice sailor will discover that there is a special camaraderie at fitting-out time, and that veterans are only too willing to lend a tool or a bit of friendly advice.

Applying bottom paint to the Caribbean cruising ketch Firebird, a skipper nears the end of his annual fitting-out chores, a final step before the boat is launched.

FIREBIRD
ST. THOMAS

Picking a Finish

Planning is as important a part of painting a boat as wielding the brush. And choosing the right paints—in the right colors—may be as vital to the boat's appearance as flawless technique.

Paradoxically, the problem has been compounded by the technological improvements made in the quality of paints in recent years. Modern marine paints come in many types *(right)* for boating's many specialized uses. The new paints tend to last longer and protect surfaces better than the familiar linseed-oil-based paints. However, the new compounds are chemically complex and do not always get along together. Some may never dry completely if applied over a different type, while others actually act as paint removers. Consequently, compatibility is vital, and it is sound procedure to stick to a single manufacturer's products, and to keep a list of what has been applied.

The bright spectrum of colors offered by modern paints poses a great temptation to the yachtsman with a secret yearning to go to sea in a blaze of fire-engine red or a gleam of deep purple. However, most yachtsmen still settle for white, and the chief reason, surprisingly, is ease of upkeep. Dark colors absorb a lot of heat, which can crack and blister paint, and cause it to fade. White paint, by contrast, reflects the sun's rays. Though stains are conspicuous on a white hull, it is easier to scrub them off than those on a dark hull.

Pastels have some of the advantages of white and add a bit of color as well. But they create other problems. Pastels fade, and then are nearly impossible to match.

Even the type of finish is important. A glossy finish is sleek and handsome, but tends to accentuate small surface imperfections in the hull. Semigloss paints, while not so shiny as the glossy paints at first, may look better after a season afloat. They are softer than the glossy paints and their outer surfaces wear away in a process called chalking, eliminating stains to such an extent that some enthusiasts refer to them as "self-cleaning."

Finally, a boatman should think about what parts of the boat he paints what color. How he decides may influence his boat's appearance in ways he scarcely suspects, as is demonstrated by the pictures on the following pages.

Paints for All Purposes

Today's marine paints fall into four general categories based on the type of synthetic resin used in their manufacture: alkyds, vinyls, polyurethanes, and epoxies. A paint that serves well for one job might not do well for another, so the choice should be made carefully, following the guidelines in the chart below.

Type	Use	Advantages	Disadvantages
Alkyds	All above-water surfaces.	Comes in greatest variety of colors. Dries fast. Is relatively inexpensive.	Does not adhere to fiberglass. Is not particularly durable.
Vinyls	Primarily used for bottoms, but can be used on topsides.	Flexible and abrasion resistant. Is highly recommended for aluminum.	Tends to lift all paints except other vinyls.
Polyurethanes	Above-water surfaces. Excellent for use in areas exposed to high salinity, hot sun and pollution.	Is abrasion resistant. Easy to apply. Excellent for tropical waters.	Relatively expensive.
Epoxies	All surfaces.	Highly adhesive. Weather-resistant and durable. Excellent for ferro-cement and metal.	Poor color retention. Usually more expensive than other paints.

A white yacht, like the sport fisherman below, tends to look longer and seem larger than a dark boat. Since white paint reflects sunlight, white boats are considerably cooler inside and also underfoot. But glossy white will inevitably create glare, so a pastel color for the decks and cabin tops may be easier on the crew's eyes and temper. White surfaces also show the dirt more than pastels do, and therefore they need to be frequently washed down with a mild detergent.

The same boat, with both hull and superstructure painted a dark blue, looks smaller. Dark hulls also tend to be warmer inside and can become uncomfortably hot in warm climates. The retained heat, moreover, calls for extra maintenance, especially on wood boats.

A dark cabin on the sport fisherman makes the yacht look top heavy, destroying the sleekness of its fore-and-aft lines. This unfortunate combination may have appeared attractive in the boatyard, but on the water it makes the boat look chunky. And at anchor in the summertime, when no breeze is blowing through it, the dark-painted cabin will tend to be stuffy; on the outside, whether anchored or underway, it can be painfully hot to a sun worshiper's exposed flesh.

Long a favorite pattern of yachtsmen, the combination of dark hull and white cabin house makes a boat look solid and deeply set in the water. It is easily kept clean around the decks and cabin, while the dark hull hides the nicks and scuff marks that inevitably accumulate on the topsides of a boat that is frequently docked.

Narrow stripes of color at the waterline give the sport fisherman a racy look accenting a solid-white hull. The lower stripe, adjoining the bottom paint, is called a boot top, and is commonly used alone. It is especially sensible for a light-colored boat navigating in polluted waters, since white paint at the waterline is highly vulnerable to oil and grease stains. Two thin stripes separated by a narrow band of the topside color, as shown here, provide a sporty alternative.

A broad stripe along the sheer line is another device to relieve the uniformity of a white boat, while also setting off the hull from the superstructure. Sheer is one of the distinctive traits of a boat's design, and the color stripe emphasizes the hull's graceful lines.

The Science of Sanding

Once the paint has been selected, the boat must be prepared for repainting. If the existing paint is relatively sound, a good sanding may be all that is required. If a large area needs refinishing, an orbital power sander will speed up the work enormously. It is designed for light work, and is the least likely to do damage. It can even be used, carefully, to sand across the grain of wood, a procedure not normally recommended.

In areas too small for a power sander, hand sanding is the only answer. A sanding block *(bottom right)* will assist in this chore; it puts more weight behind the paper and keeps the pressure even. A coarse grade of paper is normally used at first, with other grades employed later *(below).*

Wearing a mask because she is taking down the toxic antifouling paint on her boat's underwater areas, a crew member hand sands the rudder. It would be possible to employ a power sander here, but with extreme care to avoid removing too much paint and damaging the trailing edge of the rudder. Other underwater areas that call for special care while being sanded down to remove old finishes are the leading edges of keels, centerboards, and spade rudders.

Choosing the Right Paper

Sandpaper for everyday marine use comes in three basic types, each divided into a wide range of grades.

Flint paper, the familiar household type, comes in five grades: extra coarse, coarse, medium, fine, and extra fine. Coarser grades are used for rough work, others for finishing.

Aluminum oxide open-coat production paper has virtually replaced flint paper for boat work. More expensive but longer lasting, it is graded by number from 36 for the coarsest grain to 280 for the finest. Grades 36 to 50 are used only on very rough, bare wood, 120 for smoothing between coats of paint.

Silicon carbide paper is both the most expensive and the finest grained. Designed primarily for sanding between coats of paint or varnish, its grades run from 80 to 500. One variety of silicon carbide paper is made with a special adhesive that enables it to be used either dry or wet. Often employed to polish the bottoms of racing sailboats, it comes in grades 220 to 600.

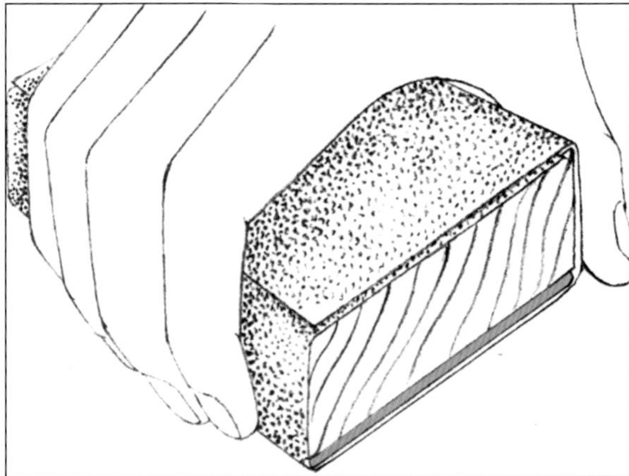

This two-and-a-half by five-and-a-half inch sanding block, three-fourths of an inch thick, fits the hand well and takes a half sheet of nine by eleven inch paper. Felt or carpet glued to the bottom helps the sandpaper to conform to curved surfaces.

Stripping Down

In the life of every boat—and owner—there comes the unhappy time when simply sanding down and painting over last year's finish will no longer suffice. If large areas of the hull are cracked and peeling, the old paint must be stripped off and a whole new surface applied.

Although much of a hull's badly worn paint can be removed with a scraper, stubborn patches will require a chemical removing agent (but never use chemical paint remover on fiberglass). When using a paint remover, apply it liberally and give it time to work, as specified by the manufacturer's label. Two or more coats may be needed. Remove the softened paint with a putty knife or scraper between applications. When all the old paint is off, the surface should be rinsed with a compatible solvent, otherwise the remover's residue may undermine the new paint. Once the hull is bare it must be primed. The proper primer depends on the surface to be covered. Wood hulls need to be sealed against the weather. Fiberglass is primed to provide adhesion for the covering coats.

Steel and aluminum boats require special care. Both metals should first be washed with an etching solution that gives the surface an adhesive tooth for the paint. Then a primer with the proper chemical base must be selected, since the wrong primer may encourage corrosion if incompatible antifouling paints are applied over them. The copper oxides in many antifouling paints can interact with a metal hull and destroy it. Paints with tin as the antifouling agent are safer. The most practical primer for either steel or aluminum is zinc chromate.

After the hull surface has been primed, all dents and cracks should be filled. So-called trowel cement is used to fill small imperfections on wooden topsides and decks; for larger areas, surfacing compounds are used. Most of these are easily applied directly from their containers. Epoxy and polyester fillers, the only fillers that stick well to fiberglass but which are used on other surfaces as well, are packaged in two containers, one of which contains a resin and the other a catalyst. The two parts must be mixed together.

Pressing the blade of a scraper flat against the hull, a boat owner removes a heavy, flawed layer of old bottom paint. When scraping a boat, long, even strokes are best; on a wood surface follow the grain. Tilting the scraper or cutting across the work at right angles should be avoided, since either of these actions will gouge the hull. Taking off paint is a task that calls for a sharp scraper; it may even be necessary to sharpen the blade as often as every few minutes.

The secret of applying primers is to use a large brush to speed up the work. Fine brushwork is less important than adequate coverage; no bare spots should be left, and on wood boats the primer should be worked in well. One or two coats of primer will be sufficient for most surfaces. However, depending on the choice of antifouling paint, a metal boat may require as many as seven coats of primer.

A boatowner uses a putty knife to mix the two parts of an epoxy compound. If too much of the catalyst or the resin is used, the mixture may harden too quickly or too slowly. In the one case, nothing can be done except to mix up a fresh batch of compound, but in the other, either a heat lamp or more catalyst can be used to speed up the reaction. But even if the compound is properly mixed, hot weather may cause it to set too fast.

The skipper at left is fairing out his hull with trowel cement, using two putty knives, one for application and the other to keep a handy supply; only small portions are usually required. Most fillers shrink slightly when they dry, so it is best to overfill the dent or crack. Depressions of more than a half inch should be filled with several layers. Each one should be completely dry before the next is added.

Toward the Perfect Coat

An indispensable part of a perfect coat of paint is the patience with which it is applied. Experience and a deft touch with a paintbrush help *(page 64)*, but what really counts is the painter's attention to details—not the least of which is deciding in advance how much paint he will need for the job *(right)*.

Another important aspect is the weather. Paint is best applied to a surface in the shade on a dry and windless day when the temperature lies between 50° and 80° F. Colder weather keeps a paint from drying, and too much heat makes paint dry too fast, leaving visible brush strokes. High humidity also keeps paint from drying; and, even in dry weather, dew may form in the early evening hours. Airborne dust, as well, can be a problem. To help overcome it some painters hose down the area around their boats before they even open a can of paint.

Preparing the paint is as important as readying the surface. Ingredients must be thoroughly mixed. Many hardware and marine-supply stores mix the paint they sell with a mechanical shaker. Nevertheless, to be certain no residue remains on the bottom of the can, a lengthy stirring by hand, or with a mixing wheel attached to an electric drill, is still advisable. High-gloss paints should be stirred, not shaken, to avoid creating air bubbles.

For best results in mixing, the thin liquid at the top of the can should first be poured into a separate container. The thicker material at the bottom of the can should be thoroughly mixed and then stirred together with the lighter paint. The "skin" that forms on the surface of previously opened paints must be removed by straining the paint through a piece of cheesecloth or a paper strainer available at marine-supply stores.

When ready to begin painting, do not carry around the full quart or gallon of paint as you work. Instead, pour a small quantity of paint into a paper container or tin that can be held comfortably in one hand. Seal the remainder as tightly as possible and set it aside.

Enough Paint for the Job

The chart below shows how much paint will be needed to put two coats on all the important areas of various-sized boats. The amounts are approximate, and have been calculated for boats that have previously been painted. For bare primed wood, amounts should be doubled. In general, a little more paint than seems necessary should be on hand; it is far better to have a bit left over than to run out late on a Sunday afternoon with the job unfinished.

Boat type	Topsides	Bottom	Boot top	Deck	Flying bridge	Interior
14' Rowboat	2 qts.	1 qt.				
14' Outboard	1 qt.	1 qt.	½ pt.	1 pt.		
18' Runabout	1 qt.	3 qts.	½ pt.	1 qt.		
20' Sailboat	2 qts.	3 qts.	½ pt.	3 qts.		
24' Runabout	2 qts.	3 qts.	½ pt.	1½ qts.		
25' Cruiser	3 qts.	3 qts.	1 pt.	2 qts.		2 qts.
32' Cruiser	2 gals.	1½ gals.	1 pt.	2 qts.	1 pt.	2 qts.
36' Sailboat	2 gals.	2 gals.	1 pt.	1 gal.		3 qts.
40' Cruiser	2½ gals.	2 gals.	1 pt.	1½ gals.	1 qt.	1 gal.

Start by test-painting a small area to ascertain how the fresh paint reacts with old paint on the surface; after a few brush strokes wait a while to see how the paint dries. If the new paint is hard to spread or dries with evident brush marks, thin it slightly with the solvent recommended by the manufacturer. Always sand lightly between coats, and bear in mind that two thin coats give a smoother finish than only one thick one.

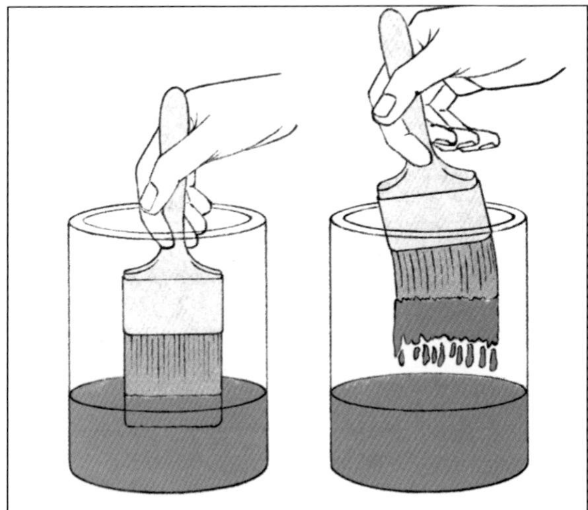

The first step in painting is to fill a container—anything from a coffee can to a special cardboard paint bucket—with no more than three or four inches of paint. To prevent overloading that might cause runs on the painted surface, only about a third of the brush should be dipped into the paint. The excess should be tapped off inside the container, rather than wiped on the rim, to prevent drips from running down the sides.

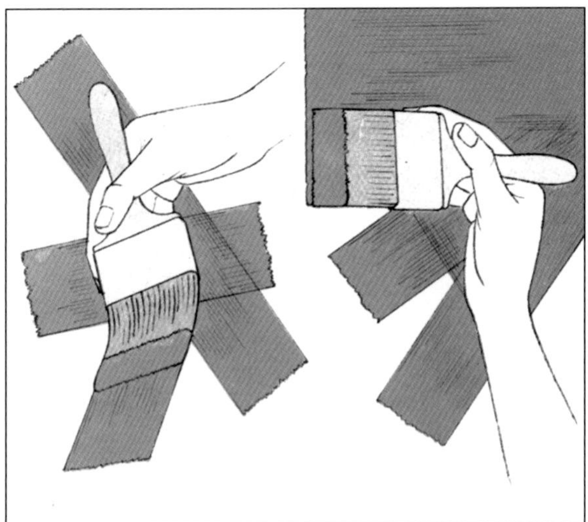

The first few strokes of paint should be brushed on in all directions *(left)*, since the purpose is to cover the surface and spread the paint evenly. But the final strokes *(right)* should run back and forth in the same line.

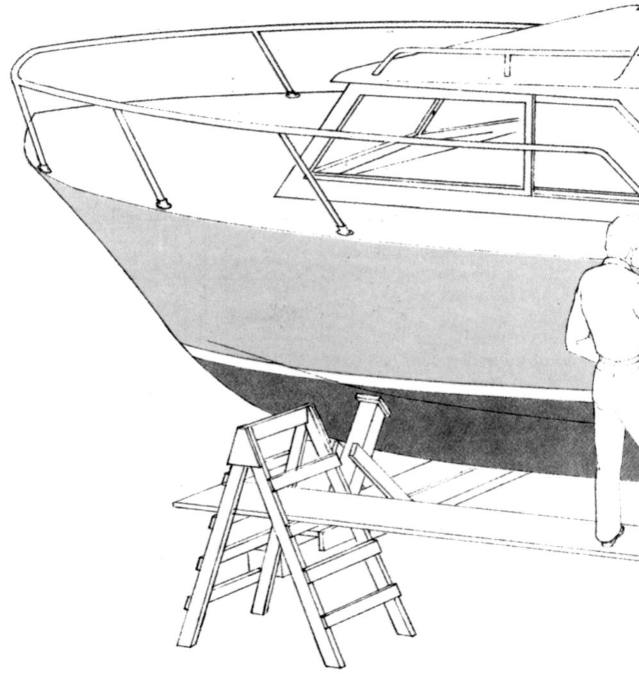

Painting a hull, a right-handed worker should move clockwise around the boat, a left-hander counterclockwise. This enables him to put his brush first onto an unpainted surface, and then finish by stroking back and forth into an already painted area, thus preventing conspicuous overlaps. It is wise to stop every so often and go back to check for drips or "holidays"—spots that the brush missed. Painting higher than shoulder level is not only tiring, but allows paint to run into the heel of the brush, overloading it. The solution is to rig a conveniently high scaffold.

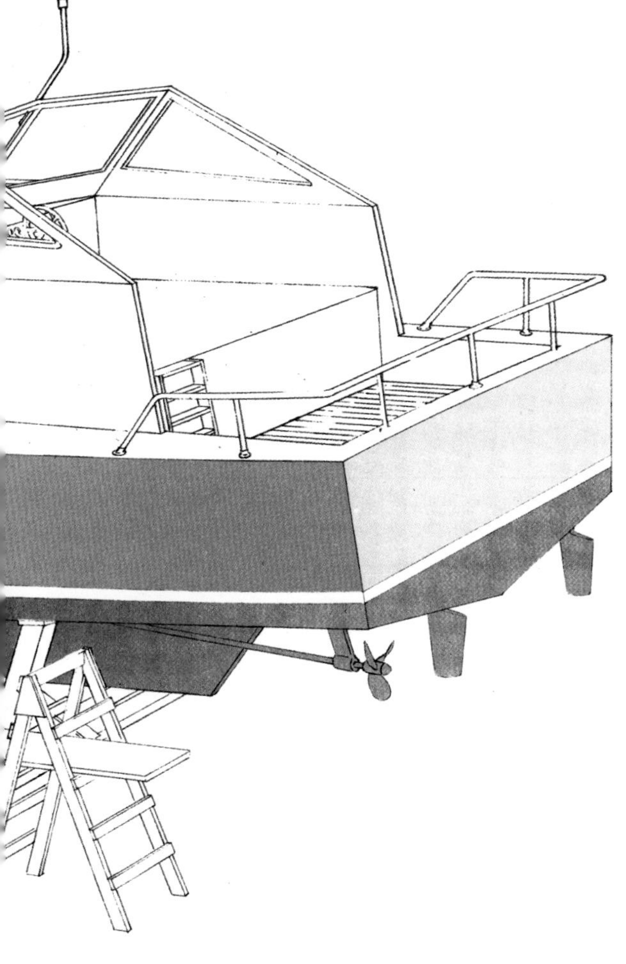

Special Tips for Decks and Interiors

Decks finished in bright or glossy paints can be hard on the eyes in sunlight and slippery underfoot in wet weather. A tan or a pastel shade will reduce glare, as will a semigloss finish. A grit can be premixed into the paint to provide nonskid footing; or a boatman can simply sprinkle sand on a freshly painted surface—although the results will generally be less uniform. In any case, such a finish can be hard to keep clean, and some boatmen prefer to put down strips of special nonskid tape where slipperiness is a problem. Wherever possible, deck fittings should be removed to paint the surfaces beneath. Nails dropped into the fittings' screw holes after the last brush stroke will assist in relocating them after the paint has dried.

Cabin interiors, where sunlight tends to be minimal, are often finished in white, complemented by varnished trim. The combination is pleasing to some eyes, though others find it not particularly restful after periods of exposure to bright sun during long intervals on deck. Some boatmen therefore opt for pastels or darker colors on interior bulkheads. Whatever the choice, semigloss or satin-finish paints provide surfaces that can easily be cleaned by sponging them down with a mild detergent. Mildew is often a problem in humid cabins; sponging will get rid of it but a more lasting defense is to stir an antimildew additive into the paint to prevent stains from forming on bulkheads or the overhead.

Brushes must be cleaned immediately after use with the manufacturer's recommended solvent; otherwise they will harden into unsalvageable junk. A heavily used brush should be worked back and forth over a few sheets of newspaper to permit the solvent to soak into the heel. If it is to be used again soon, the brush may be left suspended in a can of solvent, with its bristles hanging clear of the bottom, as shown below. If it is to be stored for more than a week or so, the brush should be washed in soap and water after being rinsed in solvent, and then tied into a paper or rag wrapping to preserve its shape.

Boot Tops and Bottoms

When the hull's topsides are gleaming with new paint, the next jobs on the painter's list are the boot top and bottom, in that order. Working from the top down reduces the chance that drips and spills will spoil work already done.

Because the boot top is so conspicuous its paint must be carefully applied. Some boats have scribe lines delineating the stripe, as on the boat at right. Otherwise, masking tape is almost essential to the job of getting straight edges. It is important to press the tape firmly down along its borders to prevent paint from seeping under it. Furthermore, the tape should be removed half an hour or so after painting, or as soon as the paint begins to set; if left longer, the tape tends to lift the paint. Drafting tape, designed to hold paper to drawing boards, is less sticky than masking tape and will lift less paint when it is removed. Special long-lasting plastic tapes, available in a number of widths and colors, can be substituted for paint.

When he turns to refurbishing the bottom of his vessel, the boatman will discover a large variety of paints from which to choose. Selecting the right one depends, first, on where the boat is kept. Salt water is a fertile environment for barnacles, grasses, and slime. In a warm climate there are marine worms intent on dining off the bottom, and various algae that will attach themselves to the boat are present even in fresh water. Antifouling paints that contain substances poisonous to these marine organisms are therefore required.

A soft, copper-rich antifouling paint is often used in warmer waters and on large or deep-keeled yachts that cannot be hauled frequently. Small racers, at the other extreme, are often hauled after each contest; their bottoms may be finished with a hard, smooth topsides paint. Metal boats, wherever kept, are best off with one of the bottom paints that contain tin as the antifouling ingredient *(page 61).*

Painting a boot-top stripe is a delicate task, even with the aid of a guiding scribe line like that incised into the wood hull of the boat below. The brush should be a new one about one inch wide; alternatively, a sash brush, designed for such careful work, can be used. The painter works up to the scribe line; slips above it can be wiped off with the solvent recommended by the paint manufacturer. Slips at the bottom will be covered over by the bottom paint.

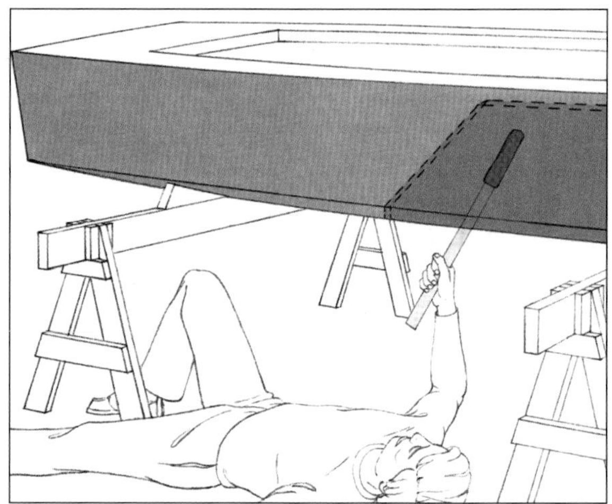

A rag wrapped around a stick is as good a tool as any for getting antifouling paint into the centerboard trunk—a confined area especially susceptible to marine growths. Some boatowners work with long-handled brushes, operating from either the top or the bottom.

Painting

Painting with a roller, as the sailor above is doing, is a satisfactory technique for applying antifouling paints to the bottoms of nonracing boats. Such bottom paints tend to be thick and messy; the roller gets the job done in a hurry, and gives an adequate though slightly pocked finish. When the job is done, the roller sleeve can be discarded. Painters who prefer to use brushes for bottom painting often buy cheap ones for the job, and retire them afterward.

The Beauty of Brightwork

To many a sailor, nothing embellishes a boat's appearance so much as the natural beauty of wood. But most bare wood is fatally vulnerable to the ravages of sun, salt, and water, and it must be protected with varnish. Only one wood generally used in boat construction is rugged enough to survive the marine environment unprotected—teak, which demands only a minimal amount of maintenance *(right).*

Brightwork, as varnished areas on boats are called, requires work—and a lot of it. Preparation of the surface is crucial. Old varnish, if blistered or chipped, must be stripped away, and the wood beneath it bleached and sanded.

In applying the finish, favorable working conditions are all-important. Varnishing should be done only on a warm, dry, windless day; humid weather will produce a cloudy finish. As with painting, the work should not be performed in direct sunlight, which might cause uneven drying and wrinkling. And because a wet coat of varnish will capture any particles in the air, a boatman must make sure that no one in the vicinity sands or kicks up dust while the finish is drying.

Good brightwork deserves care. When possible, it should be hosed down with fresh water and covered to protect it against the sun; frequent retouching may also be in order.

Brightwork can be functional as well as eye-pleasing. Wood masts and booms are often varnished so that any cracking—which might go undetected under paint—will be instantly visible.

A few yachts, like the luxury cruiser at left, appear to be composed almost entirely of creamy teak and varnished wood. Such an effect is not easily achieved; as many as seven coats and endless hours of work were required to create this glossy finish.

Special Care for Teak Decks

Teak, a golden hardwood that grows in the Far East, seems especially created for use on boats. Most often employed for decks, trim and handrails, it resists abrasion and contains a natural oil that renders it virtually proof against rot. Though no finish is needed, some owners paint or varnish teak; but the oil in the wood causes adhesion problems, and a new coat is necessary sooner than would be the case with another wood. Most skippers allow teak to weather to a handsome sandy buff.

Both grease and gasoline will mar the glow of unfinished teak—as will any oily foods that are spilled by the crew—but teak cleaners can effectively restore the wood's looks. Most commercial cleaners can be applied in one step and then rinsed with fresh water. The strongest cleaners, however, come in two chemical parts, which are applied separately: a strong base that acts as a harsh soap, and a mild acid that neutralizes the base. Both should be handled with rubber gloves, and neither must be permitted to splash on paint or fittings. Teak sealers like the one being applied below offer a more lasting solution to the problem of staining; they fill the pores of the wood and make cleaning easy. Most sealers can be applied with a rag *(below)*, an easier task than painting or varnishing. Two treatments a season will prevent drying and splitting, and will bring out the natural color of the wood.

Badly weathered brightwork must be stripped to the bare wood before new varnish can be applied. The first step *(above)* is to brush on paint-and-varnish remover. Only a small area at a time should be covered so that it can be thoroughly scraped down before the remover dries out and ceases to work.

Scraping of the old varnish begins when the finish bubbles and lifts away from the wood, usually about 15 minutes after application of the remover. The wood must be scraped with the grain, and the scraper kept sharp; otherwise the effort needed to take off the varnish might produce surface gouges.

The Dos and Don'ts of Varnishing

Flawless surfaces and a dust-free environment are the keys to a successful varnish job. Some more specific tips are suggested below.

Brushes: A brand-new brush is best for applying varnish. Never varnish with a brush that has been used for painting; even minuscule paint particles will ruin the job. Old or cheap brushes are fine for applying varnish remover; they can be thrown away afterward.

New wood: Thorough sanding is required, for even the builder's light pencil marks will show up under clear varnish. To achieve an unblemished, satin-smooth surface with such open-grain woods as oak or mahogany, use a paste filler; it can be thinned and applied with a brush. When the coating of filler begins to dry—after 15 minutes or so—wipe across the grain with a piece of cloth; this will ensure that filler is deposited in the grain channels. A minimum of four coats of varnish, sanded in between, is required on new wood.

Badly weathered surfaces: Even after stripping with a remover and scraper, blackish exposure stains may remain in the wood, and a bleach will be needed. Using the recommended solvent, rinse off all traces of the bleaching agent before varnishing.

Thinning: Expert varnishers dilute the first coats with solvent so that the finish soaks into the wood—in effect serving as a primer. Subsequent coats are undiluted.

When brightwork is in reasonably good condition, like the varnished nameboard shown here, it need not be stripped down to bare wood to be refurbished—but it still needs attention. The boatman at left is using fine sandpaper to remove all the gloss from the board's surface; his goal is a dull, or matte, finish. Imperfections are not always visible at this stage, but a rubdown with a solvent-moistened rag will reveal blemishes that are in need of further sanding.

To clean away all dust before varnishing, experts use a tack rag like the one above; it can be bought at a marine-supply store or made from cotton, linen, or cheesecloth. The cloth is dipped in warm water, wrung out, sprinkled with turpentine or recommended solvent, and wrung again. A tablespoon of varnish is then dripped on it. When dry, the sticky rag will remove every trace of dust.

Slowly pouring off enough varnish for the job into a smaller container, the boatman strains out impurities through a stocking. He treats the varnish carefully to avoid creating any air bubbles that would mar the finish. For the same reason, a varnish brush should never be scraped off on the can's rim.

Laying on the final coat, the boatman loads his brush fairly heavily and glides it across the work, using as few strokes as possible and always moving the brush in the same direction. Once the varnish is thus "flowed" on, it should not be worked over.

What's in a Name

The final touch before the pleasant moment when a boat slides into the water for the season is putting on its name. Some boatowners paint it on freehand, a method that demands a good sense of composition and plenty of patience. A less risky approach is to first trace out the name with "transfer" letters—the reverse of stencils. For professional-looking results, the transfer letters—obtainable at art-supply stores—should be used in conjunction with the three-stage technique described opposite.

The same technique is just as valuable to boatmen who opt for the simplest and most popular name-affixing method of all—decals, which can be attached to the boat in a trice. Decals commonly come in white, black, or gold, and, like transfer letters, are available in several shapes and sizes. They are easy to remove—if the skipper wants to fly in the face of the ancient superstition that changing a boat's name is bad luck. Too often, however, they drop off by themselves.

Boatmen seeking more permanent solutions sometimes choose plastic letters that are secured to a hull with screws or glue. Hand-carved nameboards serve the same purpose, and do so with peerless splendor. But the craftsman who can make one is rare—and expensive.

Most pleasure boats carry their name on their transoms—usually centered, although some skippers prefer it off to one side. The boat's home port or yacht club affiliation is often written out below the name. Modern sailboats with small or reserved transoms sometimes bear names on the topsides, about halfway aft and just below the rail. The bow is normally reserved for registration numbers.

Freehand lettering calls for the sort of rapt concentration the boatman above is giving to her dinghy's transom. A steady hand, in this case supported by a forearm, is not enough. The painter has prudently worked out the composition on paper, chalked horizontal guidelines on the transom to keep the letters level and of a uniform height, and outlined the letters with chalk before going to work with a brush. Slips can usually be wiped away with a rag and solvent.

Compositional errors can be avoided by laying out transfer letters or decals on a piece of tracing paper rather than directly on a boat's transom. First, draw a vertical center line on the paper; this will help position the name on the transom. Next, draw a horizontal baseline to ensure the name will be level. Trace the transfer letters or mark the position of the decals, then affix two pieces of tape to the top of the sheet of tracing paper.

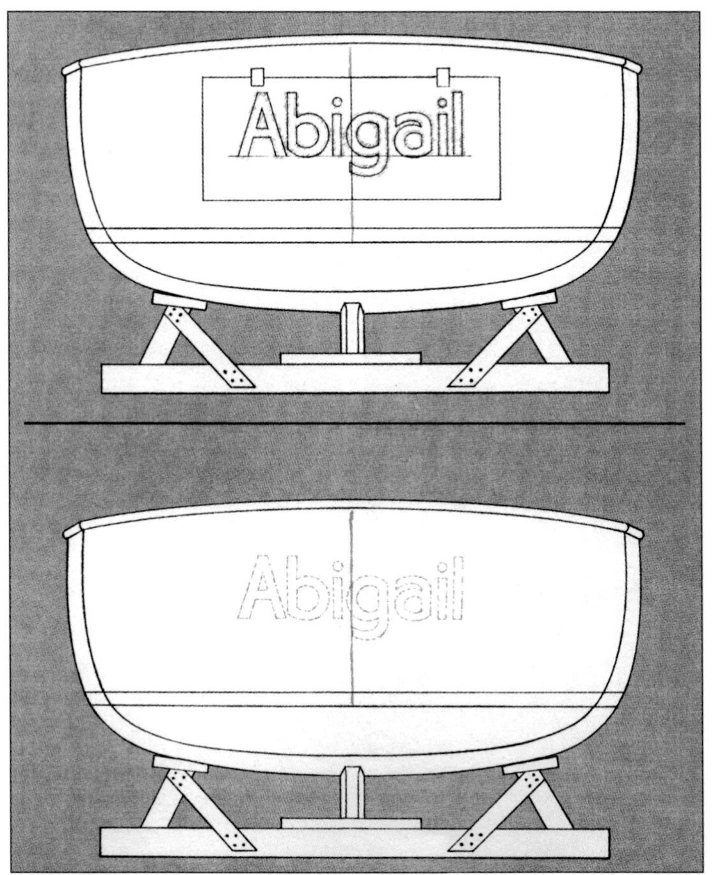

Apply chalk to the back of the tracing paper. Then, with the chalk and a ruler, draw a vertical line at the center of the boat's transom. Place the paper's center line over it, then slide the paper up or down to the desired height and attach the tape. A wide motorboat stern may look best with the name in the middle, whereas a wineglass-shaped sailboat counter may be happier with the name just below the rail.

With a felt-tipped pen or a blunt pencil, trace over the lettering on the tracing paper; the chalk on the back will transfer the markings to the transom. Then remove the paper; apply the decals or fill the letters with a fine brush.

CHAPTER 3: Engine Upkeep

The motor that drives a boat—be it outboard, gasoline inboard, or diesel—is fundamentally like its counterpart in a motorcycle, car, or truck. Indeed, the larger marine versions of these automotive power plants are frequently built around the very same engine blocks. But propelling a boat creates unique demands. Boat engines are run at nearly full speed as much as 90 percent of the time.

To cope with the strains of running full blast for hours, boat engines are made with many heavy parts, and this added burden means that the power plants are more than ever dependent on dirt-free fuel lines and a plentiful supply of cooling water. Therefore, the routine checking of fuel and oil filters becomes an essential step in preventing serious damage to the engine of a boat.

Marine engines, moreover, are constantly being knocked about as a boat slams into a wake, bounces over wind-driven chop or careens around a turn—and motion and vibration take their toll. The buffeting that a marine power plant sustains can knock finely tuned parts out of adjustment, back off important nuts and bolts, and snap fuel lines. Because boat engines have this tendency to take themselves apart, a large portion of preventive maintenance consists of nothing more than an occasional trip around the engine with a screwdriver and a wrench, trying connections, and tightening things up before some crucial part is lost in the bilge or irreparably damaged.

A gasoline inboard has certain special liabilities—its location, for instance. Tucked away, as it generally is, in the deepest portion of the hull, an inboard motor helps to keep a boat stable. But the engine compartment is the first place to flood—in some cases, with highly corrosive salt water—and the last to fully air out when the boat is bailed. This latter difficulty is potentially dangerous. Gasoline fumes, being heavier than air, tend to settle in the bilge, waiting for a lighted cigarette, a backfire, or an erratic spark from the ignition system to set them off. Such an explosion is invariably calamitous, since a mere teacup of gasoline, when vaporized, is six times as powerful as a stick of dynamite and could totally destroy the biggest yacht. Thus, inspecting the carburetor's flame arrester, checking the sight glass that warns of trouble in the mechanism of the fuel pump, and examining the fuel lines of an inboard for frays, cracks, and leaks are critical exercises, not only for the motor's health and longevity, but for that of the crew as well.

A boat, finally, does not gently roll to a stop when the motor quits. Instead, it remains at the mercy of the winds, the tide, and the rocks it may fetch upon—and an anchor may be the first tool that is needed for on-the-spot engine repairs when the boat is adrift.

Hunkered over his transom, the skipper of a sloop performs a routine maintenance chore: changing a spark plug. For a complicated job, he would remove the motor from the transom.

The Accessible Outboard

Because of their simplicity of construction and ease of access, outboard motors are well suited to maintenance by amateur boatmen. A typical outboard in the 45- to 65-horsepower range, shown opposite with its cowling removed, is made up of hundreds of separate and finely machined parts. Yet it is as sturdy as a power lawn mower and barely more complex, and a modicum of care can keep it in sound running order for 10 years or more.

One of the most important aspects of outboard upkeep consists of quick inspections for such troubles as loose wiring and especially the exterior part of the fuel system, shown here in blue for emphasis. In addition to external maintenance, regular checks on the engine's innards—and the fuel tank's, too—will help ensure smooth operation. Spark plugs will last longer and operate more efficiently if they are periodically cleaned of all energy-robbing deposits of carbon, oil, or corrosion *(page 78).* The fuel-pump filter shown opposite should be cleaned every three months, and the fuel tank should be flushed annually. A thorough flushing involves disassembling the tank; it cannot be easily emptied from the filler opening because of a slight lip on the inner side.

The most frequent maintenance job of all is lubrication. Most of the internal components of an outboard receive constant lubrication from the clean-burning, medium-weight oil that is mixed in with the fuel. But the gear case calls for a lubricant of its own, and regular infusions of oil or grease are necessary at numerous points on the outside of the engine.

The owner's manual is an invaluable ally in outboard maintenance. It offers a detailed guide to the construction of a particular engine; it supplies diagnostic advice for various performance maladies; and it helps the average boatman distinguish between jobs that he can manage and those that demand expert attention.

An outboard motor should get at least a cursory inspection every time it is used. Check for fastenings that may have been loosened from constant engine vibration; running the engine during inspection may reveal trouble spots. Examine spark-plug cables and other wires for worn insulation that could cause shorts; while electrician's tape makes a good temporary repair, defective wires ought to be replaced. Look for leaks in rubber fuel hoses on the engine and from the fuel tank; heavy-duty vinyl tape will seal links in an emergency, but again, the hoses should be replaced. Clean mud and grass from the cooling-system intakes to prevent overheating. Examine the propeller and have it repaired at a boatyard, or replace it if it is badly dented.

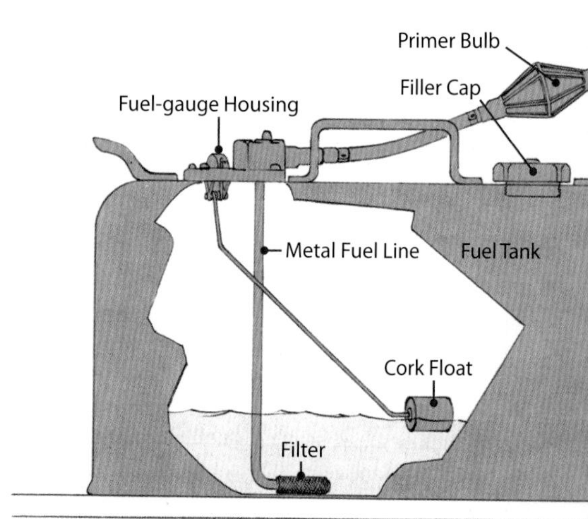

To flush the fuel tank, remove the screws holding the fuel-gauge housing and the metal fuel line to the top of the tank; then carefully lift out the entire assembly. Invert the tank to drain out all the fuel, then thoroughly flush the tank with gasoline to remove any gummy residue of old fuel. Before reassembling, check the fuel gauge's cork float, replacing it if it has become saturated, and rinse the filter at the lower end of the interior metal fuel line with gasoline.

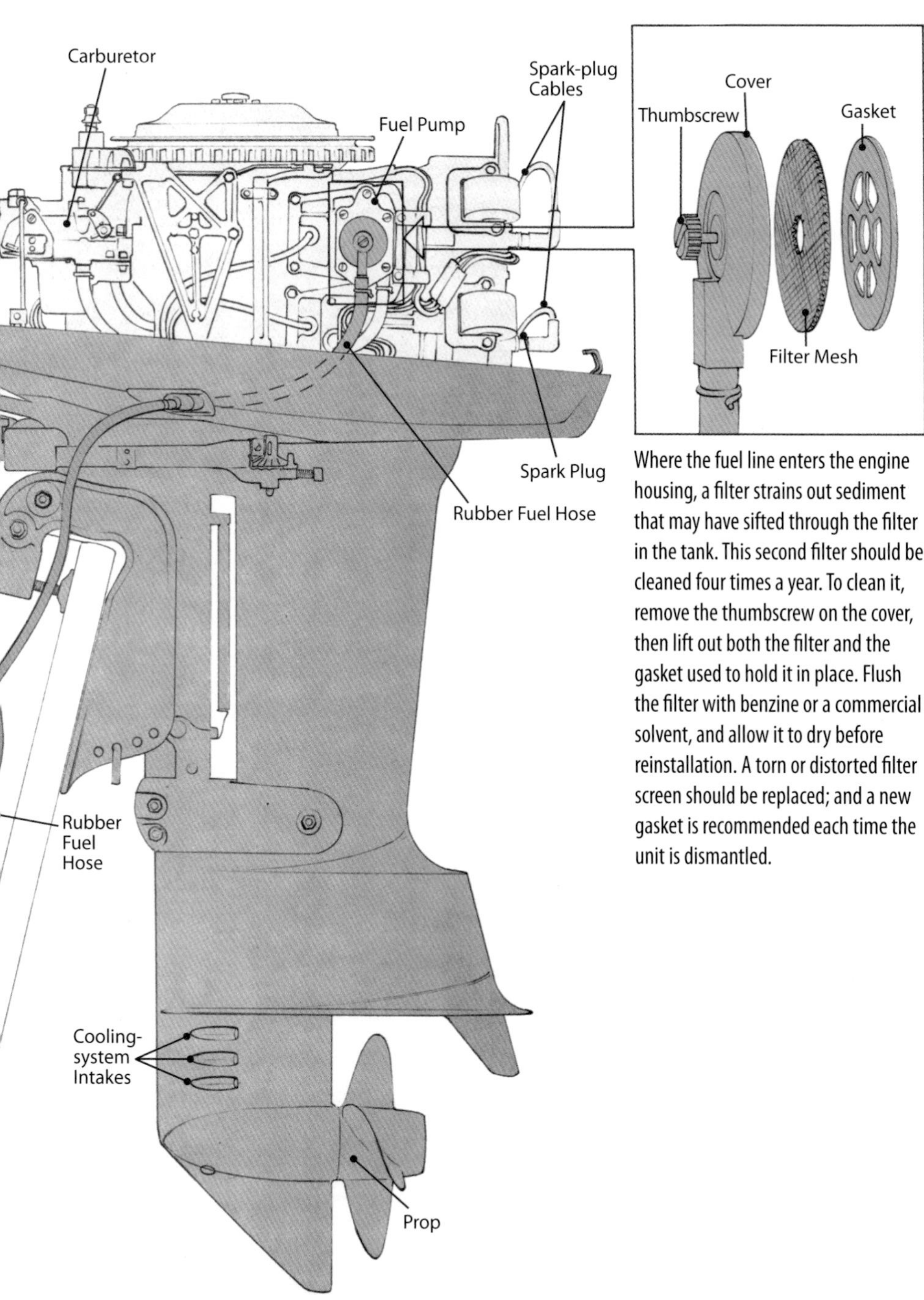

Where the fuel line enters the engine housing, a filter strains out sediment that may have sifted through the filter in the tank. This second filter should be cleaned four times a year. To clean it, remove the thumbscrew on the cover, then lift out both the filter and the gasket used to hold it in place. Flush the filter with benzine or a commercial solvent, and allow it to dry before reinstallation. A torn or distorted filter screen should be replaced; and a new gasket is recommended each time the unit is dismantled.

The Ills of Spark Plugs

Spark plugs ignite the fuel in an engine's cylinder by sending bursts of electricity between two electrodes separated by only a few hundredths of an inch. Since any deposits on the electrodes will impair ignition efficiency, the plugs should be removed and inspected about once every three months. If the electrodes are coated with oil, caked with carbon, or just discolored from ordinary wear and tear, the plug can be cleaned by soaking it in kerosene and scrubbing it with a wire brush. If, however, the electrodes are pitted *(far right)*, the plug must be replaced.

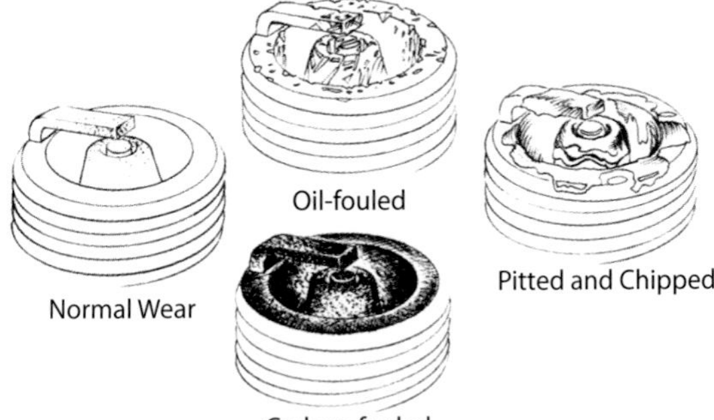

Before installing a plug—new or just cleaned—check the gap between the electrodes to be sure that it meets the specifications in the engine manufacturer's manual. The requisite tool, available at auto-supply stores, is a feeler-gauge, equipped both with blades of varying thickness and with tiny levers that can be used to bend the side electrode to the proper position. If the gap is too wide or narrow, adjust the electrode until the right-sized blade slips into the opening, touching both sides but not jamming. Screw in the plug by hand; tighten it with a torque wrench.

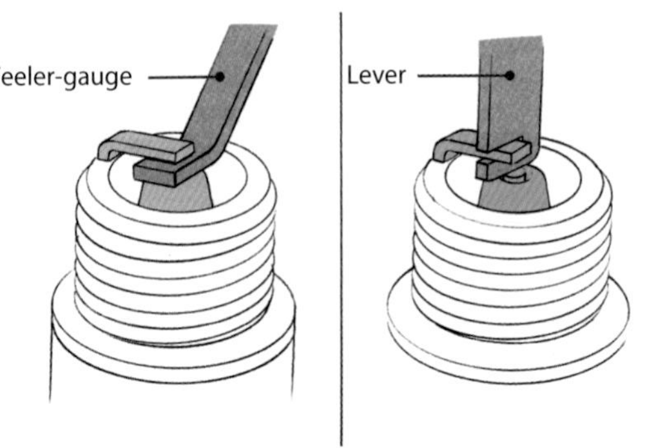

A High-powered Plug

In their quest for more reliable engine performance, outboard manufacturers have adopted a new kind of plug that provides an extra-hot spark; it is not interchangeable with old-style plugs, for it requires the added power of a modern capacitor-discharge ignition system. Called a surface-gap plug, the new design lacks a side electrode. Instead, the spark jumps horizontally across the face of the plug—spreading out from a center pin, which acts as one electrode, to the rim, which serves as the other. A surface-gap plug is inspected and cleaned in the same way as a conventional plug *(above)*, although there is no spark gap to adjust. Replacement is necessary when the rounded center electrode either becomes worn to a sharp point or no longer protrudes higher than the rim.

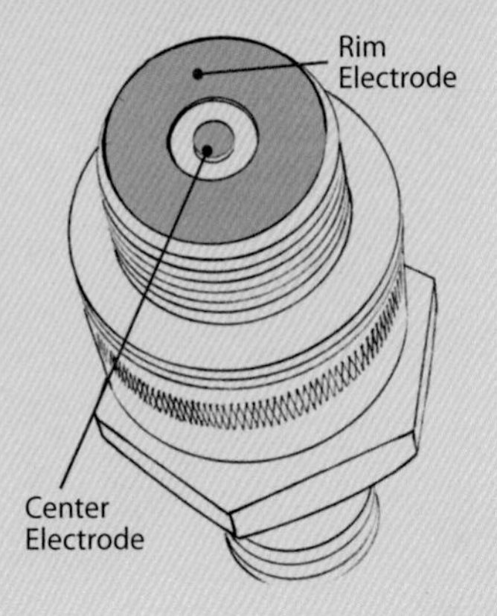

Flushing an Engine

A yearly flushing of an engine that is operated in salty or silty water will protect the cooling system from corrosion, and will clear deposits from intake valves as well. A small outboard can be cleansed by running it inside a barrel or drum partly filled with fresh water *(right)*. After firmly clamping the motor to the side of the drum, put a board behind it to reduce splashing. Run the motor at idle speed for about 10 minutes, so it has time to pump water around the system.

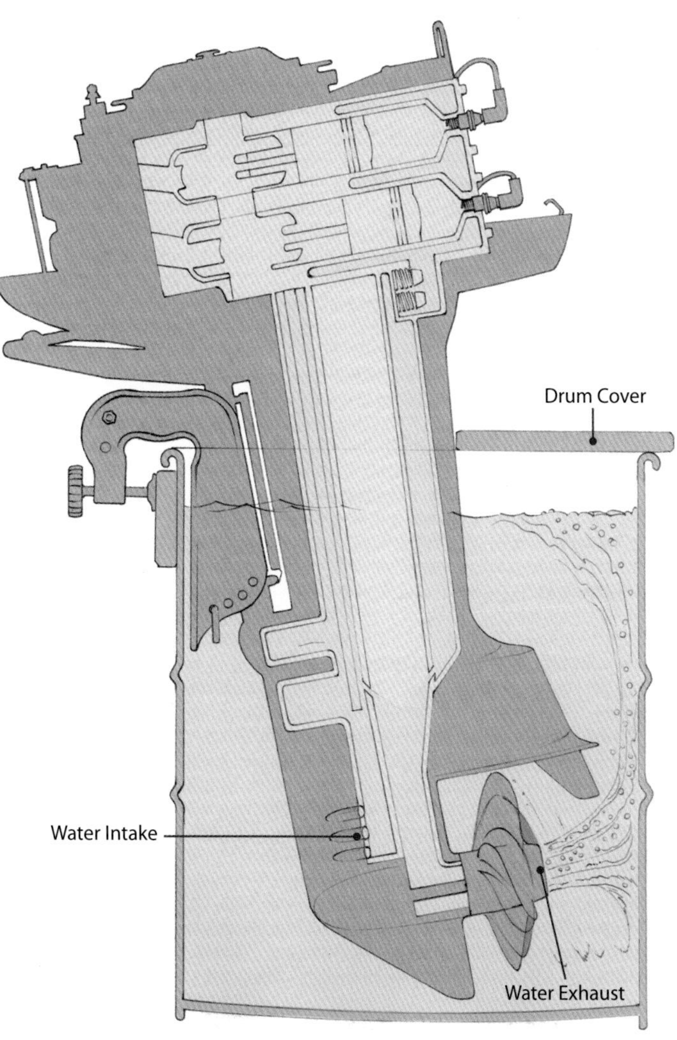

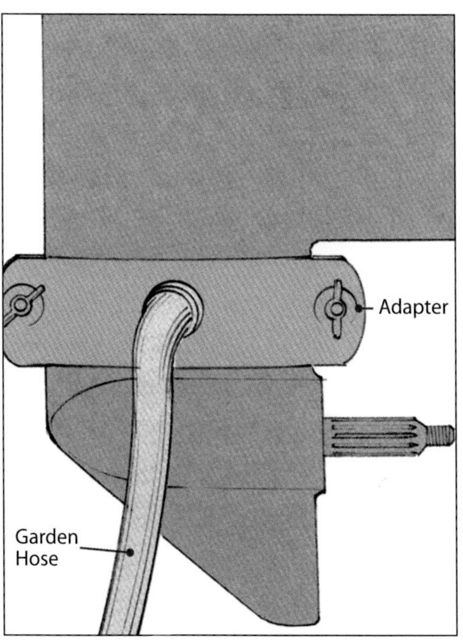

Some outboard engines are too large to be lowered into a drum. However, they can be easily flushed while mounted on a rack, or tilted up on the boat, with a garden hose attached to the water intake, using a special adapter *(above)* available at marine-supply stores. Since the engine will be operated in the open air, remove the propeller for safety. Operate the engine no faster than idle speed until clear water runs from the exhaust.

A Lubrication Program

Three basic types of lubricants—oil, grease, and a heavy-duty compound for the gear case—combat friction and corrosion in outboard engines. They must be replenished at regular intervals, for grease and oil eventually wash or wear away from most parts, and gear-case lubricants become contaminated with particles of metal chipped from the gears during normal use. When servicing an outboard, check the owner's manual for the recommended grades of lubricants. Different engines may require oils of differing viscosity; or the manufacturer may specify lubricants that have anticorrosion additives.

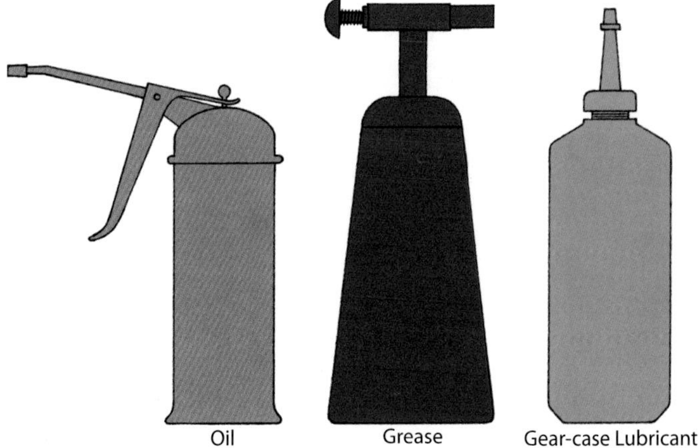

Where and When to Lubricate

The chart right lists lubrication points found on most outboard motors; it also specifies the proper intervals for servicing in either a fresh-water or salt-water environment. The colored and numbered dots correspond to those accompanying the engine diagrams opposite. Color indicates the type of lubricant required—blue for oil, red for grease, and green for gear-case lubricant. Blue and red dots at the same lubrication point mean that some manufacturers call for oil there, while others specify grease.

Lubricant	Lubrication point	Lubrication interval	
		Fresh water	Salt water
1	Safety-switch cam	60 days	30 days
2	Throttle-shaft bushings, gears	60 days	30 days
3	Swivel bracket	60 days	30 days
4	Safety switch	60 days	30 days
5	Starter lockout	60 days	30 days
6	Magneto linkage	60 days	30 days
7	Gear-shift linkage	60 days	30 days
8	Shift lever and shaft	60 days	30 days
9	Tilt-lock lever	60 days	30 days
10	Clamp screws	60 days	30 days
11	Motor-cover latch	60 days	30 days
12	Throttle-shaft bearing	60 days	30 days
13 13	Throttle-cam follower	60 days	30 days
14 14	Carburetor linkage	60 days	30 days
15 15	Starter pinion, gear, and shaft	60 days	30 days
16 16	Propeller shaft	60 days	30 days
17 17	Choke shaft	60 days	30 days
18	Gear case	Once a season	Once a season

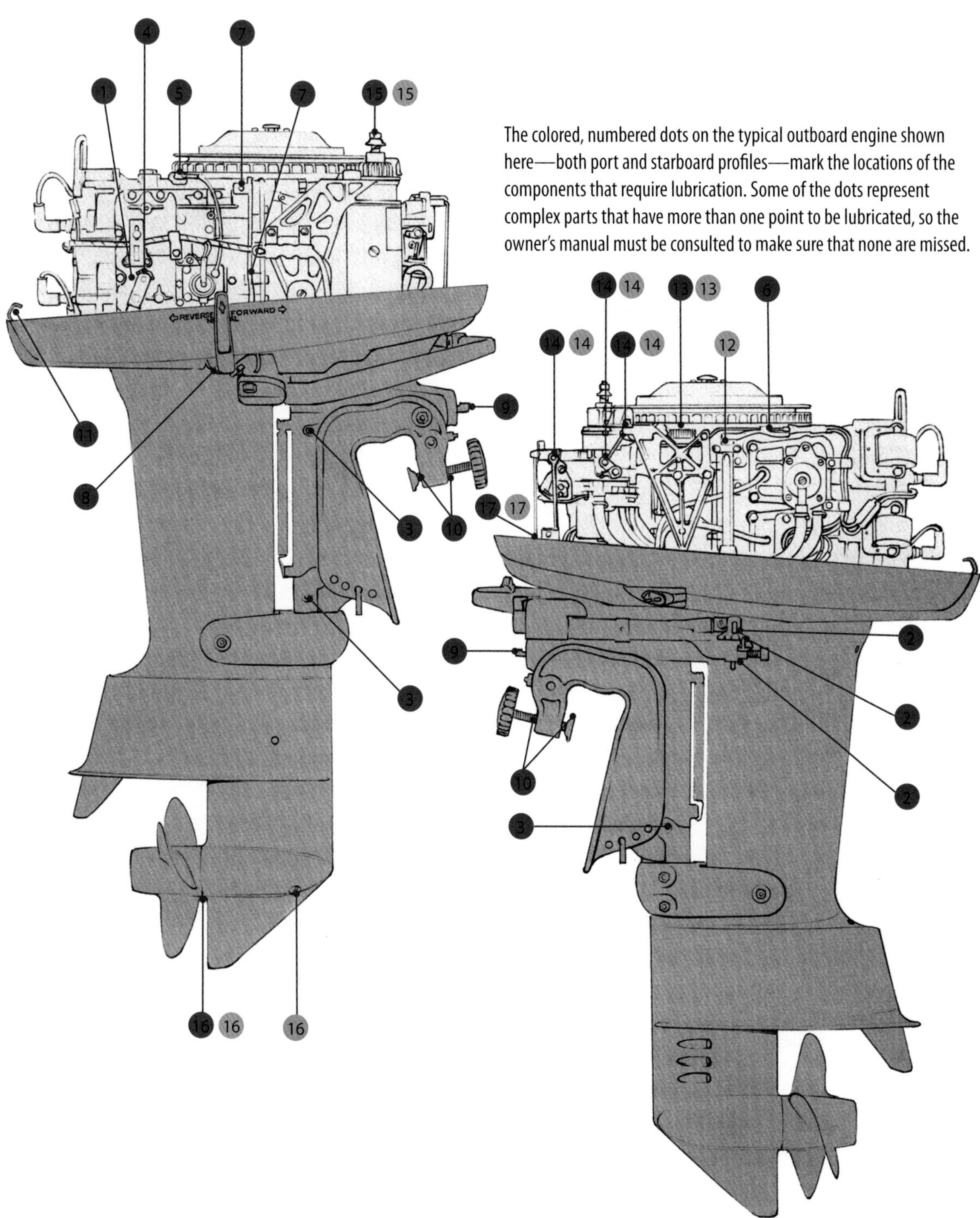

The colored, numbered dots on the typical outboard engine shown here—both port and starboard profiles—mark the locations of the components that require lubrication. Some of the dots represent complex parts that have more than one point to be lubricated, so the owner's manual must be consulted to make sure that none are missed.

The Gasoline Inboard

A modern gasoline inboard, like the 190-horsepower model shown here, has certain distinctive features that set it apart from automobile engines and require a small extra measure of maintenance. The most conspicuous of these is the two-stage cooling system; it pumps sea water aboard to cool a circulating reserve of fresh water, which, in turn, cools the engine. Another distinctive feature is the flame arrester, a cylinder of steel mesh mounted atop the carburetor to trap backfire flames that could ignite fumes in the engine compartment. To further guard against explosions, the inboard will often have a device called a sight glass *(page 84),* which signals a leak in the fuel pump.

Routine care for a seagoing cooling system consists of checking the condition of the belts that drive the two water pumps, and making sure that the fresh-water reserve tank is brimful at all times. The flame arrester must be removed every 50 hours and soaked in kerosene or benzine to dissolve accumulated carbon deposits. Fuel-pump trouble revealed by the sight glass can usually be fixed by replacing a single part, the fuel-pump diaphragm.

In most other respects, looking after an inboard hardly differs from tending an auto engine—except that the penalties of inattention may be more severe. Any long cruise should begin with a thorough inspection of the motor. Check the electrical system for frayed wiring and loose connections. Test the tightness of hose clamps in the fuel or water systems with a screwdriver; gently squeeze or probe the hoses themselves to find any soft spots caused by deterioration. And make sure that the various lubrication needs of the engine *(page 89)* have been met.

Every 250 hours, the inboard should be turned over to a professional mechanic for a tune-up. At this time, request that it be steam-cleaned of dirt and oil to expose any spots where rust or corrosion may be taking hold. Scrub off such spots with a wire brush, then touch them up with primer and paint.

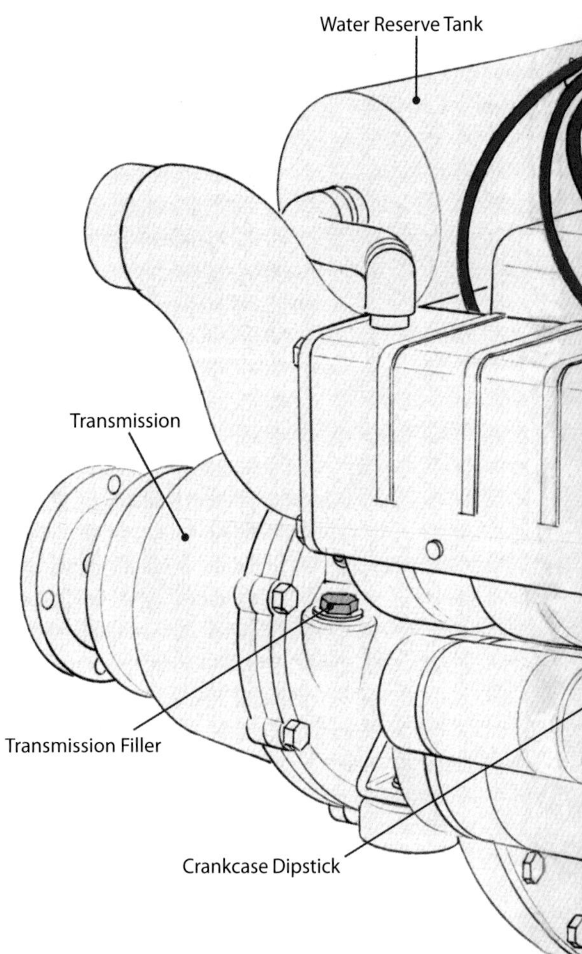

In this view of a typical inboard gasoline marine engine, the components that the boatman should learn to inspect and maintain on a regular basis, as explained on the following pages, are color-coded according to their function. The parts dealt with in fuel-system maintenance are shown in orange; those in cooling-system maintenance are in green; those in ignition-system maintenance are in red; and those in lubrication servicing are shown in blue. Other connected parts are labeled for emphasis.

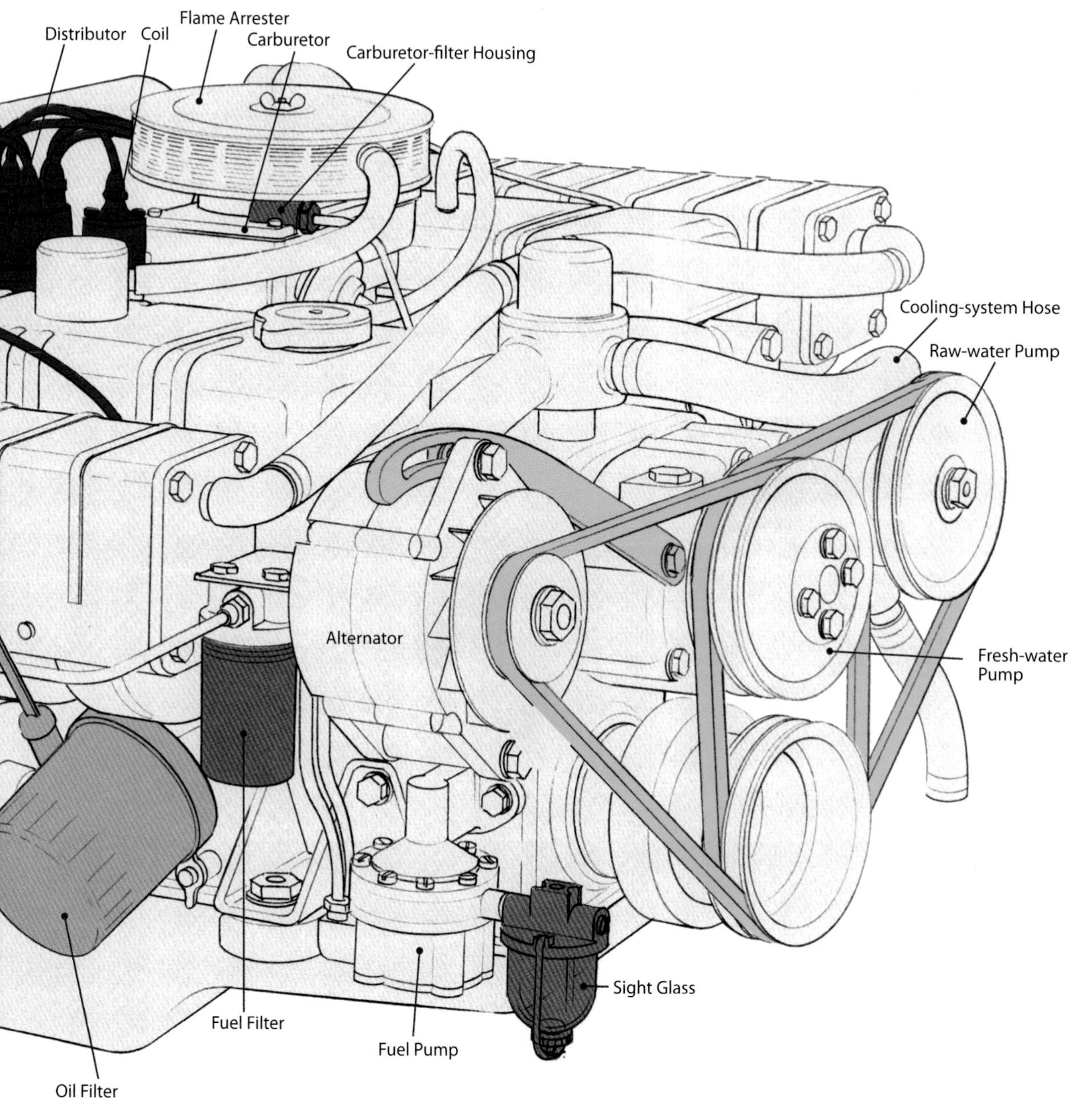
Distributor
Coil
Flame Arrester
Carburetor
Carburetor-filter Housing
Cooling-system Hose
Raw-water Pump
Alternator
Fresh-water Pump
Sight Glass
Fuel Filter
Fuel Pump
Oil Filter

Replacing Filters

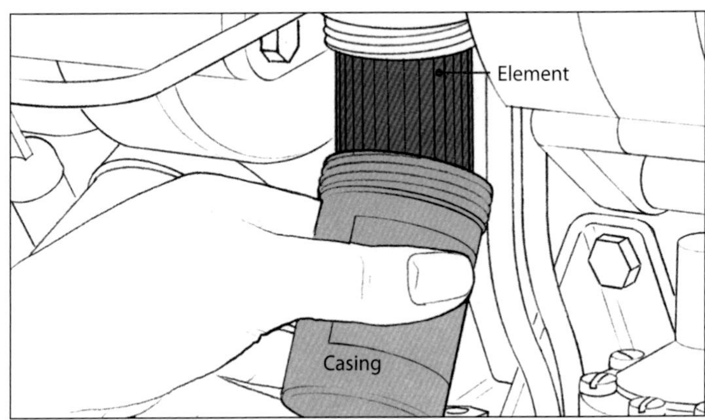

Attached to every inboard engine along the fuel line is a primary filter, which rids gasoline of impurities as it travels to the fuel pump. This filter should be changed after every 100 hours of engine use. To remove the element, first unscrew the filter casing—using a wrench if necessary. Take out the element and its gasket and discard them. Before installing a new element and gasket, rinse the casing in benzine or a commercial solvent. Insert the new element and casing, as shown. Start the engine; if leaks appear around the casing, lighten it more securely.

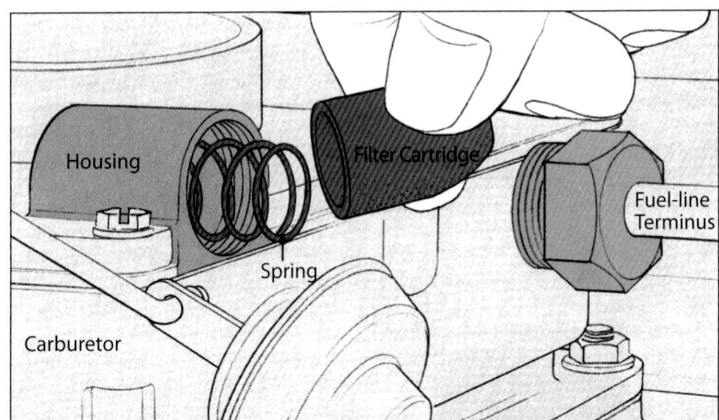

The carburetor filter, a small fitting located at the point where the fuel line enters the carburetor, should be replaced after every 50 hours of engine use. Begin by disconnecting the fuel-line terminus from the carburetor with a wrench. Pull the terminus back from its connection slowly; the filter cartridge is held against it by a spring and must be grasped as it pops out. Discard the cartridge; rinse the spring, terminus, and housing in solvent; insert a new cartridge and assemble.

A Vital Checkpoint

Marine fuel pumps are often equipped with a simple but ingenious warning device called a sight glass that allows the boatman to spot trouble in his fuel-pump mechanism. This glass should be looked at whenever the engine is started. If it remains empty after start-up, the fuel pump is functioning normally. But if the diaphragm within the pump has ruptured as a result of wear, fuel will run into a tube beneath the diaphragm and, through it, into the sight glass. Replace a ruptured diaphragm by removing the screws from the fuel-pump housing; the diaphragm lies directly underneath the housing. A malfunctioning fuel pump is a hazard on a boat, since gasoline escaping from the system will collect in the engine compartment and the bilge.

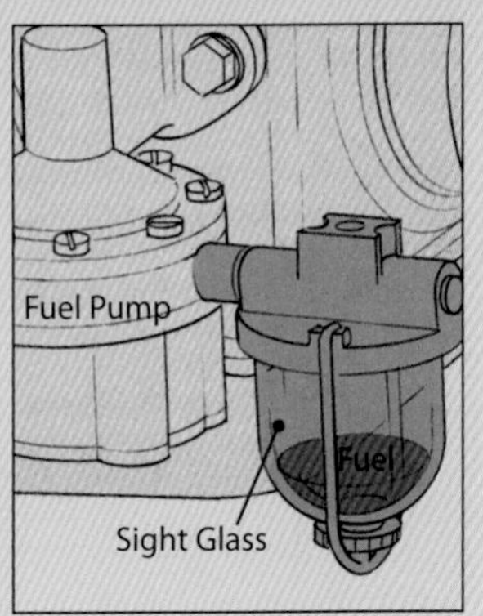

Adjusting Belts

Belts running off the drive shaft power the cooling and electrical systems. If the belts are too loose, the system will not work efficiently; if too tight, they will wear out, crippling the engine. Ideally, a belt should have from one quarter to one half an inch of play (dotted line) when pressed firmly with a thumb at the midpoint between the pulleys. Make this thumb test after every 50 hours of engine use, and adjust the belt to the correct tension as shown below.

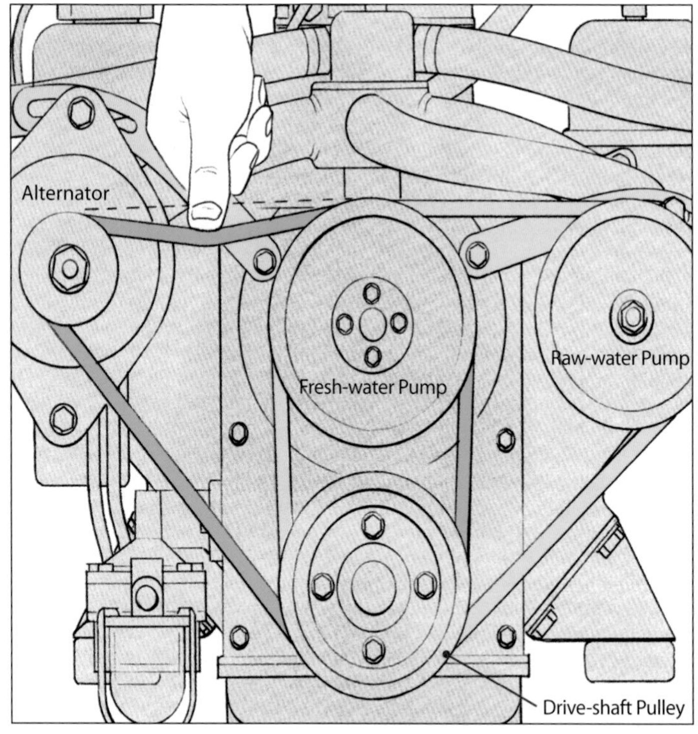

If the electrical system's belt is slack, it should be tightened by moving the alternator along the slot in the mounting bracket. Loosen the mounting nut with a wrench and then take up the slack in the belt by prying the alternator away from the engine with a long sturdy tool, such as the wrench shown here. Secure the mounting screw and test the tension again to be sure that the adjustment is adequate. The sea-water pump can be moved in the same way to adjust its belt.

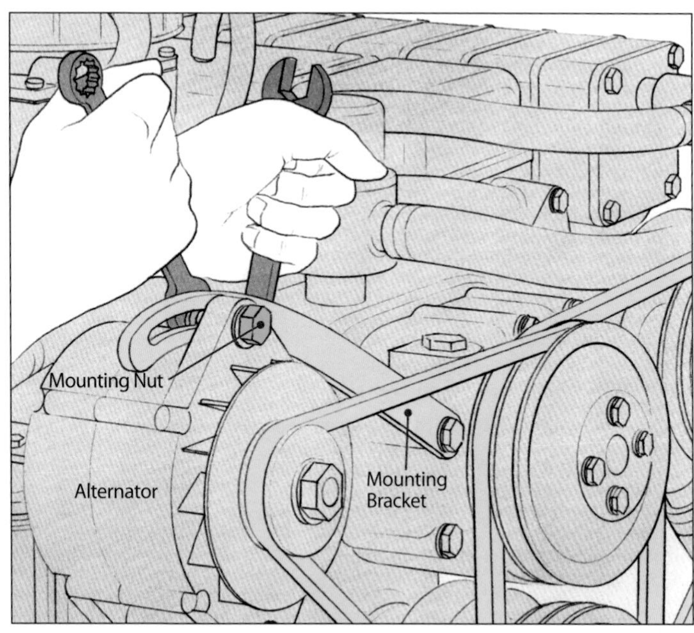

Engine Upkeep

Distributor Care

An inboard engine's distributor, together with the coil, helps create high-voltage bursts of electricity, then parcels out this power to the individual spark plugs. To work properly, it must be kept clean. After every 250 hours of engine use, remove the plastic distributor cap by snapping its clips open with a screwdriver. Wipe dirt and oil from the inside of the cap with a dry paper towel. If the cap is cracked, it must be replaced.

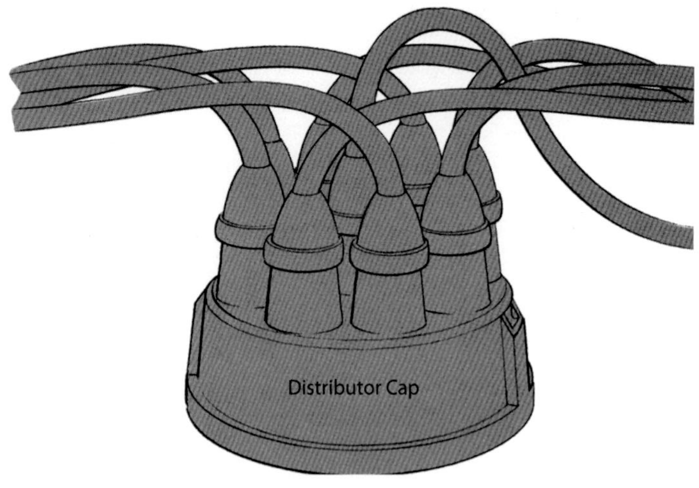

In the distributor, two tungsten contacts called breaker points open and close rapidly as a rotating cam strikes the outer point's mounting, or breaker arm. The points must be clean and smooth to do their job efficiently—activating the coil. To check, pry back the arm with a screwdriver. If the points show only grayish deposits, buff them lightly with an ignition file *(below)*, obtainable at auto-supply stores. Replace pitted points.

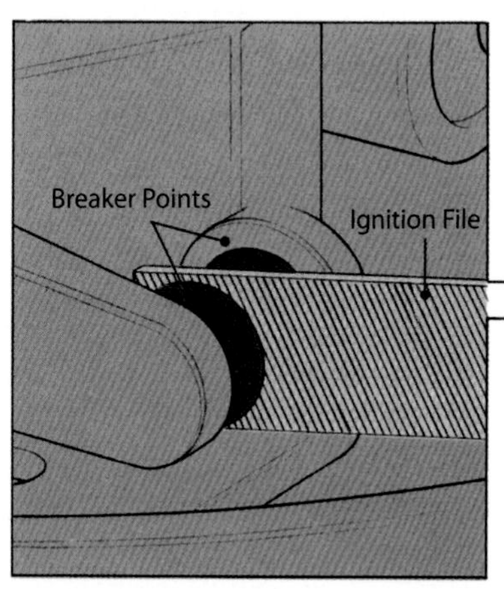

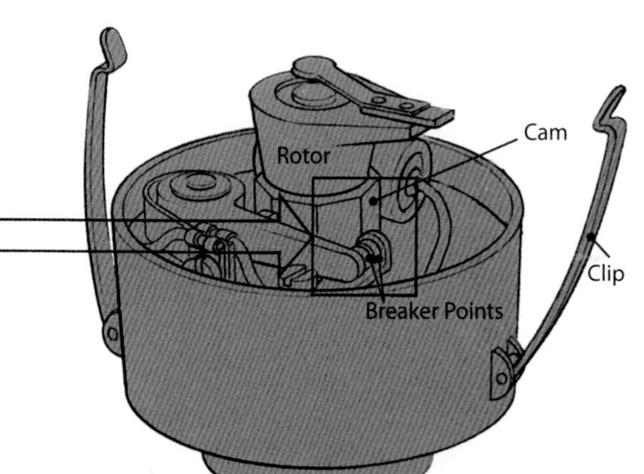

After the breaker points are cleaned, the gap between them should be checked. Begin by pulling the coil cable from its connection in the center of the distributor cap. Then, using a wooden clothespin as a guard against shock, hold the end of the cable about a quarter of an inch from a clean area on the engine block, and have a helper turn on the ignition and crank the engine. A thick spark should leap from the cable to the engine if the breaker points are properly gapped. If the spark is weak and yellow, reset the gap by the method given on the opposite page.

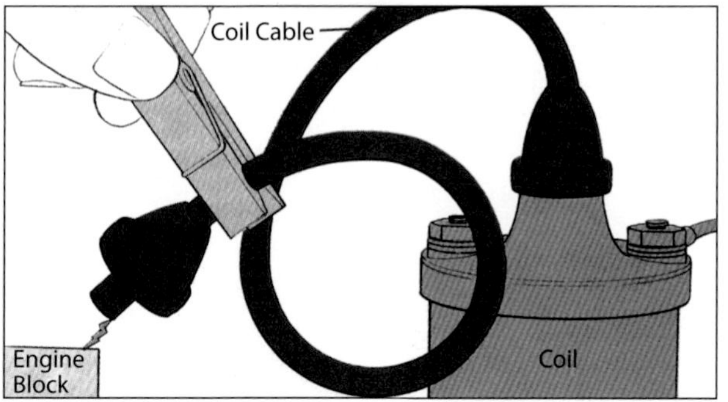

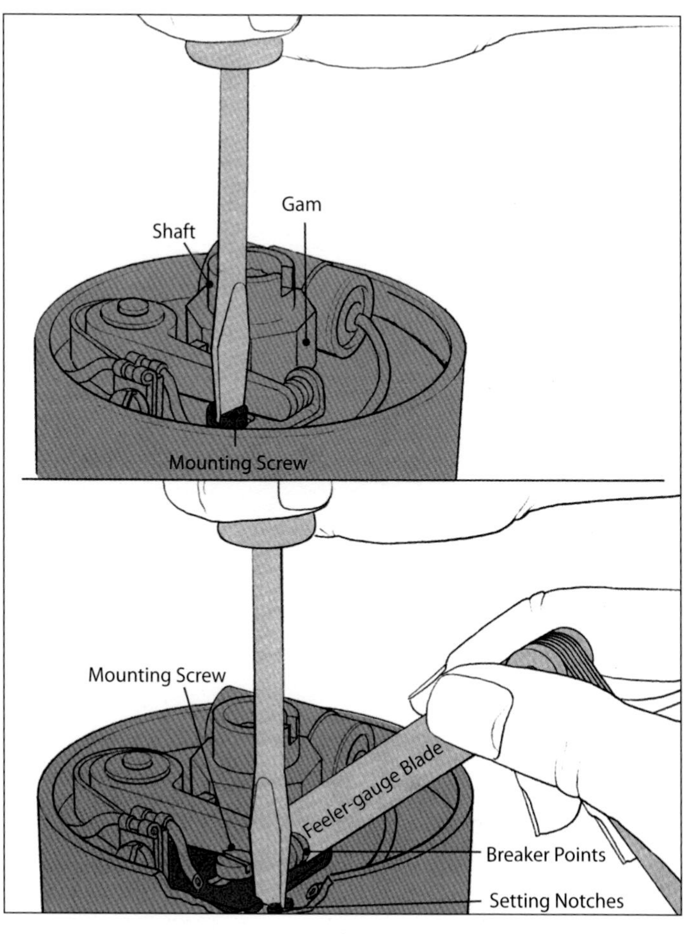

To set the distributor breaker points to the correct gap, first remove the rotor by simply lifting it off the top of the distributor shaft. Next, have a helper crank the engine until the rotating cam has opened up the gap to its fullest extent. Then loosen the mounting screw that holds the inner point secure.

Consult the owner's manual for the correct gap, then select a feeler-gauge blade of that thickness and slip it between the points. Next, insert a screwdriver between the setting notches and twist clockwise. This will open the points wider than the thickness of the feeler blade. Now turn the screwdriver in the opposite direction until the points just touch the blade on either side. Remove the blade and carefully tighten the mounting screw, then slip the blade between the points again. If the gap has altered as the screw was tightened, repeat the adjustment.

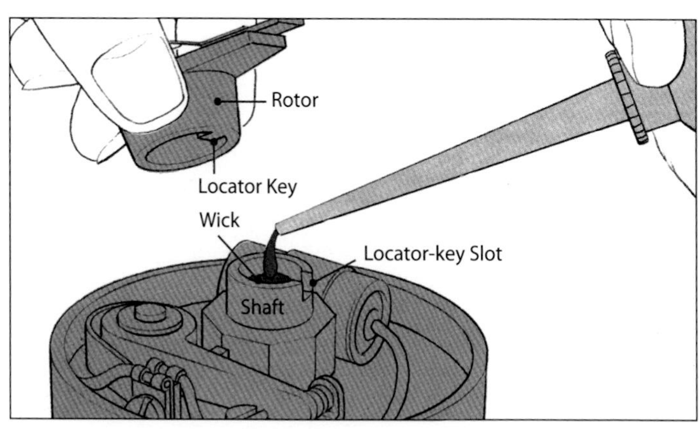

Before slipping the rotor back in place, lubricate the wick—the oil-absorbent felt inside the distributor shaft—with three drops of engine oil. Wipe off any spillage with a clean rag. Align the locator key with the slot provided for it on the shaft, press the rotor into place, and fasten the distributor cap.

Changing Oil and Filters

The crankcase oil in an inboard gasoline engine should be changed after every 50 hours of engine use. Most inboards are mounted just inches above the bilge and there is little or no room to drain them from beneath—as is the common practice with auto engines. A crankcase suction pump, electrical or manual, is required for the job. Before draining, run the engine until it reaches normal operating temperature, then turn it off and let a minute or so pass, permitting the sediment to settle. Remove the dipstick and insert the pump hose in its place. Draw out the old oil; then refill.

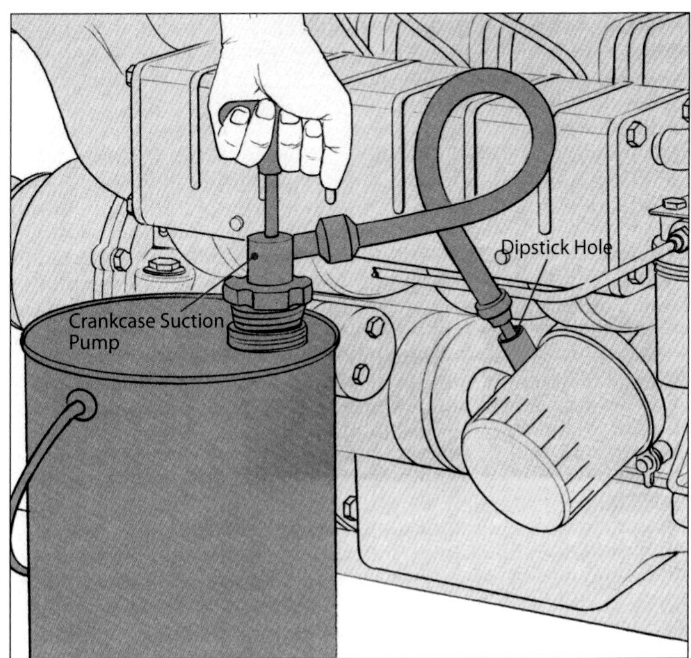

In some large powerboats, the engine is set above a cavity that permits crankcase oil to be drained downward into a pan. Run the engine until warm, turn it off and remove the crankcase drain plug. In some cases the pan may have to hold seven quarts of oil—although four quarts is more typical.

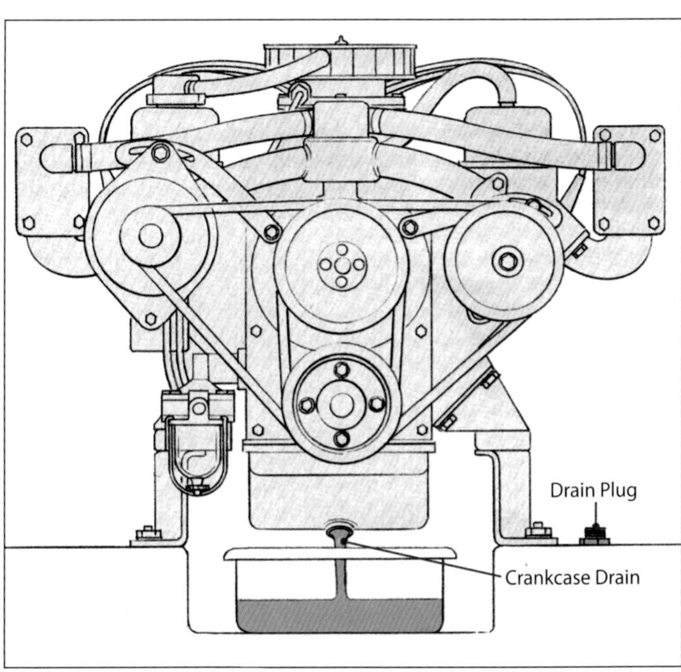

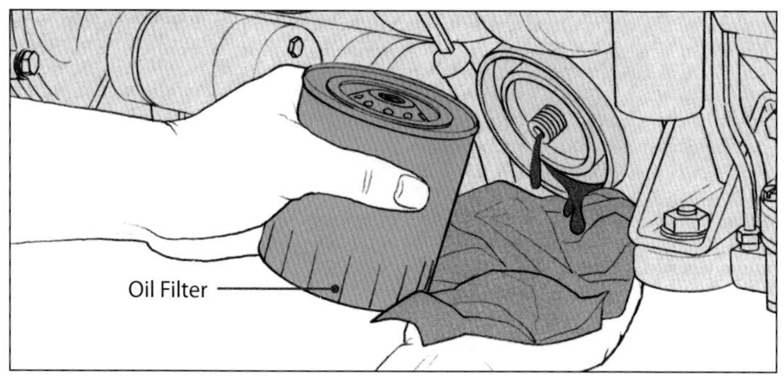

The oil filter, a cylindrical fitting jutting outward at the side of most gasoline inboards, should be replaced every time the engine oil is changed. Usually it can be unscrewed by hand, but if it is corroded in place, a strap wrench will free it, or a screwdriver can be hammered sideways right through the filter and used as a lever to turn it. During removal, hold a rag beneath the filter to catch oil. Tighten the new filter by hand; a wrench could strip its threads.

Where and When to Lubricate

To check your engine's lubrication, consult the owner's manual for recommended servicing. Then draw up a schedule showing the types of lubricants, the amounts needed, and the frequency of treatments. (The entries at right are for a typical inboard.) After each servicing, record the date—or the reading on the engine-hour meter—and check the log regularly to see if lubrication is due.

Parts	Lubricant	Amount	Interval
Distributor	Medium-weight engine oil	Five drops	Every 25 hours
Transmission-control linkage	Light engine oil	Five drops	Every 25 hours
Crankcase	Medium-weight engine oil	Four quarts	Every 50 hours
Hydraulic transmission	Transmission fluid	Two quarts	Every 100 hours
Distributor wick	Light engine oil	Three drops	Every 250 hours

Servicing the Transmission

Nestled behind an inboard engine, the hydraulic transmission is often overlooked during the round of maintenance chores. The boatman should perform two kinds of maintenance—replenishing the fluid in the housing and changing it every 100 hours. To check the level of fluid, remove the filler nut and inspect the dipstick that is attached to it. Note the appearance of the fluid. Normally, transmission fluid has a reddish tinge; if it appears milky, water may have leaked into the system, and a specialist should be consulted.

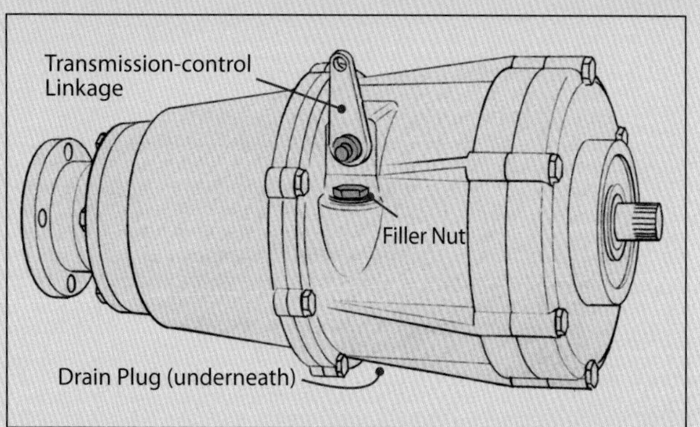

The Sturdy Diesel

Diesel engines have a well-earned reputation for running smoothly with less care than other types of power plants. There are two reasons. Most diesels are built to heavy-duty specifications that help to ensure their durability; typically, a 50-horsepower diesel like the one at right will run four times longer between major overhauls than a gasoline engine of equivalent power. In addition, a diesel engine is designed to operate without either a carburetor or an electrical ignition system. Consequently, it has fewer parts to wear out or break down.

Taking the place of a carburetor is a device called a fuel injector, which sprays precisely measured charges of vaporized fuel oil into each cylinder through a fine-gauged nozzle. The fuel vapor enters the cylinder just as the piston reaches the top of its stroke, compressing the air inside. This compression, which may reach as high as 500 pounds per square inch, raises the air temperature in the cylinder to about 1,000° F.—well above the flash point of the fuel. Thus no electric spark is needed to ignite it.

Despite its rugged construction, the diesel is not entirely maintenance-free. Crankcase oil must be changed at regular intervals, as prescribed in the engine manual. Drive belts for the alternator and water pump must be checked for wear and proper tension by the procedure shown on page 85. The cooling system must be kept brimming with fresh water. In addition, the fuel system (outlined in blue, at right) must be serviced periodically. Otherwise, specks of dirt and sediment in the diesel oil may clog the narrow channels in the fuel injector and nozzles.

To guard against clogging, a set of primary and secondary filters in the fuel lines trap minute dirt particles. The primary filter also removes water droplets suspended in the fuel—the result of moisture condensing inside the fuel tanks. This water accumulates in the bottom of the filter housing, which should be drained regularly during periods of normal engine use. In addition, after every 200 hours of operation, the filtering elements in both the primary and secondary filters should be replaced and the fuel pump cleaned.

Instructions for performing these tasks begin on page 92. Before starting, be sure to close the main valve in the fuel tank. This prevents fuel from siphoning out of the tank and running into the bilge when the pump or filters are opened.

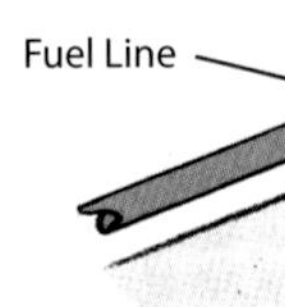

Engine Upkeep

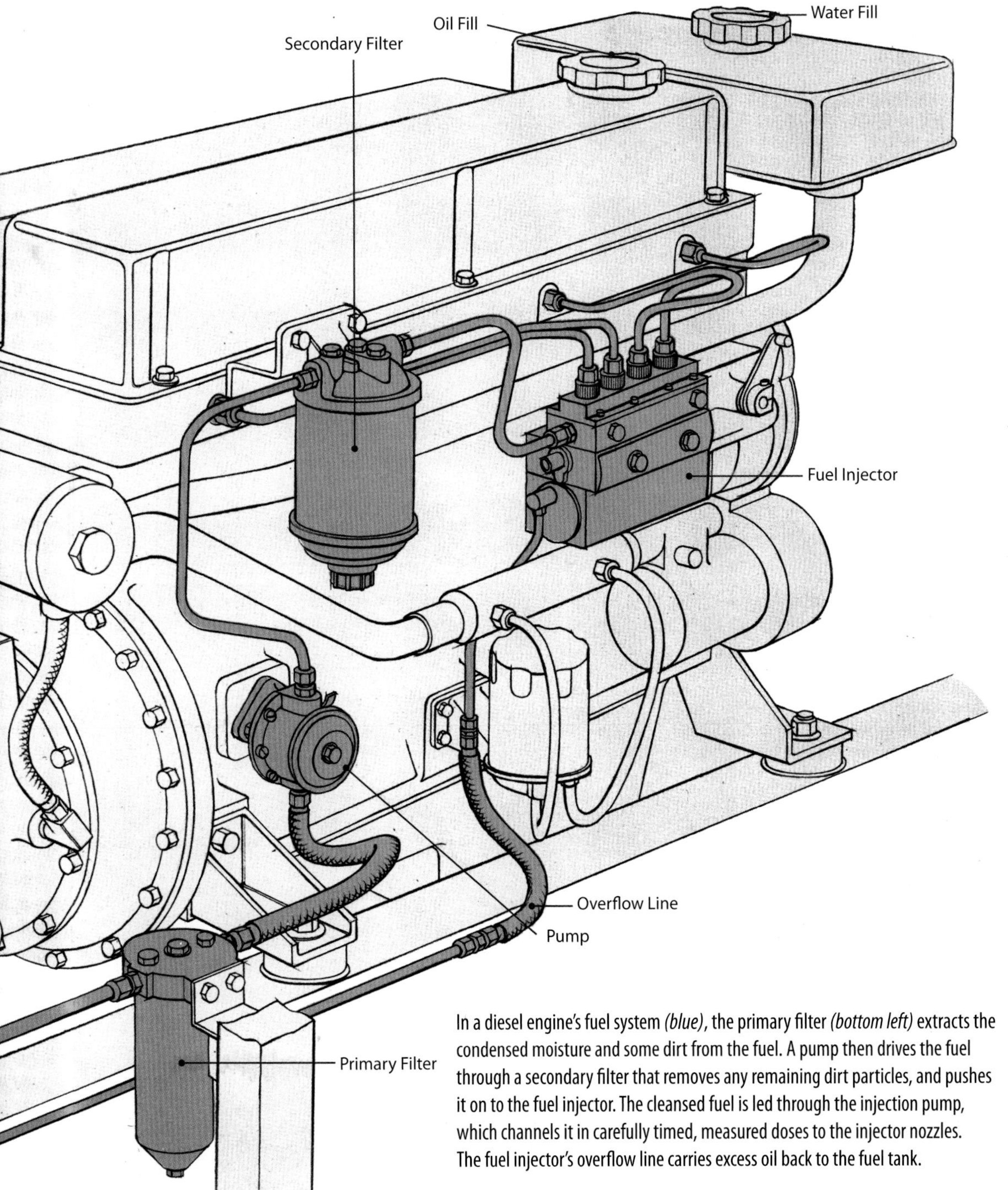

In a diesel engine's fuel system *(blue)*, the primary filter *(bottom left)* extracts the condensed moisture and some dirt from the fuel. A pump then drives the fuel through a secondary filter that removes any remaining dirt particles, and pushes it on to the fuel injector. The cleansed fuel is led through the injection pump, which channels it in carefully timed, measured doses to the injector nozzles. The fuel injector's overflow line carries excess oil back to the fuel tank.

Filters for Diesel Fuel

The diesel-engine components shown on these pages perform a series of related functions—cleaning impurities out of the fuel, pumping the fuel from the tank and injecting it into the cylinders. When any of the components is taken apart for cleaning, air enters the system. Unless it is bled off, the engine will lose power.

First, loosen the bleed screws atop the primary filter one at a time, manipulating the lever on the fuel pump until pure fuel seeps around each screw in turn. Repeat this step at each of the bleed screws on the secondary filter. Then progress to the final bleed screws on the fuel injector. (The fuel pump has no bleed screws, since its pulsating diaphragm forces air out toward the other fittings.) When pure fuel oozes out of the right-hand bleed screw on the injector, the job is complete.

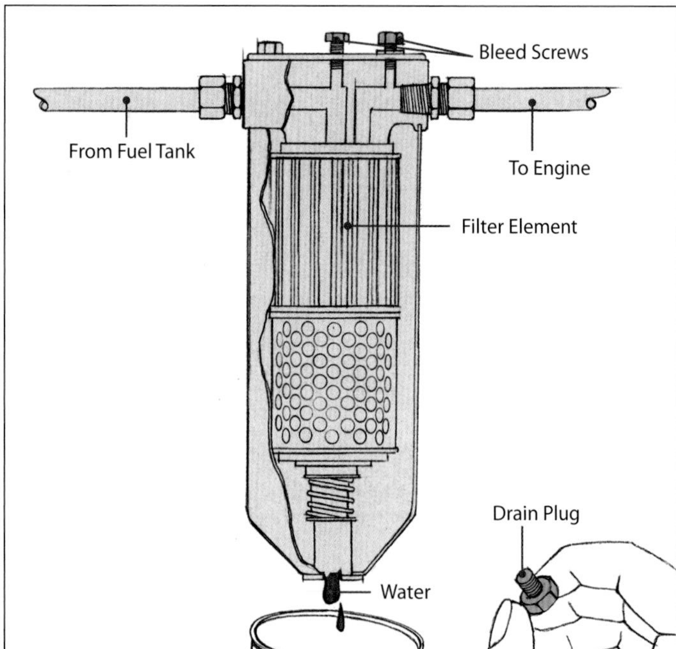

Two maintenance tasks are performed on the primary filter, which separates water from the fuel. After each tankful of fuel is used up, unscrew the drain plug and catch the moisture in a cup until pure fuel seeps out. Every 200 hours of engine use, dismantle the filter and change the element. Both tasks admit air, and the system must be bled.

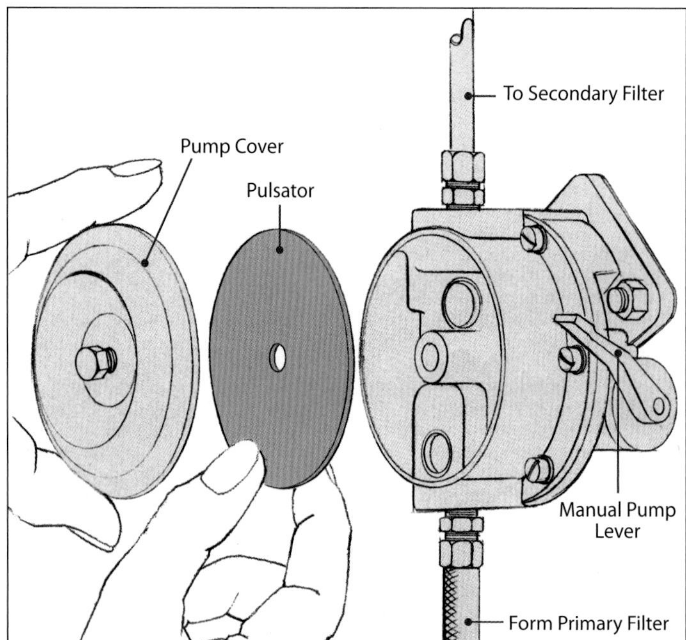

To clean a fuel pump, first remove its cover and the rubber pulsator, which helps pump fuel at a steady pressure. If the inside of the pump is caked with dirt, have the entire mechanism cleaned and rebuilt by a mechanic. Any small amounts of sediment, however, can be carefully removed with a toothpick. If the pulsator is punctured or cracked, it must be replaced. Flush the fuel-pump cover with fuel and rebolt it over the pulsator. Then bleed the entire fuel system.

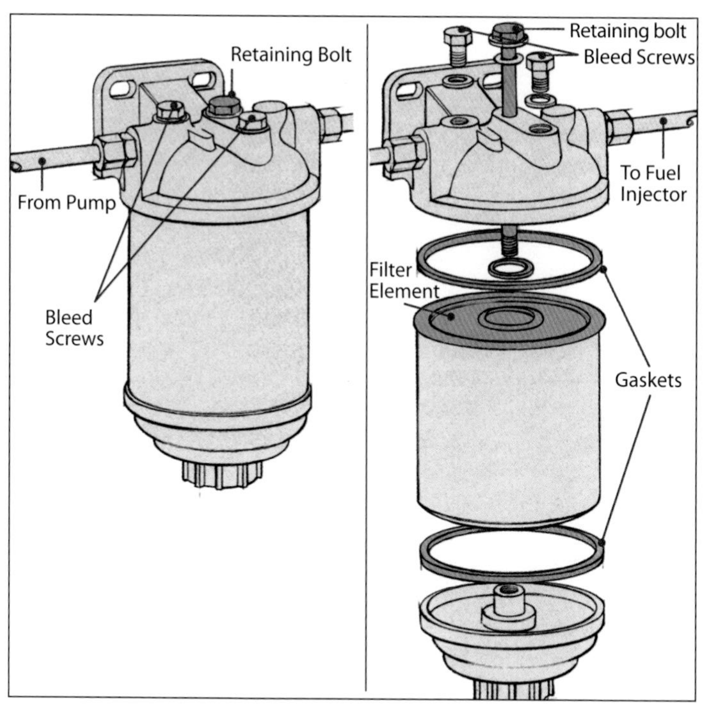

To change the element of a typical secondary fuel filter (shown both assembled and dismantled at left), undo the retaining bolt that lies between the two bleed screws atop the filter. Removing the bolt frees the filter element and the gaskets. Install new gaskets whenever the filter element is changed. (The element in the primary filter is changed in the same manner.) Then bleed the system.

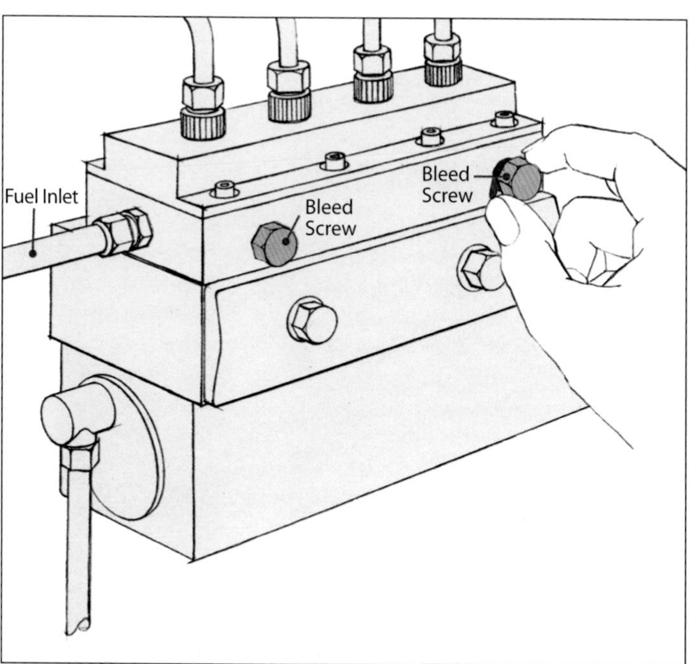

Although the fuel injector is not routinely dismantled by a boatman for maintenance, it must be included in the bleeding process, since air tends to diffuse throughout the fuel system when any part of it is opened. Thus the injector should be bled every time any element of the fuel system is cleaned. As with the filters, loosen the bleed screws and work the pump until pure fuel runs out of the opening, and then tighten the plug.

Caring for the Control Systems

Any boatman who has muffed a landing at a crowded dock because a steering cable jammed or because his engine would not shift into reverse knows the hazards of neglecting maintenance of a boat's controls. Sometimes the consequences can be fatal, as when an outboard skipper was hurled into the water when a flawed steering shaft broke and his speeding runabout swerved abruptly. The unmanned boat then circled and fatally slashed the man with its propeller.

On small boats, the various control mechanisms are simple, accessible and thus easy to maintain. On larger craft, the networks of steering, clutch, and throttle connections that link a boat's command station to its rudder, carburetor, and transmission are often partly concealed beneath a gunwale or in a remote recess of the bilge. But their relative inaccessibility is no excuse for neglect. A boatman must attend to them just as diligently as he would to his engines, sails, or hull. Some of these fixtures may be subjected to extreme wear and strain. For example, when a powerboat makes a hard turn at 10 knots, every square foot of rudder surface meets nearly 300 pounds of resistance. The cables, blocks, and connections of the entire steering system must be in top condition to endure such strain. Clutch and throttle connections encounter less stress, but they are under steady pressure from vibration, particularly where their terminals attach to the engine. These terminals may fracture, jam, or slip loose.

Any serious damage to the controls calls for professional attention. But the real key to safety in controls is preventive maintenance—tightening a clutch cable terminal, lubricating a pedestal steerer's sprocket *(right),* or repacking a leaky stuffing box, the through-hull fitting above the rudder. Constant and thorough inspection will ensure that the crucial chains of communication between a boat handler and his craft remain intact and responsive.

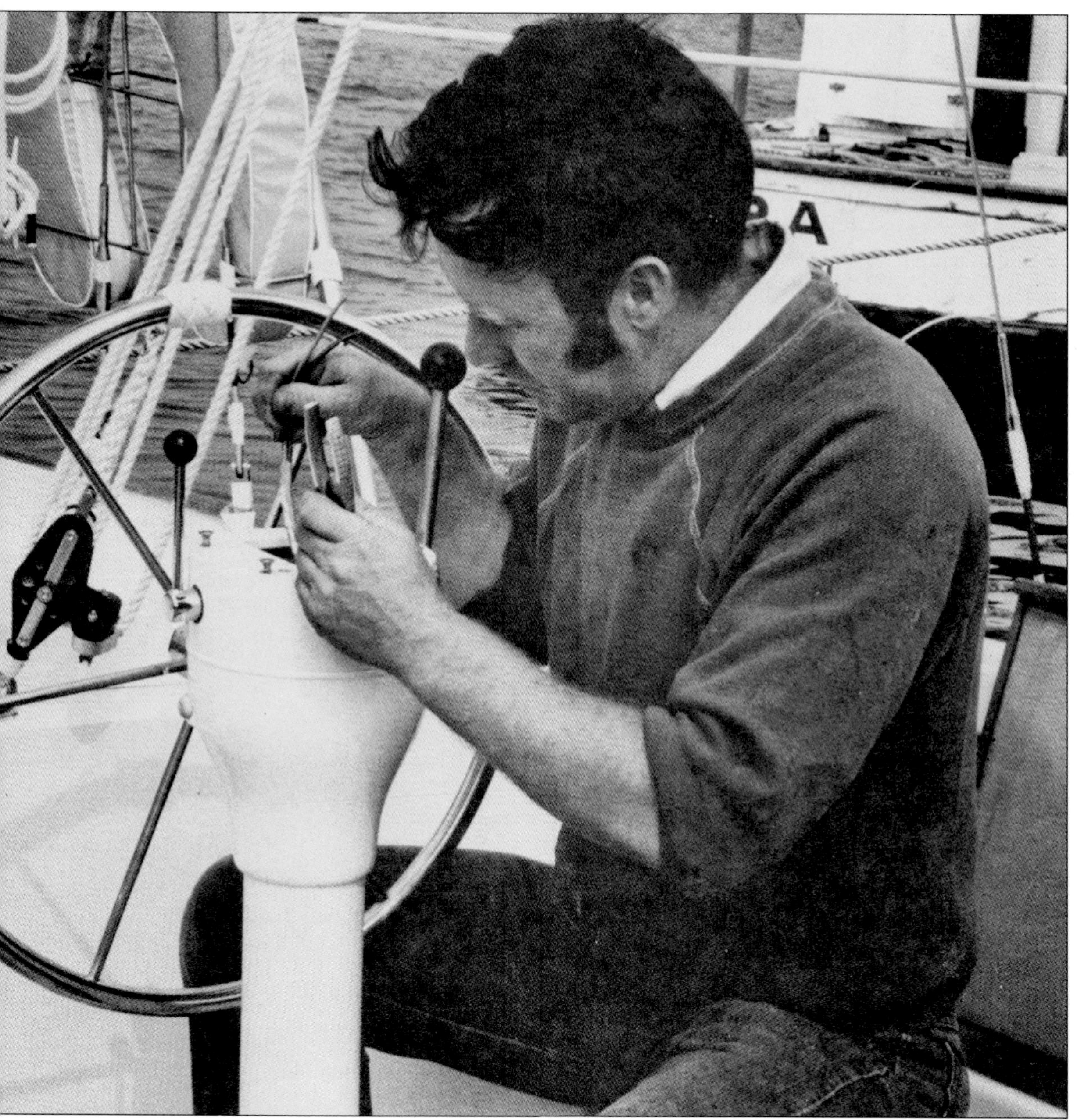

Having removed the binnacle that houses his compass, a boatman inspects the vital equipment beneath—the sprocket and chain of his boat's pedestal steerer. This device translates the rotary motion of the wheel to a direct pull on the cables controlling the rudder *(page 98)*.

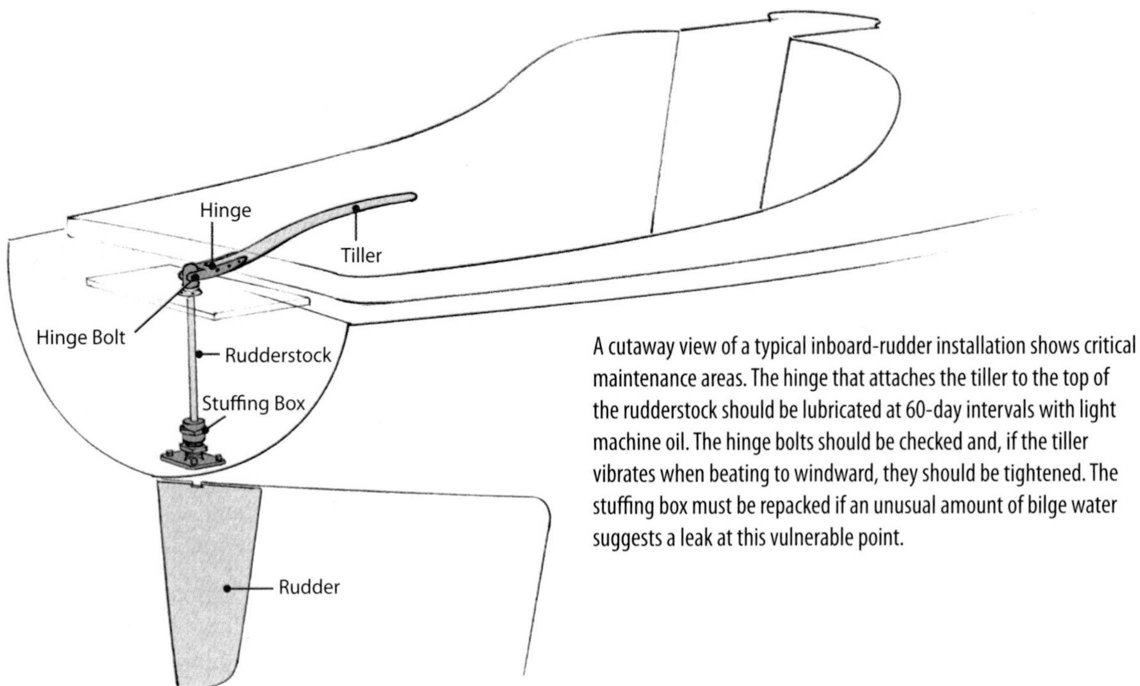

A cutaway view of a typical inboard-rudder installation shows critical maintenance areas. The hinge that attaches the tiller to the top of the rudderstock should be lubricated at 60-day intervals with light machine oil. The hinge bolts should be checked and, if the tiller vibrates when beating to windward, they should be tightened. The stuffing box must be repacked if an unusual amount of bilge water suggests a leak at this vulnerable point.

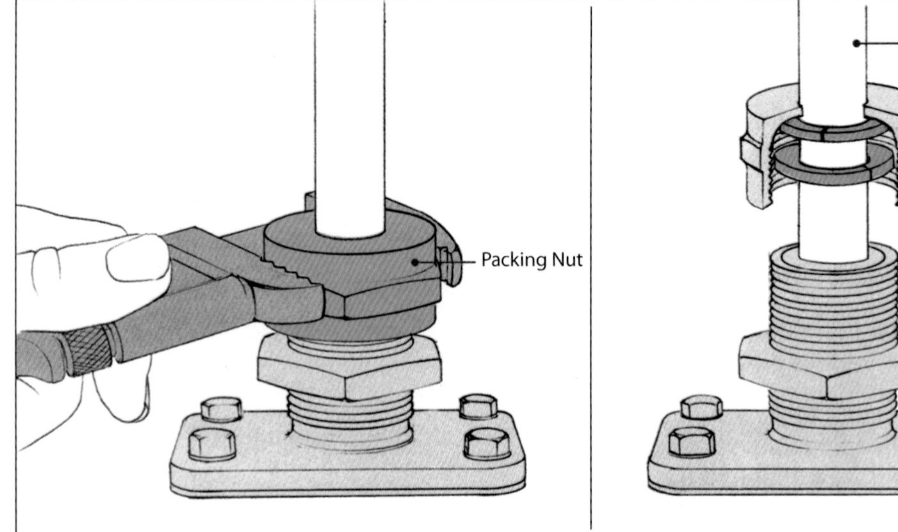

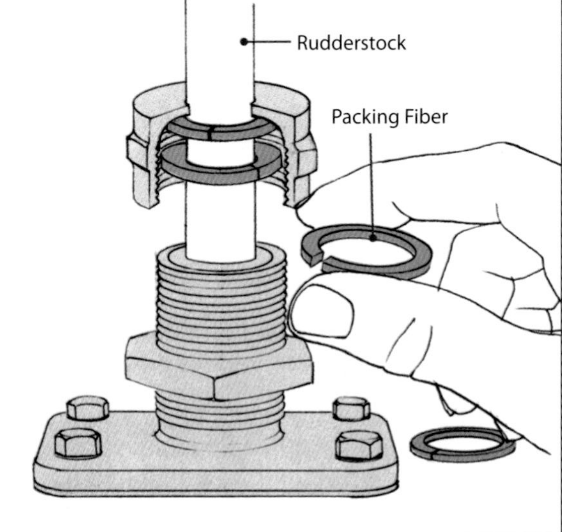

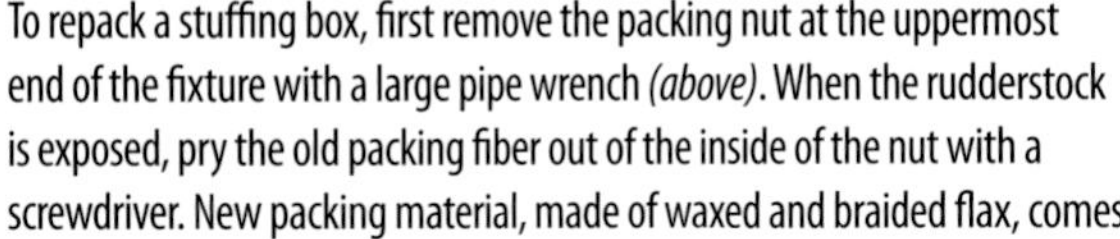

To repack a stuffing box, first remove the packing nut at the uppermost end of the fixture with a large pipe wrench *(above)*. When the rudderstock is exposed, pry the old packing fiber out of the inside of the nut with a screwdriver. New packing material, made of waxed and braided flax, comes in rectangular sheets from marine-supply stores; it must be cut into circular rings, slit open so they slip around the rudderstock *(above, right)*. Insert at least three rings around the stock. Then screw the packing nut tightly down on its base, or gland. Compression of the fiber makes the seal watertight.

Simple Rudder Maintenance

The commonest and simplest steering device used on sailboats is a rudder operated directly by a tiller—a design that evolved from the steering oar of antiquity. Rudder-tiller combinations come in two basic styles and one variant: outboard *(right, top),* a freely detachable design found on smaller boats; inboard *(left),* equipped with a fiber-packed stuffing box, and typically found on boats over 15 feet long; and the tube-mounted inboard *(right, bottom).*

All three designs require periodic lubrication, particularly at the tiller hinge atop the rudderstock. Rudders with pintles and gudgeons—strong metal fittings connecting the leading edge of the rudder to the transom or keel—require occasional out-of-water inspection for loose bolts and wood rot. And the skipper of any small craft should carry a sturdy oar to serve as a jury-rigged tiller in case these fittings break or the rudder is lost while at sea.

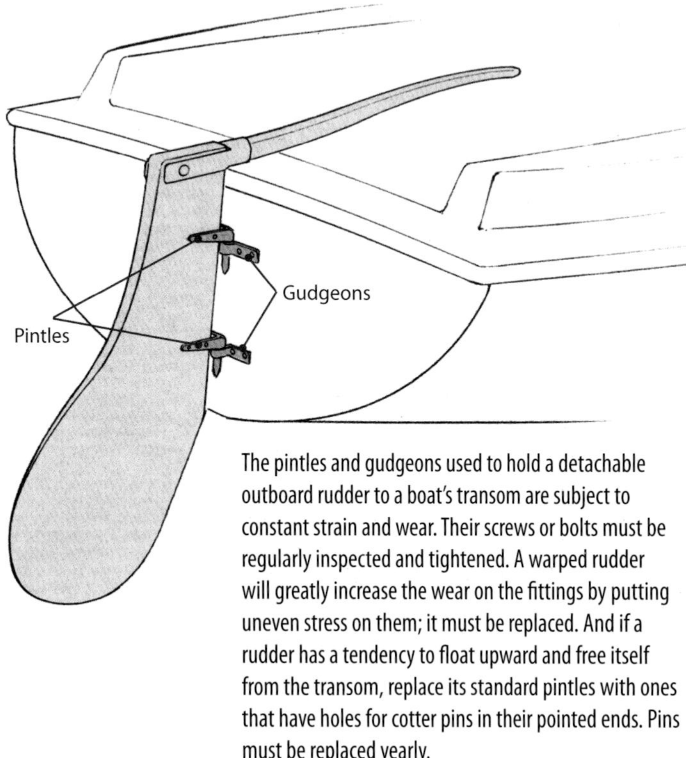

The pintles and gudgeons used to hold a detachable outboard rudder to a boat's transom are subject to constant strain and wear. Their screws or bolts must be regularly inspected and tightened. A warped rudder will greatly increase the wear on the fittings by putting uneven stress on them; it must be replaced. And if a rudder has a tendency to float upward and free itself from the transom, replace its standard pintles with ones that have holes for cotter pins in their pointed ends. Pins must be replaced yearly.

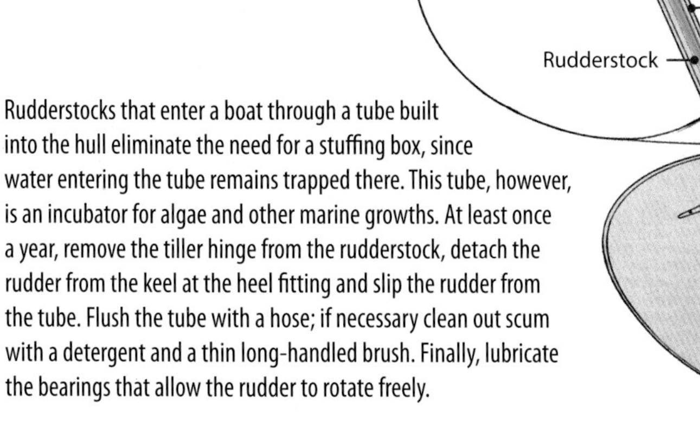

Rudderstocks that enter a boat through a tube built into the hull eliminate the need for a stuffing box, since water entering the tube remains trapped there. This tube, however, is an incubator for algae and other marine growths. At least once a year, remove the tiller hinge from the rudderstock, detach the rudder from the keel at the heel fitting and slip the rudder from the tube. Flush the tube with a hose; if necessary clean out scum with a detergent and a thin long-handled brush. Finally, lubricate the bearings that allow the rudder to rotate freely.

The different components of a pedestal steering system each require care on a different schedule. Every three or four weeks when a boat is in use, squirt #30 motor oil or light machine oil into the sheave bearings. Once every year, take the boat out into open water and make a hard-over turn in each direction while a crew member below watches for looseness of the block fastenings or the cable connections. Every two years, remove the housing atop the pedestal, oil the roller chain and inject grease into each of the grease fittings atop the roller bearings. Every five years, replace the cables.

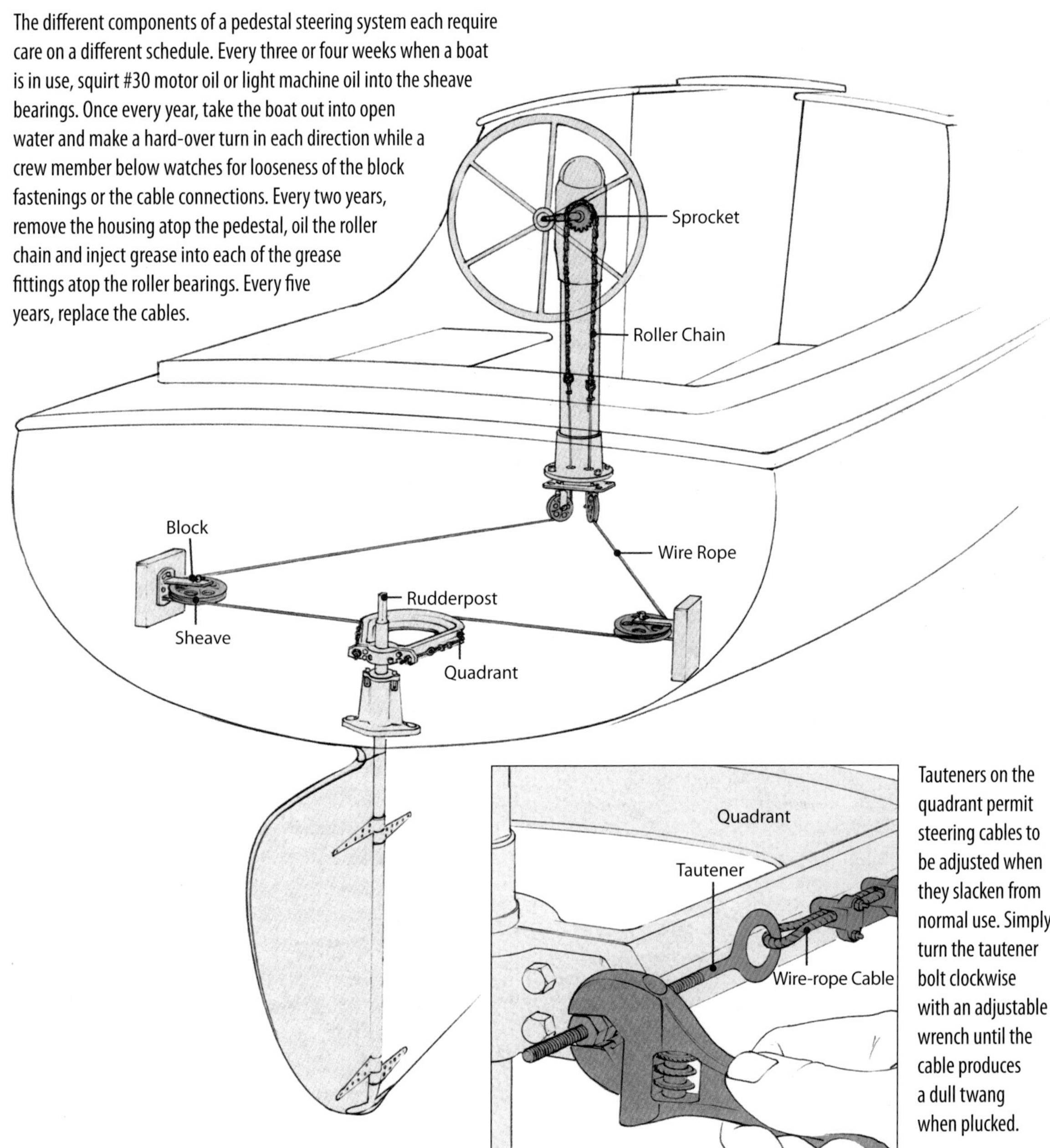

Tauteners on the quadrant permit steering cables to be adjusted when they slacken from normal use. Simply turn the tautener bolt clockwise with an adjustable wrench until the cable produces a dull twang when plucked.

Sailboat Steering Wheels

Two types of wheel-steering rigs are commonly used in sailboats over 25 feet—the chain-and-sprocket steerer *(left)* and the worm steering gear *(right).* Both types provide a boatman with some basic advantages over a tiller. Because of the mechanical advantage inherent in its design, a wheel with, say, a two-foot diameter gives the helmsman four times more turning force on the rudder than would a typical four-foot-long tiller. Moreover, a wheel can be mounted practically anywhere in a vessel, affording the helmsman better visibility and shelter than does a tiller.

The chain-and-sprocket steerer is the more sensitive of the two predominant wheel rigs but requires exceptional care. Once a month during normal use, oil should be applied to the sheaves, the moving parts of the blocks that guide wire rope from the steering pedestal to the turning quadrant.

The worm-gear rig is a plow horse by comparison—less responsive than its rival but also more hardy. If the worm steerer is lubricated at monthly intervals, it should last for decades.

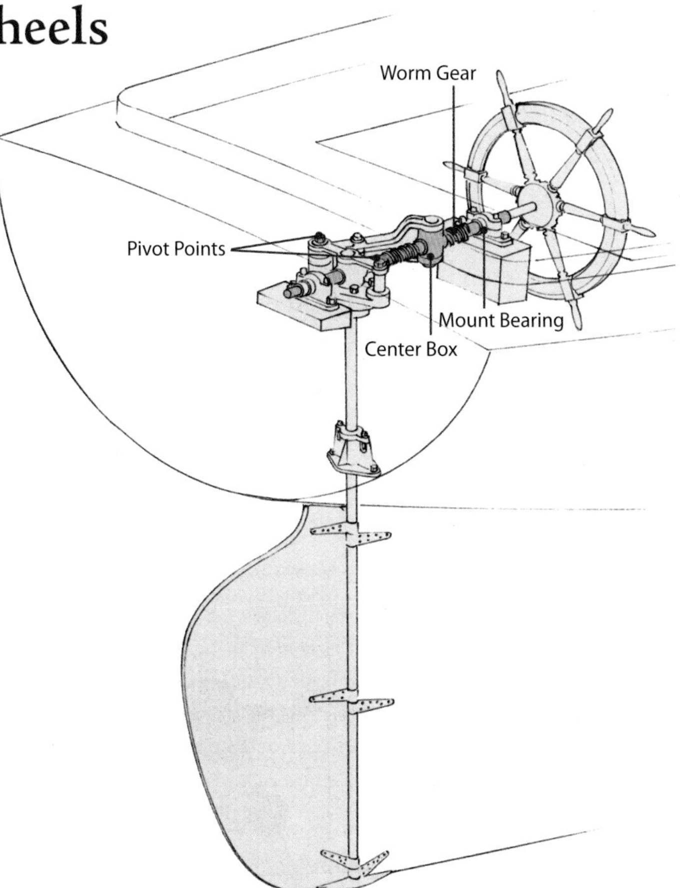

A worm gear serves to shift the rotary motion of a wheel from the horizontal to the vertical axis required to turn the rudder; in the process it is constantly subjected to turning friction. Lather it with grease at least once a month. At the same time, pump grease into the center box that supports the middle of the gear, and coat the pivot points and the mount bearings with high-grade motor oil.

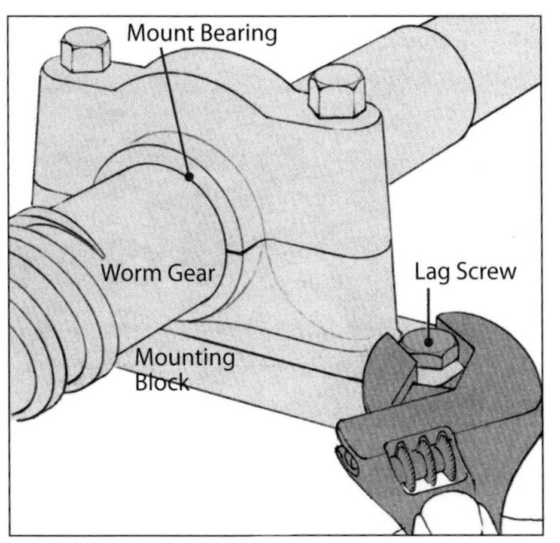

The worm gear's most vulnerable points are the lag screws that attach the mount bearings to the mounting block. These screws must be checked once a year. Tighten them with an adjustable wrench if they are loose. After tightening, shake the steering shaft; if the gear moves, it will have to be remounted—a job best left to a boatyard.

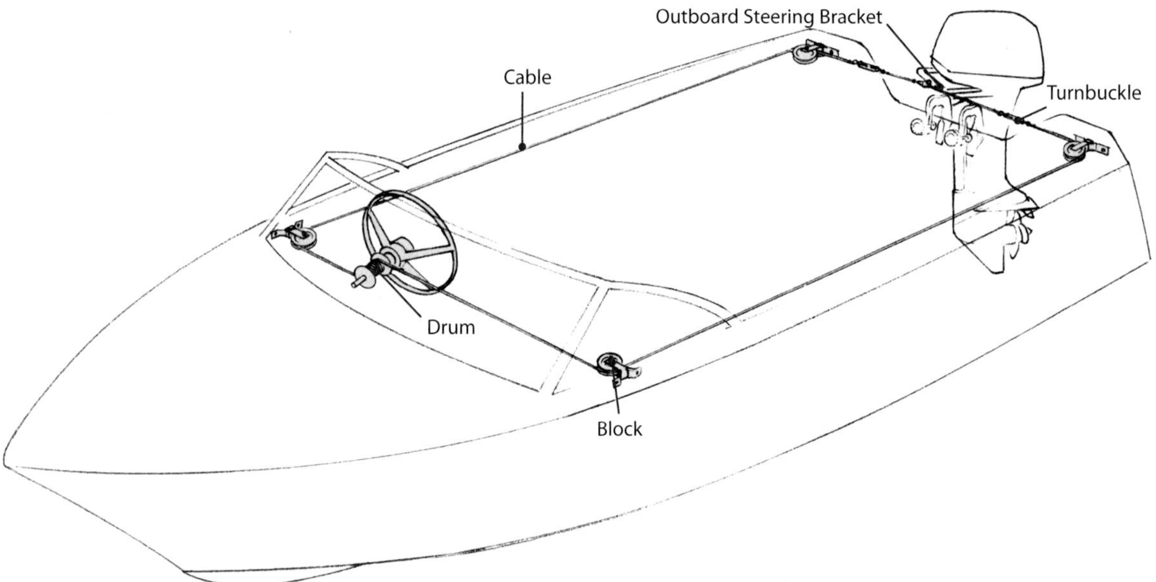

In the drum-and-cable steering system on this runabout, a turn of the wheel winds up and releases cable by equal amounts in opposite directions, pulling the outboard's steering bracket to one side or the other. The system is vulnerable in several ways. Cable may stretch from hard usage. Blocks are subjected to great stress by the cable's pulling force. And a block's mounting may be worked loose by a flexing hull or by the engine's vibration. All fittings on the system should be checked and tightened regularly, and the cable tension should be kept properly adjusted, as demonstrated below.

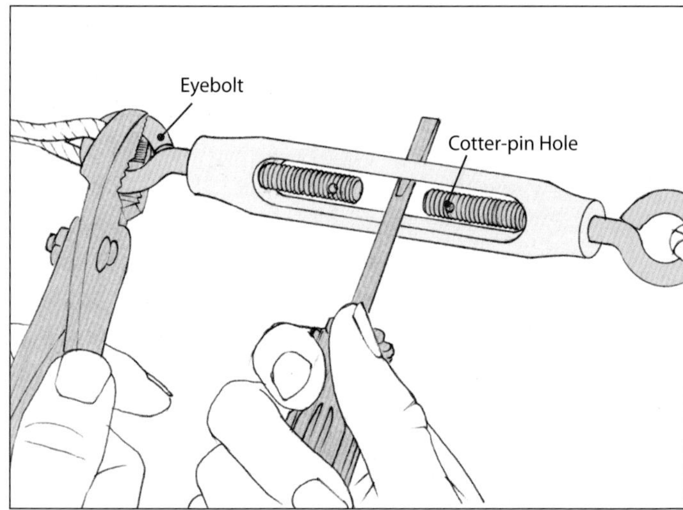

The tension in a steering cable is adjusted by twisting a turnbuckle to take up or give off slack. First remove the cotter pins from their holes in the tumbuckle's eyebolts. Grasp one eyebolt with a pair of pliers; then, using a screwdriver as a turning lever, rotate the turnbuckle. When the adjustment is completed, reinsert the cotter pins and wrap tape around them to cover their points.

Powerboat Steering Gear

Except for the smallest outboards and the slowest launches, virtually all powerboats have wheel steering. Where a sailboat in the 30-foot range can be managed with a tiller, the helmsman of a powerboat half that size moving at more than 10 knots needs a wheel's mechanical advantage to control his craft; a tiller with equal turning power would be impractically long.

Wheel-steering systems for powerboats come in three basic designs: the drum-and-cable rig shown on these pages, usually employed for outboards; and the rack-and-pinion and hydraulic systems explained on the following two pages.

Of the three, drum-and-cable controls are mechanically the least sophisticated; in fact, any boatman can easily devise such a system with parts available from marine-supply stores. It also requires considerably more care than the other two steering systems—both of which are composed of factory-finished parts and may contain their own internal lubrication. However, such maintenance tasks as adjusting cables with a turnbuckle, checking a drum-and-cable rig for weakened blocks or mending an override on the drum can be quickly executed because the system is exposed and accessible.

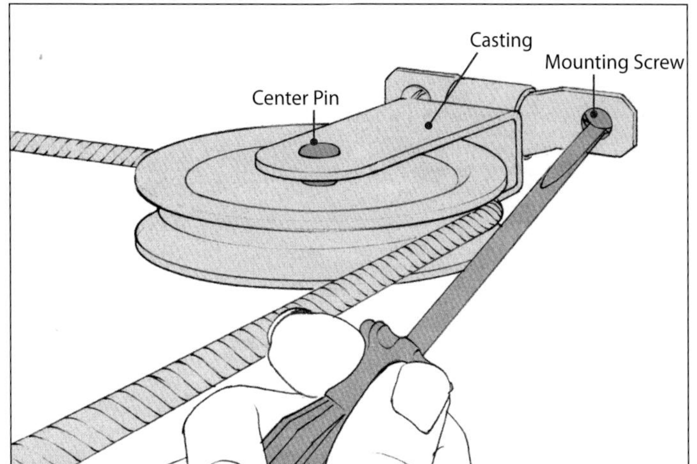

Blocks on drum-and-cable rigs are frequently made of relatively weak, thin metal castings—as are their center pins. Both tend to crack or break easily. Moreover, if the blocks are mounted with screws (or fiberglass-tape mountings), rather than bolts, they may spring loose during a sharp turn. Every month or so, check the block castings for signs of damage (replace immediately if any cracks show) and test the tightness of the mounting screws. Many boatmen replace the screws or fiberglass mountings with through bolts.

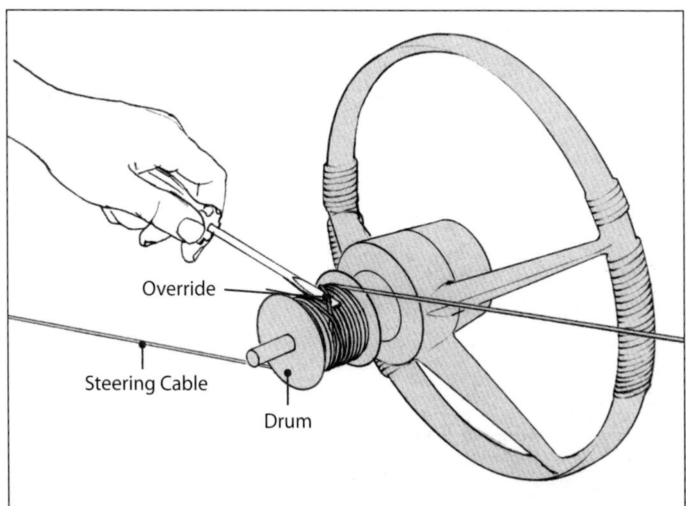

When the steering cable stretches, an overriding turn may develop on the wheel drum and cause the cable to jam. Loosen the turnbuckle to slacken the cable, and pry off the override with a screwdriver. If more than one turn has gone astray, it may be necessary to detach the cable at the turnbuckle to get enough slack so the cable can be rewrapped.

In rack-and-pinion steering, rotary motion of the helm is translated into linear motion and carried, by a cable led through a plastic conduit, to a lever on the rudder. The system is easier to install than drum and cable, and its flexible cable can be led virtually anywhere in the boat. Rack-and-pinion steering is also ideal for multiple control stations, as is shown here. Finally, the cable does not slacken with use, and therefore it has no turnbuckles for adjustment.

Flying-bridge Station
Main-cabin Station
Conduit
Lever
Rudder

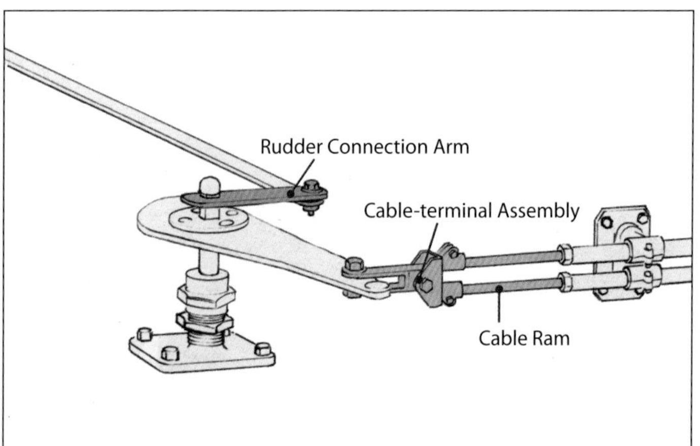

The principal maintenance points of a rack-and-pinion steering system are the cable connections on the rudderpost. A dab of grease should be applied every 60 days to the cable-terminal assembly, the cable ram, and the rudder connection arm. At the same time, all movable fittings in the rudder area should be checked for loose bolts, signs of corrosion, and any damage from vibration.

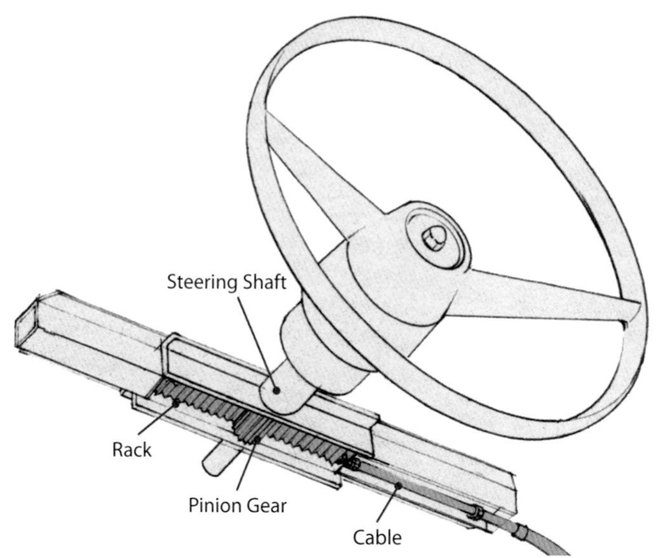

In a rack-and-pinion system, a pinion gear attached to the end of the steering shaft meshes with teeth on the horizontal rack. A turn of the wheel forces the rack sideways, pushing or pulling the cable running to the rudder terminals. No regular maintenance is required for the rack and pinion, but if the wheel operates roughly, slide the rack out of its trough and apply high-quality grease to its toothed surface.

A Hydraulic Boost

Hydraulic steering, designed for powerboats over 30 feet, differs significantly from both the drum-and-cable and rack-and-pinion systems in that it utilizes a basic power source other than human muscle. The heart of the system is a pump powered by the engine and mounted at the steering wheel. Depending on which way the wheel is turned, the pump forces oil-based hydraulic fluid—stored in a central reservoir—through one or the other of a pair of metal tubes leading toward the rudders. There, a cylinder manipulates the rudders by extending or retracting its piston arm in response to the varying fluid pressure. A relief valve helps control the pressure of the fluid.

Like the rack-and-pinion steering, hydraulic steering permits multiple steering stations—and has some additional advantages all its own. The system is designed so that the fluid exerts pressure only on the rudder, never the helm. Hence the wheel always moves easily.

Maintenance of hydraulic steering is best left to a professional, for the critical parts are complex and delicate. However, the skipper should check the tubing periodically for leaks; loss of fluid could incapacitate the system.

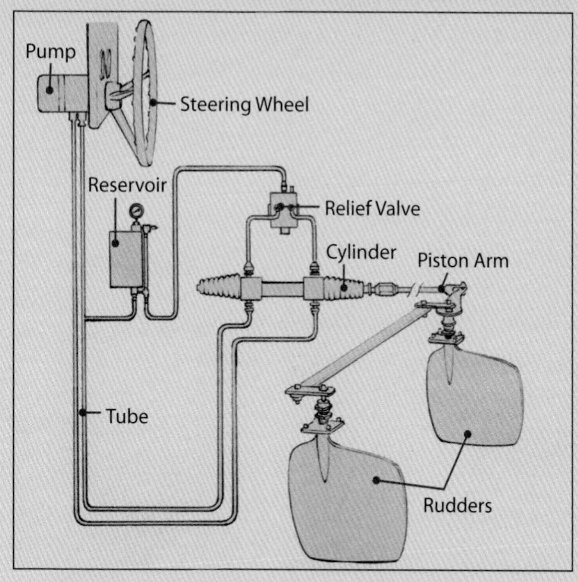

Propulsion Regulators

Complementing the steering system's directional control is another set of controls that regulate the progress of a boat backward or forward through the water. These engine controls ordinarily are activated by a pair of levers mounted in the cockpit or on the bridge. One of them, the clutch lever, engages the gears, the other is for the throttle. The levers are mechanically connected to engine and transmission terminals either by rigid rods—common on older boats and even some modern ones if the distance to be spanned is short—or by flexible cables for more remote command stations.

Both sets of controls operate in an uncomplicated, straightforward fashion. When the throttle lever is pushed forward, a valve in the carburetor is opened and the boat moves faster. And since a boat—unlike an automobile—has no variable gear ratios, a boat's clutch lever has only three positions: forward, neutral, and reverse. This simplicity pays a dividend in reliability. Given regular attention, the controls can survive corrosion and constant vibration to enjoy a long life—perhaps as long as the boat's.

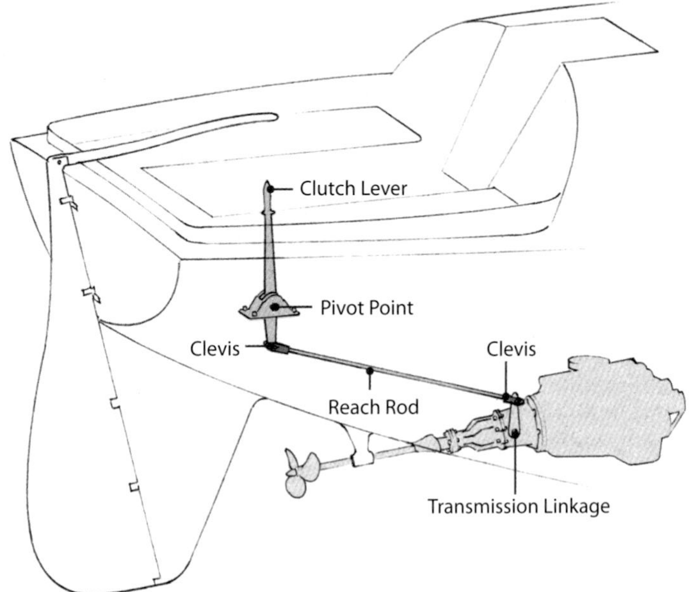

On a sailboat, the clutch-control lever for the auxiliary engine is linked to the transmission by two connecting joints, called clevises, and a sturdy pipe called a reach rod. Lubricate the pivot point every 60 days with light machine oil, and inspect the clevises and their pins for corrosion or vibration damage; replace them if necessary.

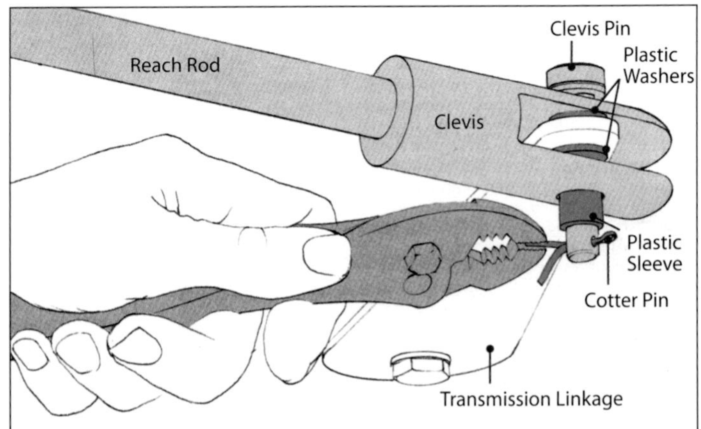

Since reach rods are usually made from durable bronze and engine parts from cast iron, galvanic corrosion can occur where the reach rod couples with the transmission-control linkage. To prevent this, the pin of the connecting clevis may be insulated with a plastic sleeve and washers to protect the joint. These plastic parts should be changed every year, as should the cotter pin.

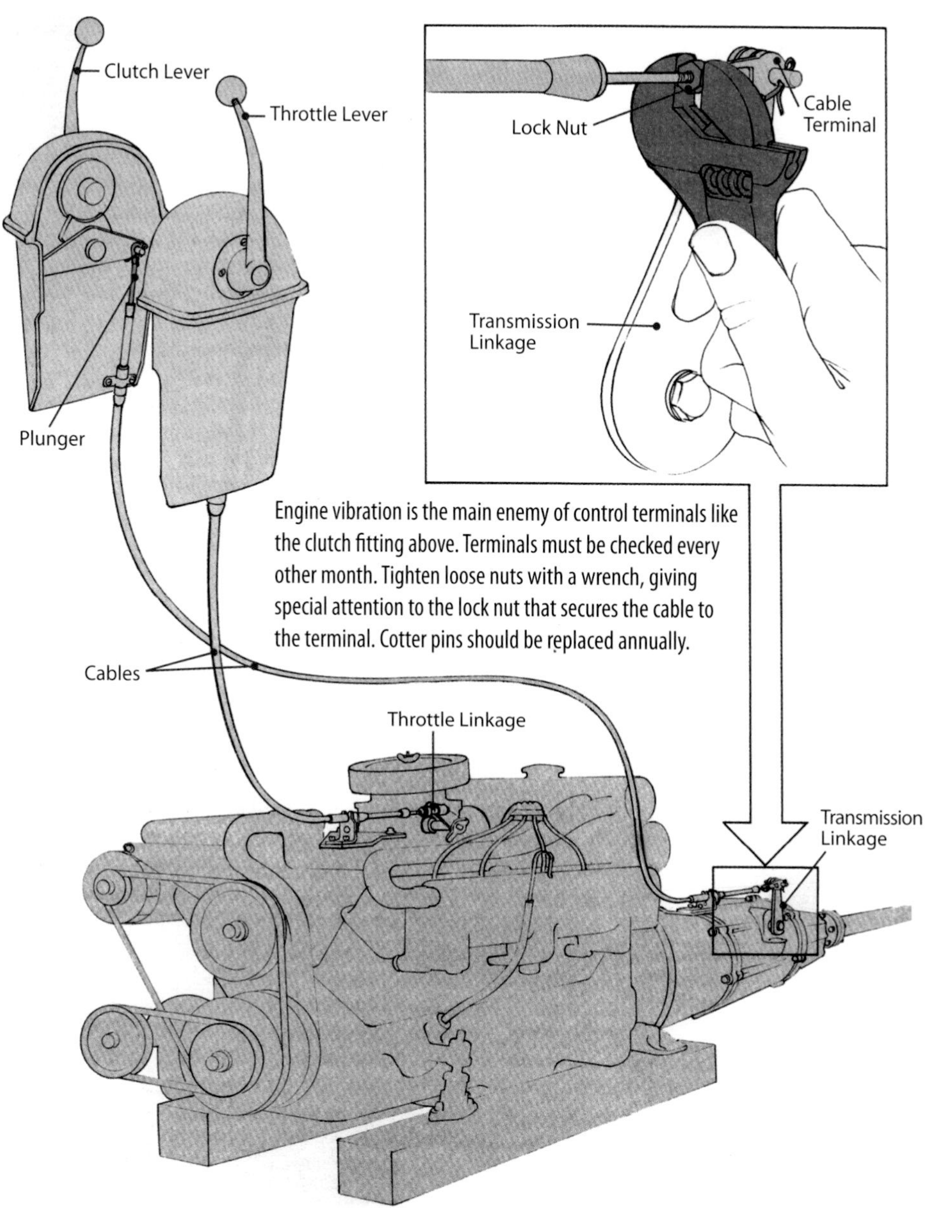

Engine vibration is the main enemy of control terminals like the clutch fitting above. Terminals must be checked every other month. Tighten loose nuts with a wrench, giving special attention to the lock nut that secures the cable to the terminal. Cotter pins should be replaced annually.

The control system above has individual clutch and throttle levers housed side by side in a single case *(shown opened)*. The levers are connected to the engine by flexible, stainless-steel cables sheathed in plastic. Every month, all moving parts—including the plungers inside the lever case—should be wiped with machine oil. If the levers and case are hit by salt spray, wash them clean with fresh water. A coating of oil or wax will help insulate them against corrosion.

CHAPTER 4: Belowdecks

A boat can possess a well-maintained, sound hull and the most graceful lines that ever came off a marine architect's drawing board—and yet be a floating misery if it is neglected below-decks. In the snug world below are arrayed the fixtures and mechanisms that supply, among other things, electricity, air and water, and systems for removing waste. Though these amenities may come respectably close to matching the comforts of home, they are harder to come by and to keep up on a boat than ashore. Electric power must be stored aboard or tapped from a slipside source. Fresh water must be carried along in tanks. Even fresh air for ventilation must be let in and out without at the same time admitting a load of spray. And the conduits, connections, tanks, and batteries that provide these things must be kept in A-1 condition.

The marine environment adversely affects belowdecks equipment with the endless rolling of a boat, whether it is moored or underway, and will wear out things that would be almost indestructible ashore. Hoses, ducts, doors, clamps, and all hinged fastenings must consequently be regularly checked and adjusted, lest they flex or flail themselves to destruction. Batteries and heavy tanks must be strongly secured to keep them from breaking loose and damaging a boat's hull.

Dampness is a particular plague to electrical systems. Sloshing bilge water, condensation, and spray entering through open ports can short out unprotected circuitry. Stray currents, connecting any ungrounded fittings through watery bilges, can rapidly reduce even the finest marine metals to so much crumbly rust by galvanic corrosion.

And shipboard electricity may also be highly dangerous. Although the 12-volt DC system that most boats use when they are underway cannot deliver a serious shock, the 110-volt AC dockside power is potentially lethal. A spray-soaked crew member who is standing on a wet cabin floor is in the same jeopardy as the householder who has just stepped from the shower and is about to turn on the bathroom light.

But though the belowdecks world has its share of hazards and inconveniences, it can also be cozy and livable. A dramatic boost in boating pleasure and convenience can be achieved by simply wiring in an extra storage battery for a bonus of power, or adding a light above a navigation table, or installing a mushroom vent *(page 123)* over an area that is poorly served by the other ventilation ducts. And sometimes even the crudest stopgap measure will pay off handsomely. For instance, some boatmen who are all too experienced with the fitful ways of marine toilets suggest stowing a tennis ball nearby. Jammed down the drain, it makes an emergency stopper when a backed-up head starts to flood over.

A boatman belowdecks on a power cruiser replaces a valve on his bilge pump. Above him is a green bilge blower to rid the adjoining engine compartment of gasoline fumes.

Electric Power Afloat

On virtually all pleasure boats the basic electrical system is a direct current, or DC, system (represented by the red and black wires at right). While some of the current originating from the battery goes straight to the ignition system, the rest flows into a unit called the DC service box. The box then parcels out current to such fixtures as the running lights, cabin lights, bilge pump, depth finder, and so on.

Many boats also carry a second, auxiliary system of alternating current, or AC *(orange wires),* which is operated at dockside only, by plugging into an electrical outlet ashore. The AC power, the same as that in any home, travels first to the boat's AC service box. This versatile unit is equipped with a voltage meter to warn against high or low voltages that could damage the boat's electrical equipment, and it also contains fuses to break a circuit in the event of a dangerous surge of power. From the service box, AC power goes out to conventional outlet plugs around the boat.

The DC system, however, is neither so convenient nor so simple. The peculiar nature of its circuitry allows for no outlet plugs, so that every new fixture must be wired directly back into the DC service box.

The arrangement for grounding a DC system is much more complicated than for an AC system, whose operating wires and grounding wire are all in a single cable connected to the shore. DC ground wires—technically known as return wires and indicated in black at right—are led from electric lights and other devices to the DC service box. From there, a single return wire leads to a so-called grounding point on the engine. Another return wire leads from the engine to the negative terminal of the battery, thereby completing the DC circuitry.

The engine is also linked, by means of a series of wires that are called the bonding system *(green),* to all the other major metal items on the boat, including the propeller—which connects the entire system to the water and ultimately connects it to the earth itself.

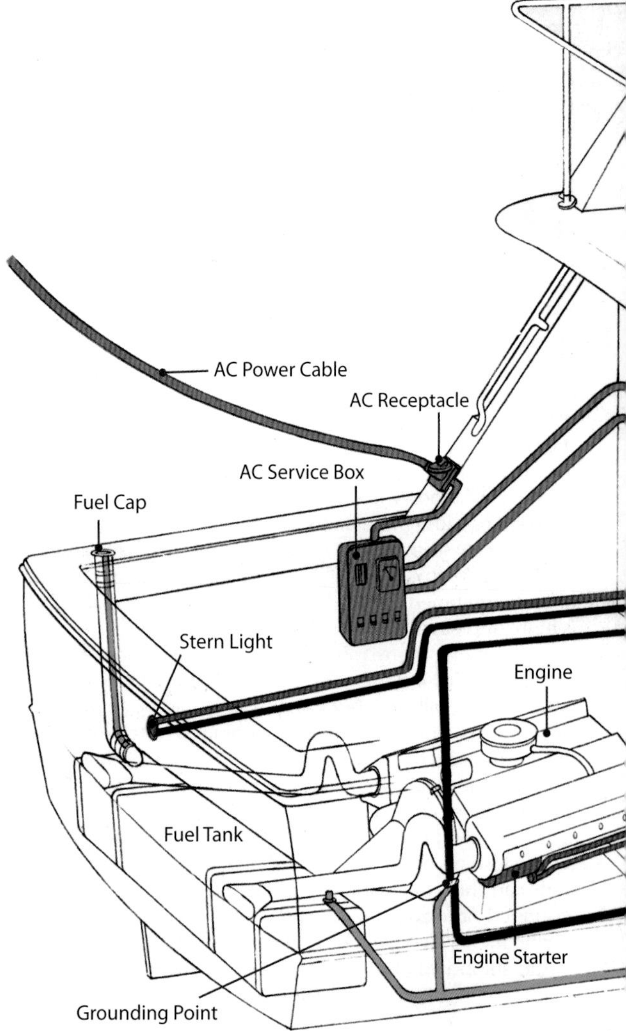

The red, black, and green wires on the power cruiser above belong to its DC system. The red ones are power-delivering, or hot, wires; black are return wires that serve both to complete DC circuits and ground them; green are bonding wires that link large metal objects together. Of the three, the bonding wires are least understood by boating novices, but they are critical to safety. Without the bonding system, these metal objects could absorb static charges or leakage from the circuitry. Connecting them neutralizes the errant electricity, thereby thwarting galvanic corrosion and radio interference—or even an explosion if a stray spark was to land near the fuel fill cap.

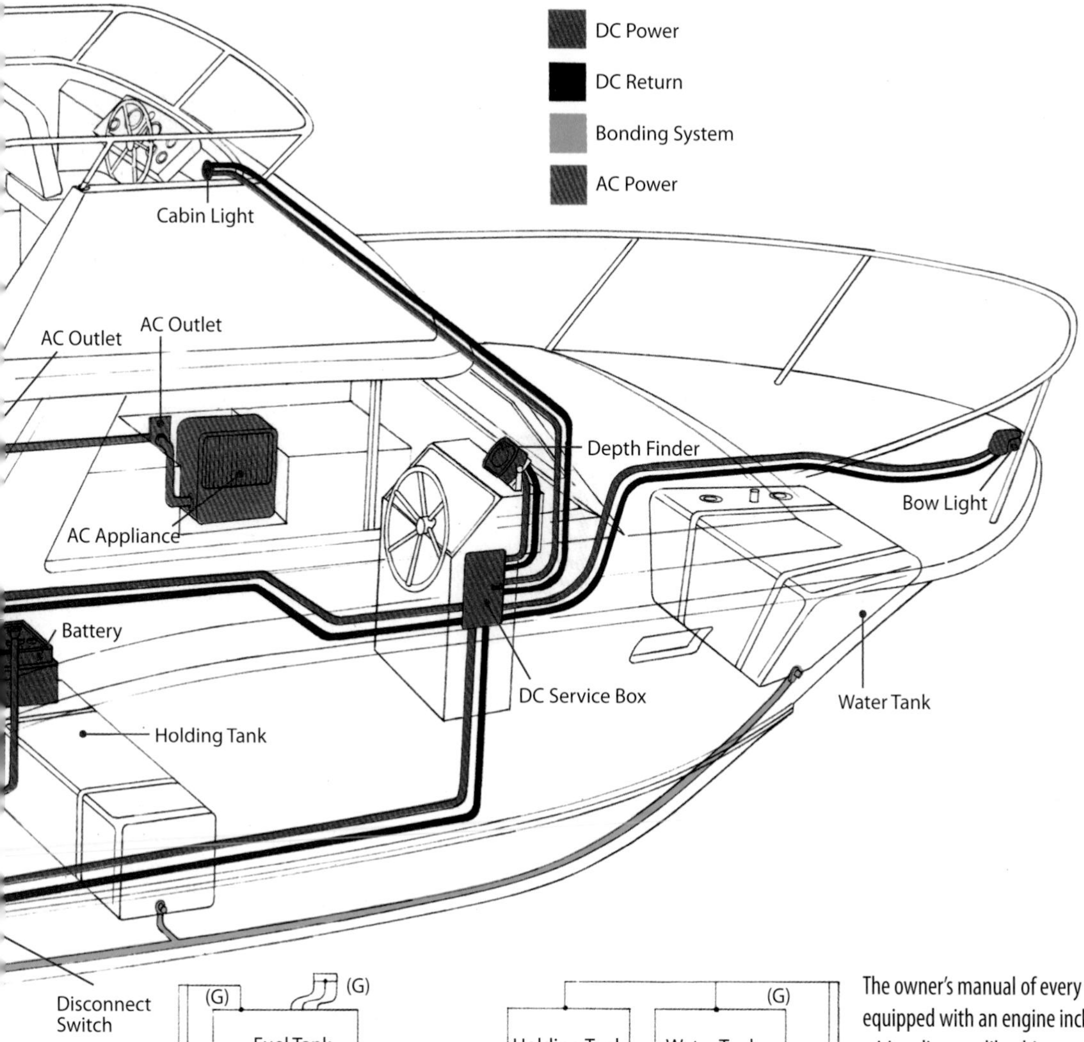

DC Power
DC Return
Bonding System
AC Power
Cabin Light
AC Outlet
AC Outlet
Depth Finder
Bow Light
AC Appliance
Battery
DC Service Box
Water Tank
Holding Tank
Disconnect Switch

(G)
(G)
Fuel Tank
(G)
Holding Tank
Water Tank
Service Box
(B)
(B)
Fuse
(R)
Starter
Battery
(R)
Disconnect Switch
Engine
(R)
(R)
(B)
(G)
(B)
Cabin Light
Bonding System

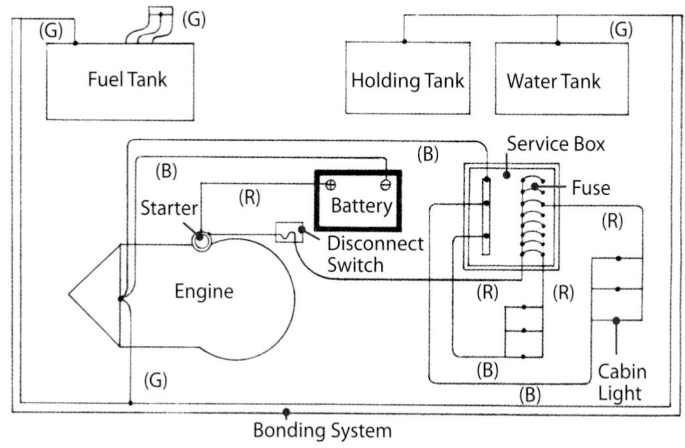

The owner's manual of every new boat equipped with an engine includes a DC-wiring diagram like this one, showing in stylized form the paths, connection points, and fuses of the wiring system. The diagram should always be kept close at hand in order to aid in troubleshooting the system. For ease of identification, the individual wires, designated by straight lines, are color-coded—here with the initials R for red, B for black and G for green—to match the colors of the boat's wires. Connection points are indicated by dots and small circles, and the position of fuses by small arches.

Installing New Gear

Any new piece of DC-powered electrical equipment, such as a depth finder or even an ordinary lamp, must be wired directly into a boat's DC service box—a basically simple task for a boatman possessing passable skill with a screwdriver and pliers. The first requisite is enough of the right kind of wire. Some appliances come with adequate wire attached. If not, a marine-supply store can usually advise a boatman on the proper wire to buy. The more power the appliance requires and the greater the distance the current must travel, the heavier the wire should be.

Before connecting the new piece of equipment, fasten it in place to avoid damage if the boat rolls suddenly—as can happen even at dockside. Next, to prevent electrical sparks during installation, turn off the battery switch, located near the battery in the engine compartment.

The wire used on boats for connecting DC appliances is actually a pair of wires bound together, each one insulated with plastic that often is color-coded to identify the positive and negative terminals. These paired wires commonly are sealed in another plastic coating that further shields them from outside contacts. Attach one wire of the pair to the positive terminal of the appliance, then the other—the return wire—to the negative terminal. Run the wires to the service box, usually located on or near the boat's steering console. Be sure to connect the wire from the appliance's negative terminal to the service box's negative terminal and the ends of the other wire to the two positive terminals. If the wires are attached to the wrong terminals at either end, the appliance may be subject to damage from short circuits.

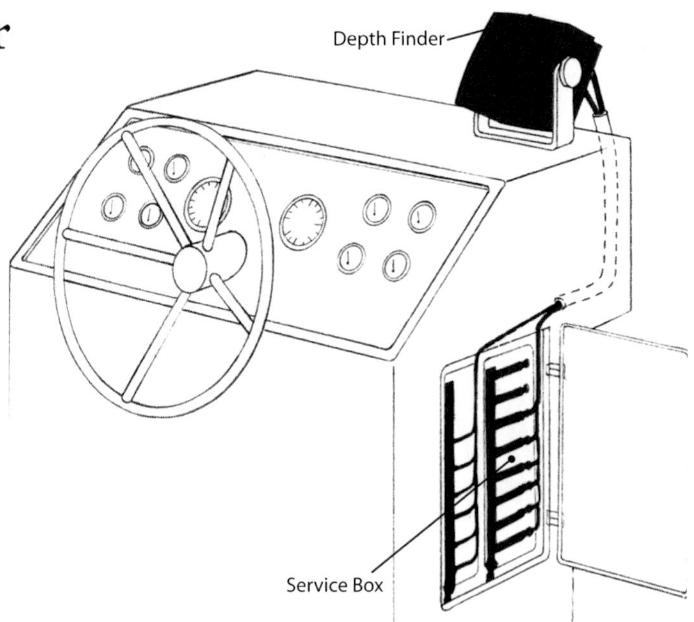

Connecting a new depth finder is usually the easiest of electrical-installation chores, since most depth finders come from the manufacturer with wires attached and the instrument is ordinarily mounted on the control console, close to the DC service box. If the new fixture is to be mounted elsewhere on the boat, the wire must be secured at least every 18 inches with corrosion-resistant metal or plastic loops or clips that are fastened in place by screws.

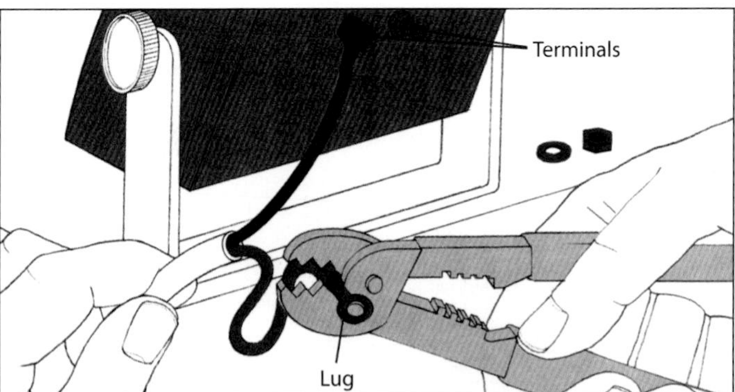

When attaching a wire to a terminal on an appliance or in the service box, always use a ring lug (*above*) rather than simply twisting the end of the wire around the terminal. The lug is less likely to pull loose and, being flat, fits the terminal more snugly and makes a better connection. To fit the end of a wire with a lug, strip one half or three quarters of an inch of insulation from the wire's end and crimp it on the lug's sleeve with pliers, or with a crimper like that shown here. Then wrap the sleeve with electrical tape.

Some Fine Points of Marine Wiring

A failure in a boat's wiring system can result in loss of power to the engine or a much-needed appliance, damage to wiring or equipment, or a potentially serious shock to the boatman himself. All wiring, connections, and switches of both AC and DC systems should be periodically checked for chafed insulation, loose connections and corroded terminals. When installing new wiring or replacing or repairing existing circuits, the boatman should keep in mind the procedures and precautions below.

- Each wire in the insulated pairs commonly used on boats should be made up of multiple clusters of fine wire strands (about 20 strands is a minimum). Such wire will resist the constant flexing, caused by the vibration of the boat, that tends to break solid wire or wire of fewer strands.
- Never connect two wires by splicing them, or by soldering them, because the vibration of the boat may rupture the connection. Instead, use terminal posts. These are small boxes, available from marine-supply stores, that contain two or three pairs of internal terminals to which wires can be attached.
- If a nut or washer for a terminal post is lost, never replace it with a version made of another metal; a steel nut on a brass terminal will induce a galvanic reaction and corrosion will result in the damp environment aboard ship.
- To prevent short circuits and shock hazard, make sure that all AC wiring has a minimum power rating of 300 volts.
- Never use ordinary metal staples to secure wiring. Not only will the staples rust but they may also pierce the insulation, creating an electrical contact between the two wires and thereby causing a short circuit. Instead, use corrosion-resistant plastic or metal loops.
- In locations that are especially damp, such as the bilge, protect the wiring with extra insulation either by wrapping electrical tape around it or by running it through flexible conduits made of polyvinyl chloride (PVC) plastic.
- Make sure that the ends of all concealed wiring on the boat can be easily reached for inspection and repair.
- Pairs of wires that pass near the compass must be kept close together; otherwise, opposing currents in the two wires create an electromagnetic field that could cause compass deviation. If the wire pairs are not bound together by their own insulation, they should be twisted around each other; this will prevent formation of the electromagnetic field.

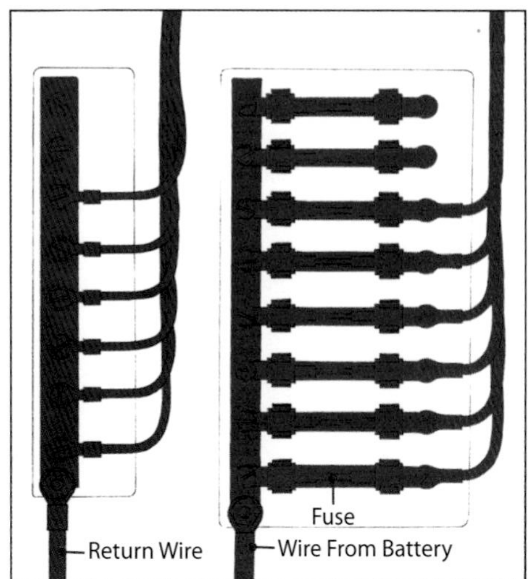

Inside the service box *(above)* are two rows of terminals—negative ones connected to a single return wire and positive terminals that connect, via fuses, to a cable leading to the positive terminal of the battery. If a surge of current overloads the system, a fuse will burn out and interrupt the circuit, thus saving wiring and equipment from damage. Circuit breakers, which serve the same function by tripping open, can be used instead of fuses; the initial cost is greater, but they can be reclosed rather than replaced when the trouble has been taken care of.

To install a second battery, begin by attaching its negative terminal to the negative terminal of the first battery, with heavy-duty cable. This grounds the new battery via the cable already leading from that post to the boat's grounding system. Next, detach the positive cable lug from the first battery; clip off the lug and wire the cable into the four-way switch. This connection, known as the common cable, will carry current from both batteries to all the DC electric gear aboard. Finally, connect the positive terminals of both batteries to the switch, as shown below.

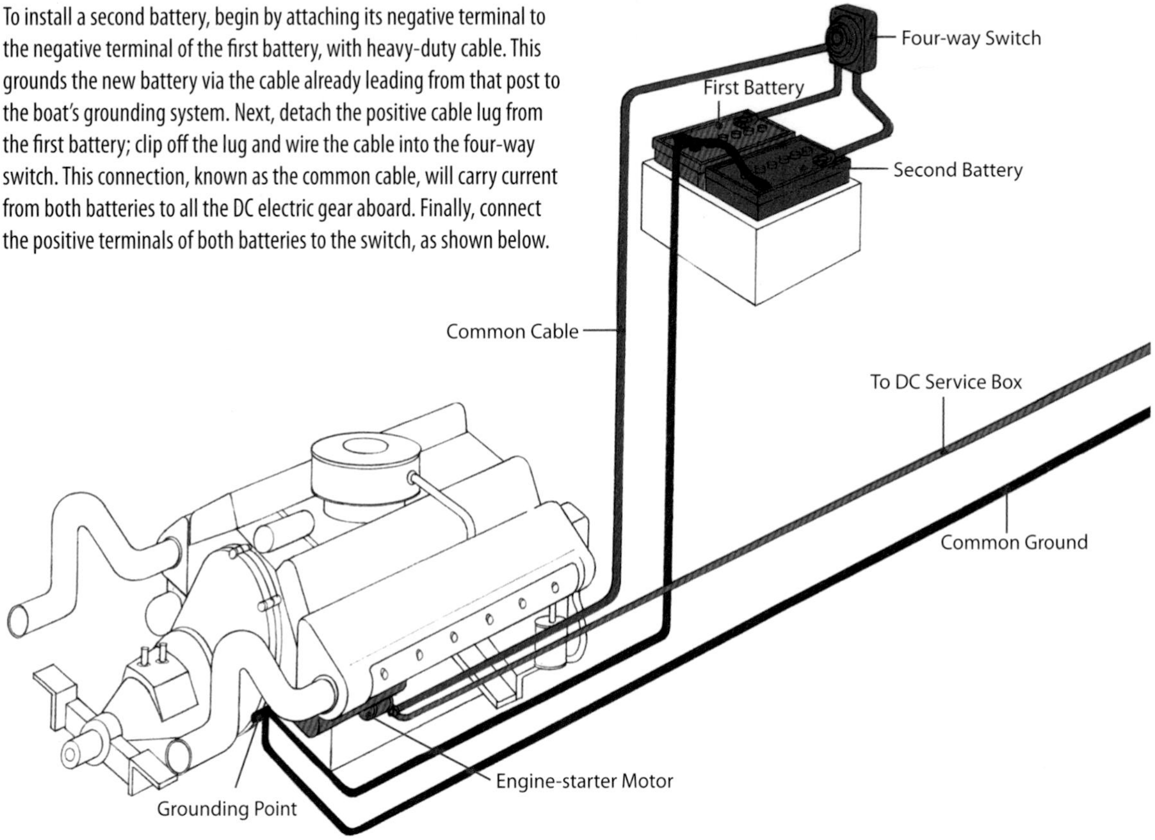

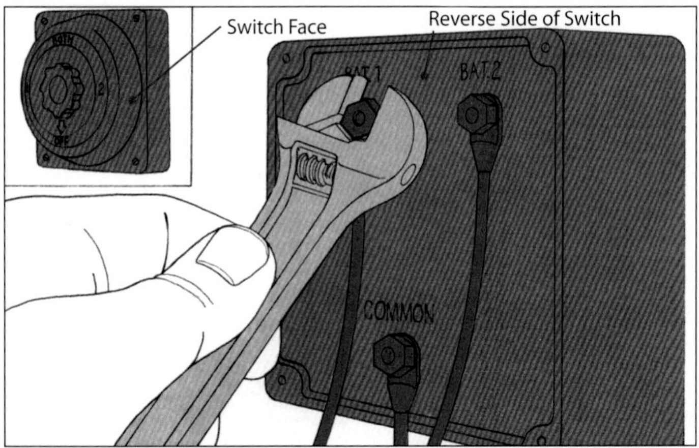

The switch used to control a dual-battery system has three terminals on its reverse side—a common terminal for the cable leading to the engine starter and two terminals for cables leading to the positive posts of the batteries. The rotating dial on the switch's face offers four different on-off possibilities: shutting off both batteries, running both (the common position), or operating one or the other. When hooking any cable into the switch, the dial should be set at "off."

Ample Current

As extra electrical equipment and electronic gear are added aboard a boat, the drain on the battery may increase to the point where demand exceeds supply. When this happens, lights will dim, electronic devices may malfunction, and the battery will crank the engine over just barely—or not at all. The battery may even go dead.

A healthy balance can be restored by simply adding a second battery to the system as shown at left, doubling the available power. To regulate the tandem power supply, a four-way switch should be installed; each setting on the switch helps to maintain the batteries in fresh condition. One position on the switch cuts off both batteries, ensuring that they will not leak their power into the DC system when the boat is not in use. Either of two other positions on the switch cuts off one battery while leaving the other in operation. The single working battery then serves as the sole power source for lights and other equipment—typically when at anchor—leaving its mate fully charged to start the engine again. A final switch setting reconnects both batteries, so that they can be brought up to full charge by the engine's alternator when underway.

During a cruise, batteries often come under their greatest strain at dockside in the evening, when lights and other electric equipment are in use—and when a boatman least wants to endure engine noise and fumes to keep them charged. The solution to that problem is to install an AC-powered battery charger *(right)*, which taps dockside current to keep both batteries at full strength.

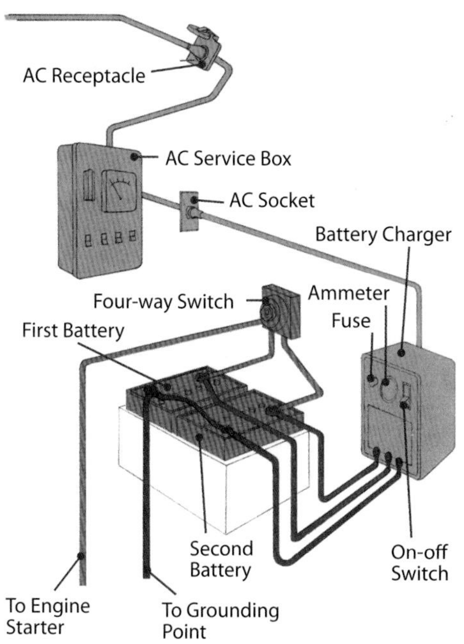

When adding an AC-powered battery charger, install the unit in a cool dry location— preferably outside the engine compartment. Attach cables from the positive terminals of both batteries to the positive terminals on the charger; then run a cable from the negative terminal of the second battery to the charger's negative terminals. Plug the charger into a convenient AC socket.

Belowdecks

A Source of AC Underway

Although the high-voltage AC current needed to run appliances like refrigerators or space heaters normally comes from dock-side, a boat's own batteries can supply a limited amount of AC power at sea with the help of a device known as an inverter. This mechanism transforms 12-volt DC current into 110-volt AC. To install an inverter, connect its positive and negative terminals directly to the matching battery terminals, using wire of at least four-gauge diameter to handle the heavy current flow. AC appliances are plugged into the electrical outlets on the face of the device. Since their power needs are great and could quickly drain a battery, operate them when the boat's engine is running—or only for very short periods when anchored or moored.

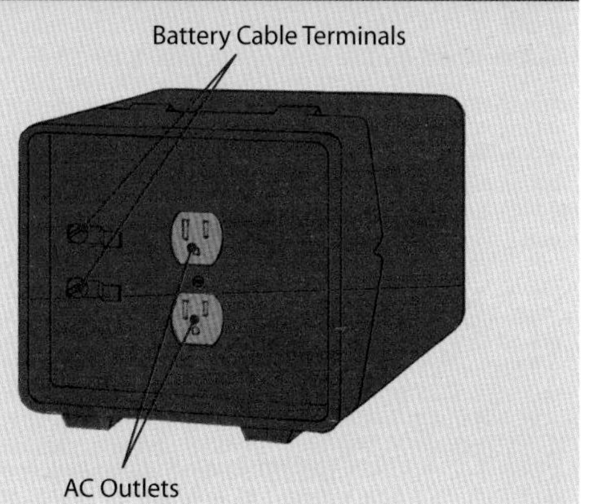

Tending the Battery

If a boat's battery is allowed to run down, not only will the engine refuse to start, but all the vessel's electrically powered safety gear—bilge pump, navigation lights, radiotelephone—will cease to function. The lifeblood of each battery cell is a solution of water and sulphuric acid, called an electrolyte, in which lead plates—the cell's positive and negative electrodes—are immersed. When the battery is fully charged, the concentration of acid in the electrolyte is fairly high. As power drains from the battery, a chemical reaction takes place, and the acid concentration decreases. Thus, by measuring the electrolyte's acidity *(bottom right)*, it is possible to tell if a battery is in prime operating condition or on the verge of failure.

Some of the water in the electrolyte may be lost during battery operation, lowering the fluid level in the cells; this will reduce the battery's efficiency and, in time, damage the electrodes. Check the electrolyte level once a month and add water if necessary. At the same time, be certain the battery is securely mounted; on a small open boat, it should be strapped into a waterproof battery box like the one above right. Be sure the terminals are clean and corrosion-free *(opposite)*.

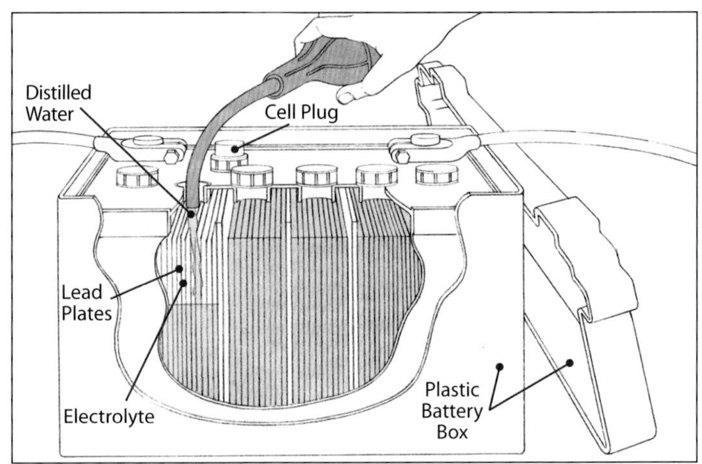

Whenever the fluid in a battery cell drops below the top of the lead electrodes, more fluid must be added; the small bulb-and-tube device shown here is a handy tool for doing this. Use distilled water if possible; otherwise, clean tap water will do. Be careful not to overfill the cells, since the overflow may corrode the battery terminals. Wipe up spills immediately, and rinse the top of the battery with a solution of baking soda to neutralize the acid in the fluid.

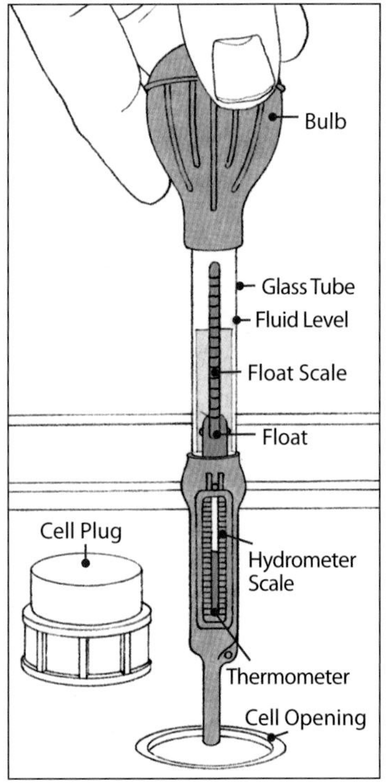

A highly accurate device for determining a battery's charge is a hydrometer like the one shown here, which measures the acid content of the electrolyte. Dip the hydrometer into a cell opening and draw fluid until the float bobs. At the fluid level read the number on the float scale. Then adjust for the solution's temperature, as indicated on the hydrometer's scale. The resulting figure is the electrolyte's specific gravity; a figure of 1.26 or more indicates a strong concentration of acid and a battery that is fully charged.

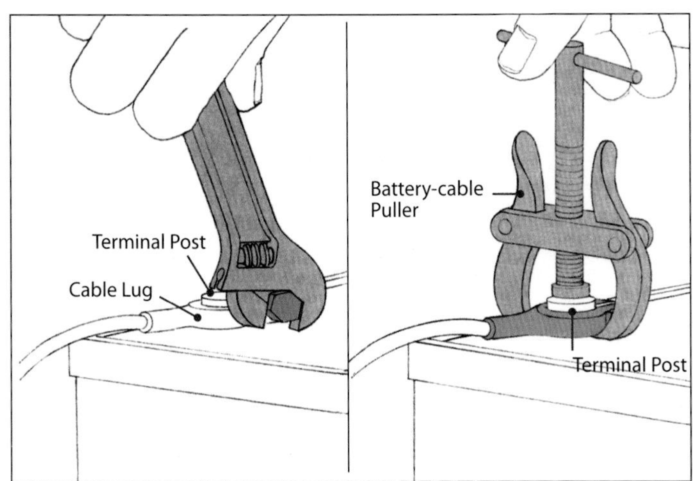

The corrosive lead sulphate deposits that tend to build up on a battery's terminal and cable connections should be cleaned off periodically. First loosen the nut that secures the cable lug to the terminal post *(far left)*. If the corrosion is so advanced that the cable cannot be lifted off easily, a tool called a battery-cable puller *(left)* may be necessary to remove it. Fit the puller around the lug and give the handle a clockwise twist; the lug will be lifted neatly off the battery.

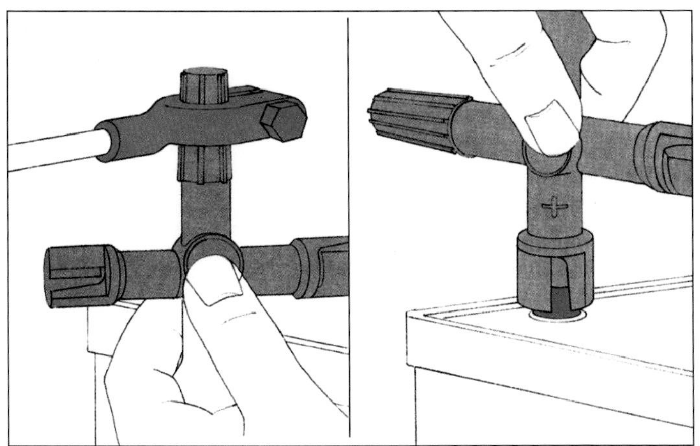

The next step is to remove any lead sulphate deposits from the lug and exposed terminal post. The most efficient tool for doing this is a device called a router, which has a ridged arm and two corrugated sockets. To scour the cable lug, simply insert the ridged arm and rotate, as shown at far left. The sockets are designed to fit over the terminal posts (they are different sizes to prevent attachment of a cable to the wrong post). A rotating motion, as shown at left, will clean the posts. If a router is not available, use a stainless-steel brush or steel wool.

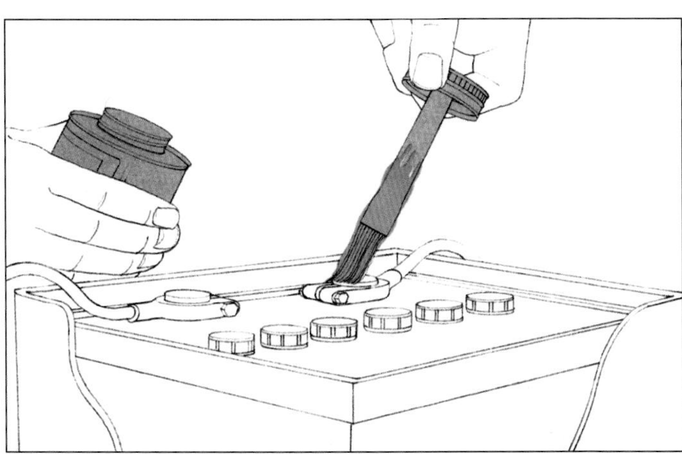

After reconnecting lugs to the posts, brush on a thick coating of petroleum jelly, or any electrically conductive paste available at marine-supply stores. This coating not only improves the electrical contact between cable and terminal but also keeps away moisture and battery acids, thus retarding a build-up of further lead sulphate deposits on the battery's electrical contact points.

Internal Water Systems

On a power cruiser or an auxiliary sailboat, four discrete plumbing systems are packed into the belowdecks area. One system supplies fresh water for drinking, cooking, and washing to a galley sink. A hand pump on the sink draws the water from a tank, usually positioned in the bow to counterbalance the weight of other heavy installations farther aft. This tank is vented, allowing air to enter as the water level changes; otherwise, a vacuum left by departing water would make pumping difficult. The waste water from the sink flows out of the boat by gravity.

A second system provides raw water for the toilet. A pump beside the toilet draws water through a seacock at the bottom of the hull and into a vented holding tank that is emptied when the boat docks at a marina.

In a third system, another seacock admits raw water to cool the engine. After the cooling water has passed through the engine block, the system's pump, powered by the engine itself, expels the water via the exhaust pipe along with the engine's exhaust gases. The fourth—and the simplest—system pumps out any water that has collected in the bilge.

To maintain this plumbing network, check all pumps periodically and keep their moving parts clean and lubricated. Replace their washers and packing at the first sign of leakage. Disassemble seacocks for inspection whenever the boat is hauled; they can also be tested when the boat is in the water by closing the seacock, uncoupling its hose, and cautiously reopening it to make sure it admits water.

Each month, flush engine coolant pipes on seagoing boats with fresh water to remove salt deposits; clogging could cause ruinous overheating of the power plant. Regularly examine all conduit hoses for leaks. And when installing or replacing a hose, always arrange it so that no kinks or sharp bends occur to interfere with flow.

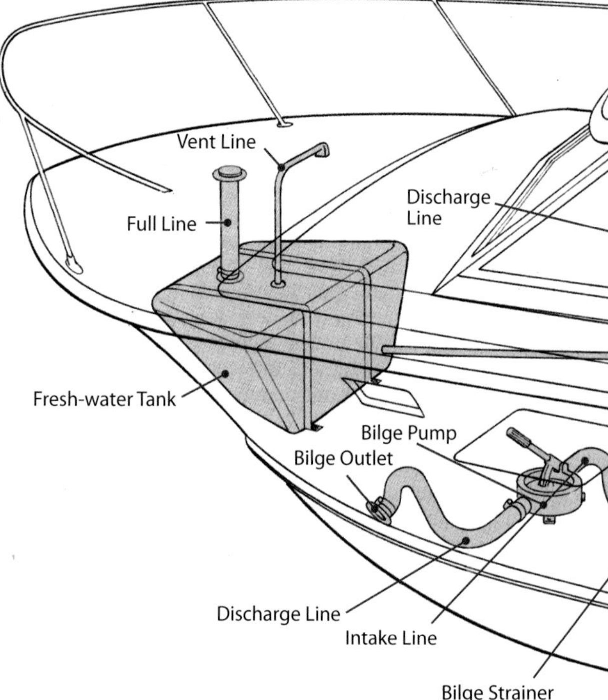

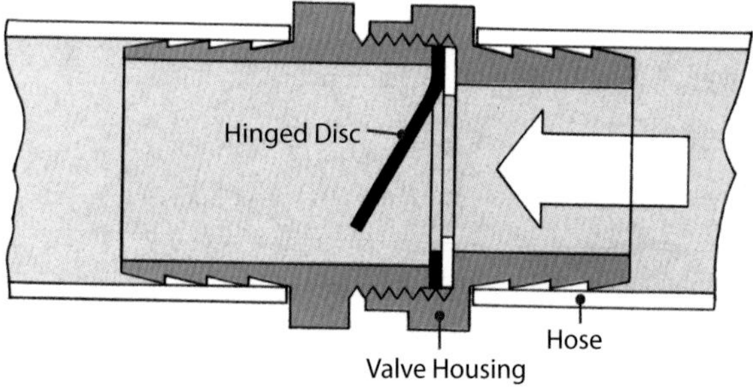

A check valve is often placed in a water line leading to a galley hand pump to prevent water from flowing backward in the line; this makes pumping easier by keeping the pump primed at all times. As shown in the cutaway view above, water *(white arrow)* traveling from right to left through the valve pushes open a hinged disc.

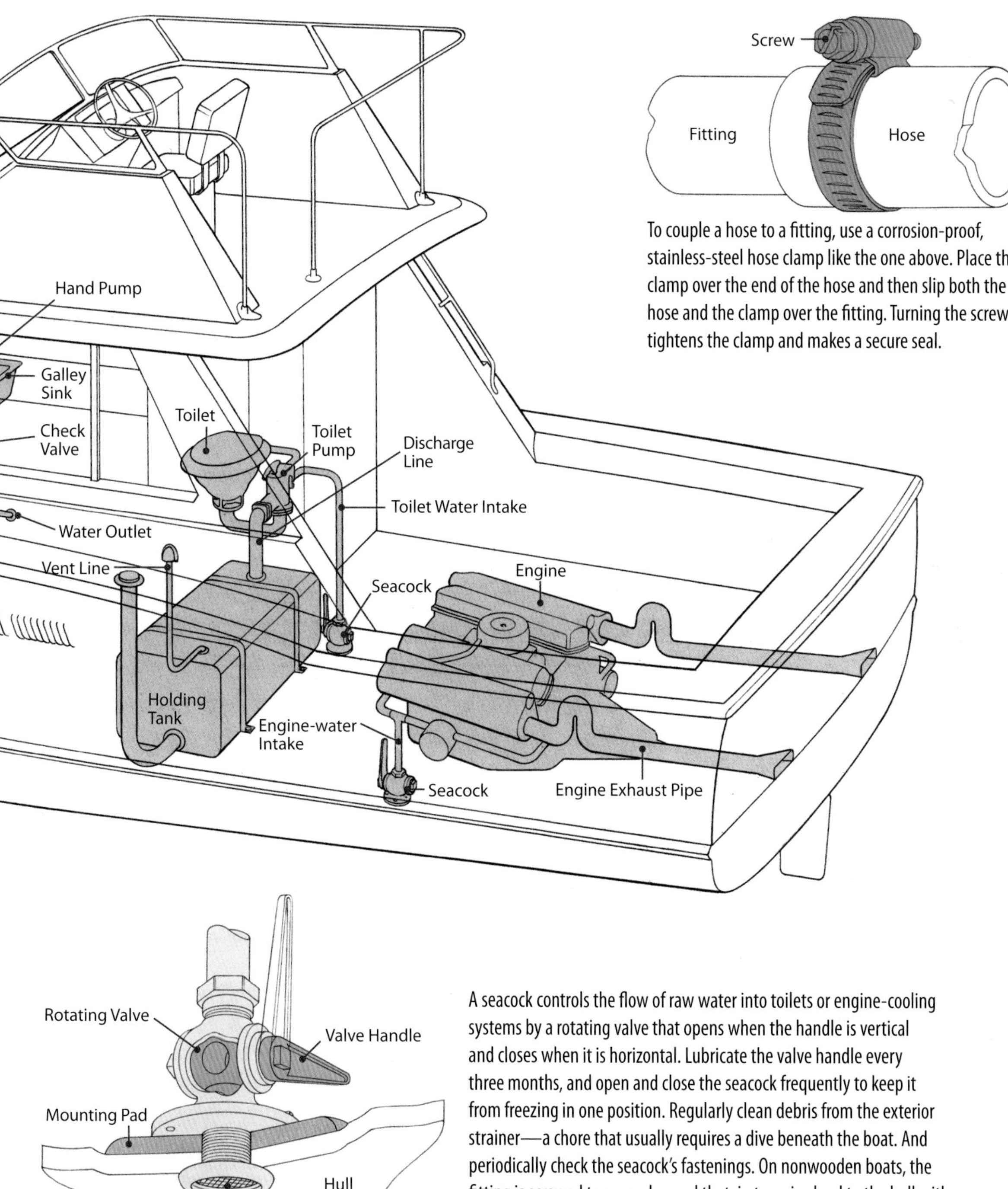

To couple a hose to a fitting, use a corrosion-proof, stainless-steel hose clamp like the one above. Place the clamp over the end of the hose and then slip both the hose and the clamp over the fitting. Turning the screw tightens the clamp and makes a secure seal.

A seacock controls the flow of raw water into toilets or engine-cooling systems by a rotating valve that opens when the handle is vertical and closes when it is horizontal. Lubricate the valve handle every three months, and open and close the seacock frequently to keep it from freezing in one position. Regularly clean debris from the exterior strainer—a chore that usually requires a dive beneath the boat. And periodically check the seacock's fastenings. On nonwooden boats, the fitting is screwed to a wooden pad that, in turn, is glued to the hull with bedding compound for a watertight seal.

The Indispensable Pump

Pumping out the bilge is one of the first maintenance tasks a sailor learns—and for the best of reasons. All boats take on some rain or sea water, and while the water seldom accumulates in quantities sufficient to sink the boat, a wet bilge can spread destruction in subtler ways—causing engine parts and other equipment to rust, eating away interior paint and generating mildew.

Two of the most efficient types of bilge pumps are shown here. One is a hand-operated diaphragm pump, the other a submersible electric model. Each can disgorge as much as 15 gallons of water a minute—enough to quickly remove any random drippage, and even to keep pace with a major leak if the hull is punctured.

Both, however, require regular care to ensure reliability. On the electrical pump, the vulnerable point is the impeller—an element composed of rubber blades that drive water through an outlet hose by rotating rapidly. These blades must be regularly cleaned (a probing finger will do) to prevent clogging. On the diaphragm pump, the handle is the weak spot, sometimes breaking off after heavy use. Lubricate it at its pivot points, and always keep a spare handle aboard.

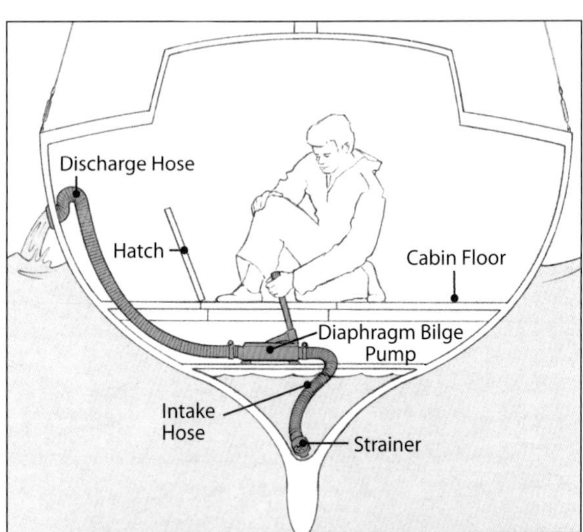

Since a manual diaphragm bilge pump is very difficult to operate when submerged, it should be installed well above the lowest point of the bilge, depending on hull conformation. And because the pump is subjected to considerable wrenching by the operation of its hand lever, it should be securely mounted. Additionally, the intake hose should extend to the deepest part of the bilge, and the hose's end should be fitted with a metal strainer to prevent the pump from being clogged. Keep the strainer clear of debris. Also, make sure both intake and discharge hose connections are tight.

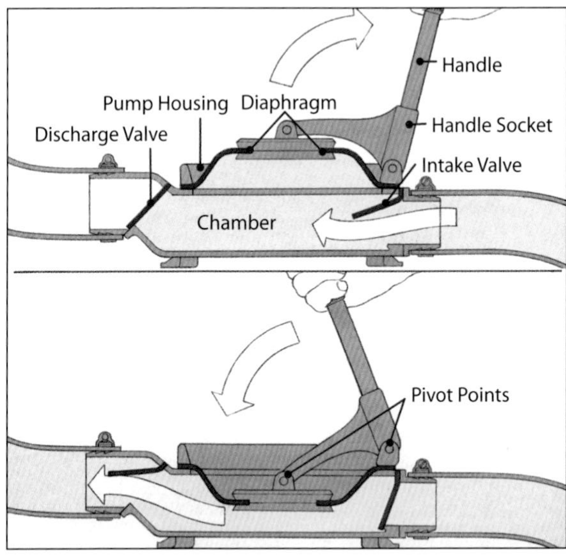

A diaphragm bilge pump is operated by a smooth but rapid back-and-forth motion of its handle. Pulling the handle back *(top right)* raises the rubber diaphragm in the pump housing; this bellows-like action draws water into the pump chamber through the intake valve, hinged to open inward only. The forward stroke *(bottom)* forces the water through the discharge valve, hinged to swing outward only. To service the pump, oil the pivot points on top of the housing and at the bottom of the handle socket. Replace the rubber diaphragm if it is leaking.

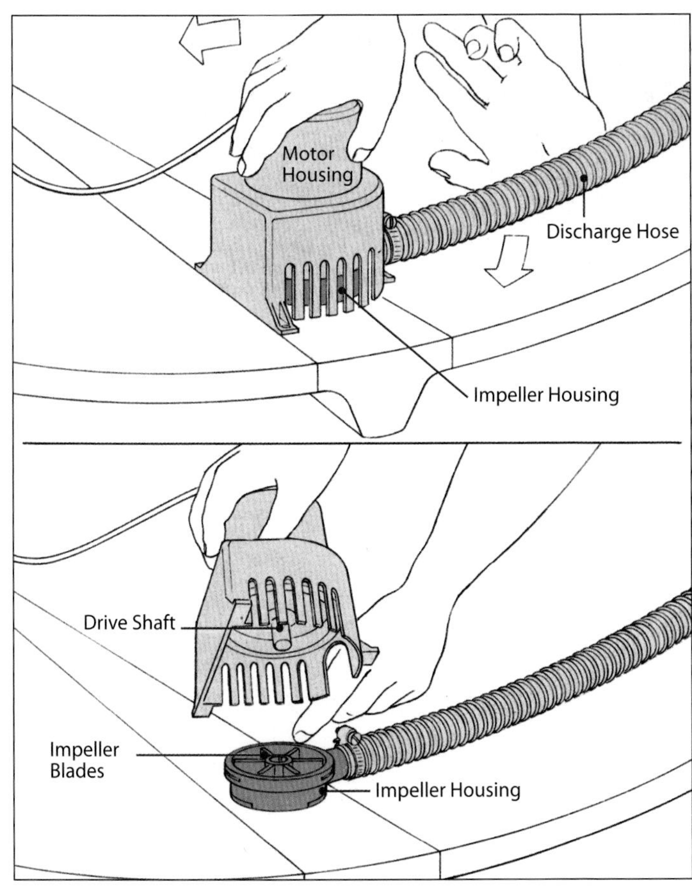

An electric bilge pump is designed to keep operating even if completely submerged. Whenever such a pump slows down or stops altogether, the trouble may be that something has clogged the impeller—the rotating element fixed in the base of the pump housing. Dismantling the pump for cleaning is a simple task, since the impeller's only connection to the motor is through the drive shaft—which is designed to be disconnected easily. A firm rap on the discharge hose will help disengage this connection, allowing the impeller and motor housings to be slipped apart *(below)*.

Once the pump has been removed, dislodge any debris or sludge from the impeller blades with a finger. At the same time, check the blades for signs of wear. If the impeller needs to be replaced, simply pull it out and insert a new one; no tools are required for the job.

A Mandatory Filter

Under the Federal Water Pollution Act that became law in 1974, the discharge of oil or oily wastes into United States navigable waters is prohibited, and offenders are subject to a $5,000 fine (boats under 26 feet are exempted). Even the small amounts of oil and sludge that accumulate in a bilge are considered harmful and are covered under the law. To comply with this regulation, cut out a segment of the bilge pump's discharge hose at any convenient point, and using hose clamps, rejoin the severed ends with a filter like the one at right. The filter houses a canister containing a mixture of polymers that trap oil while permitting clean bilge water to pass through it and overboard. After a few months of use, the canister will become saturated with oil and must be replaced.

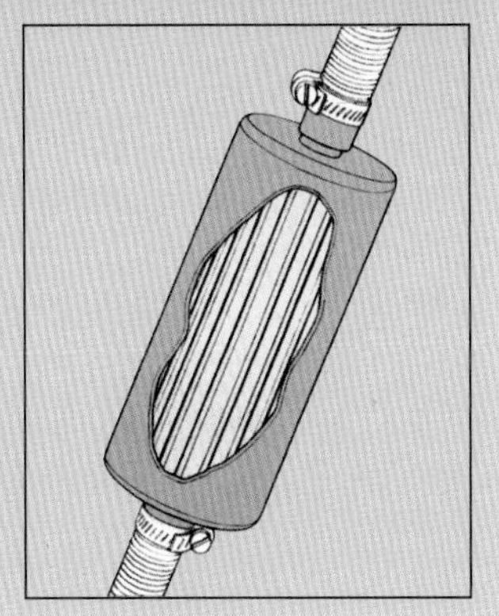

How the Head Works

Marine toilets, or heads as they are called aboard ship, come in both manual and electrical versions. The care of both types is virtually identical except that the maintenance of the motor on electric models is beyond the abilities of most amateurs. To keep the gaskets and the valves of the pumps functioning smoothly, simply pour a lubricating detergent into the bowl several times a season and flush it through the system. Check the hoses to make sure that they are sound and that their connections are tight. On electric models, regularly inspect the wiring for signs of wear and protect the terminals with waterproof electrical tape.

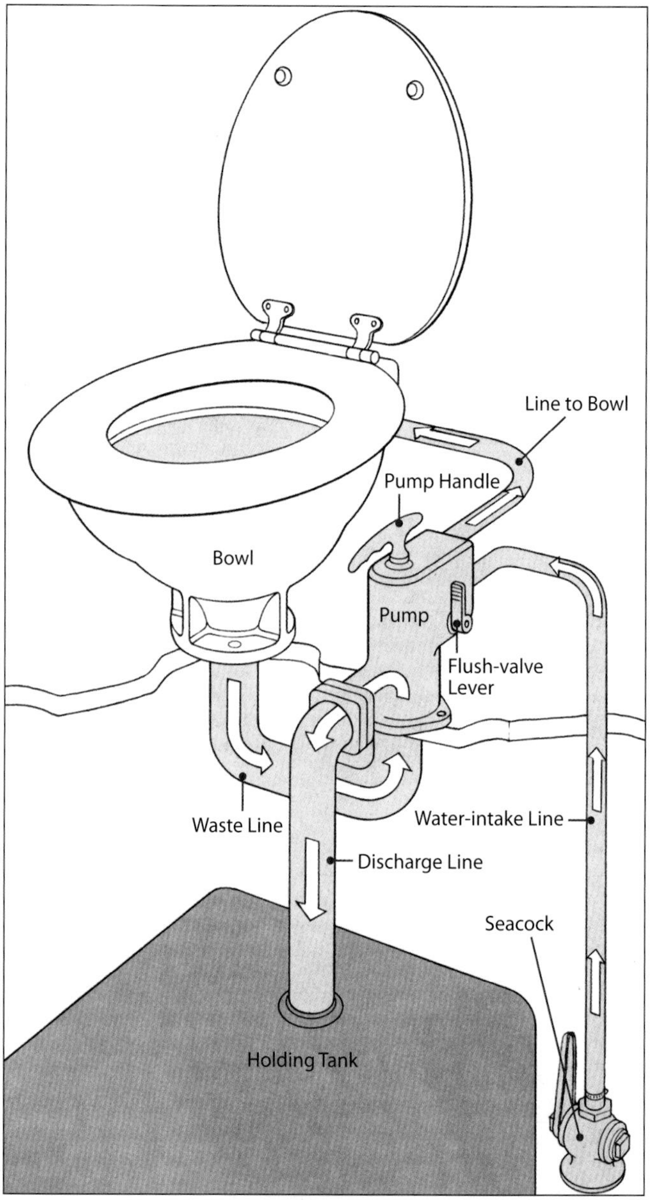

The Ancestral Latrine

On early sailing ships, the crew used the vessel's sharp prow, which was known as the beak head, as an open-air latrine. The latrine was named for its location—an appellation that still survives, even though the head came in from the cold more than a century ago.

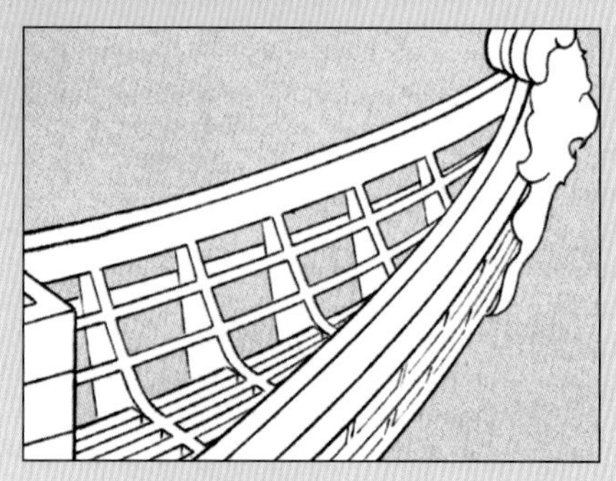

Line to Bowl
Pump Handle
Bowl
Pump
Flush-valve Lever
Waste Line
Water-intake Line
Discharge Line
Seacock
Holding Tank

In a typical hand-operated marine toilet, the up-and-down action of a pump circulates raw water and flushes waste into a holding tank when the flush-valve lever is opened *(above)*. If a manual pump handle is hard to operate—or an electric pump seems balky—be sure the seacock is wide open and there are no kinks in the intake and discharge lines. Movement of a boat underway can shut the seacock or crimp the intake line, thereby cutting off flow.

Pump Handle
Packing
Packing Nut
Outlet Valve
Flush Pipe
Clean Water
Pump Cylinder
Intake Valve
Piston Rod
Intake Valve
Joker Valve
Piston
Waste Inlet Valve
Waste Line
Discharge Line

A cutaway view of a manual toilet pump traces movement of water during the intake phase of operation and pinpoints maintenance spots. On the downstroke, as shown here, the piston draws clean water through the intake valve, while forcing waste water from the cylinder into the discharge line through the joker valve. On the upstroke, the clean water will be forced past the outlet valve and into the bowl. The upstroke also draws a new charge of water and waste from the bowl into the cylinder. The piston rod should be greased monthly and its packing nut tightened periodically to prevent leakage.

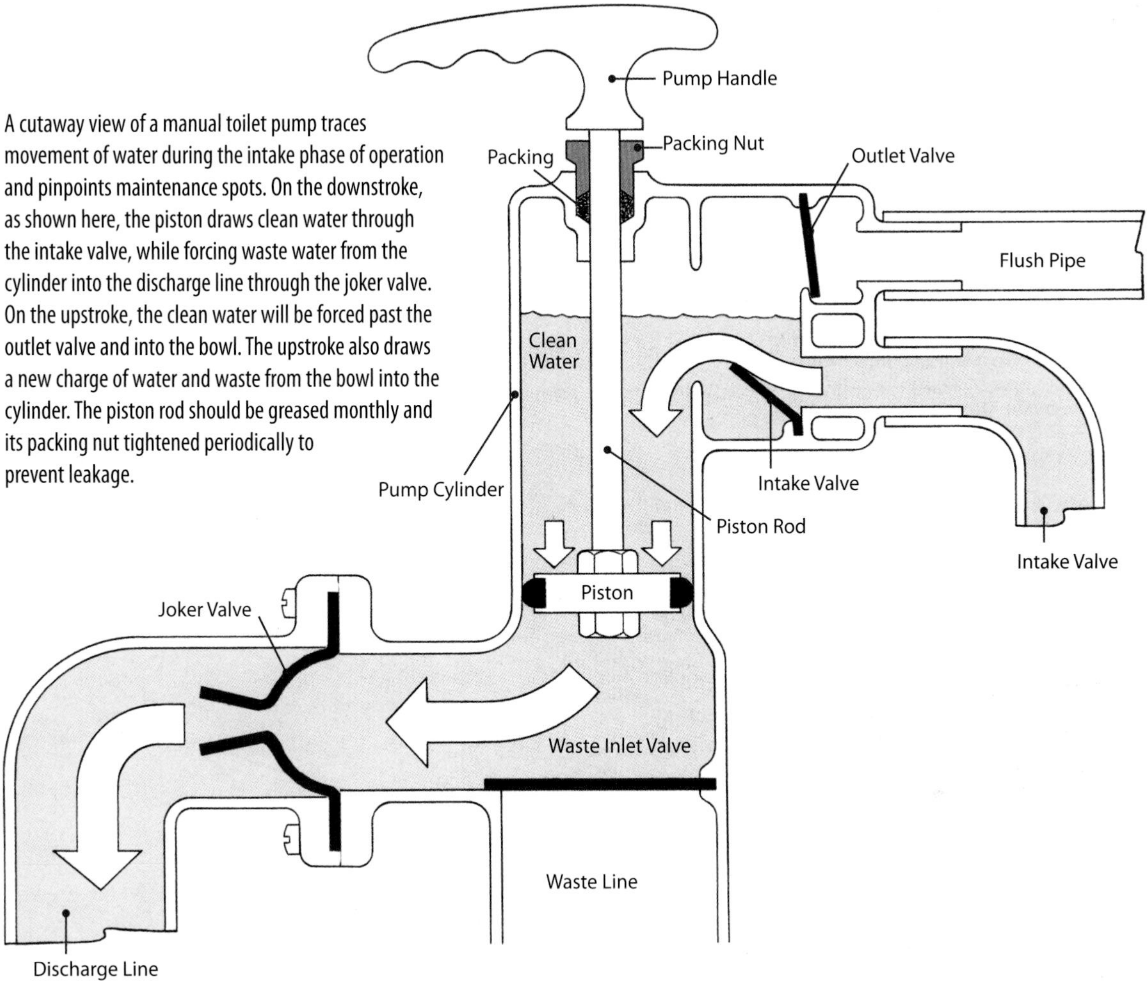

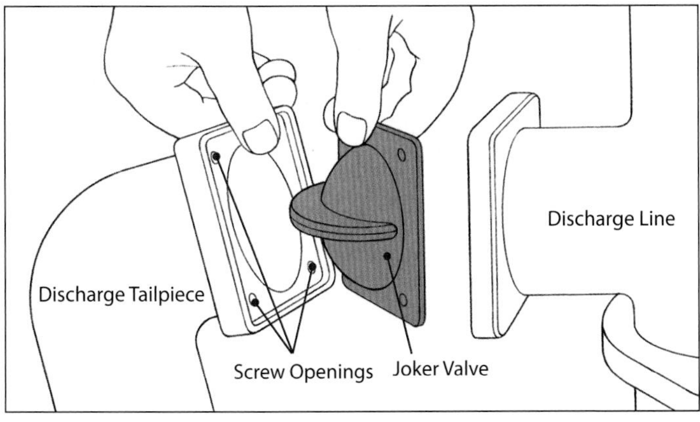

To remove foreign objects carelessly or inadvertently dropped into the bowl, unscrew the discharge tailpiece from the discharge line and lift out the rubber joker valve. If the valve is in sound condition, wipe it clean and reassemble the unit; otherwise, replace it.

Fresh Air Below

No boat will remain in comfortable, safe operating condition unless properly ventilated. Without a steady supply of clean fresh air belowdecks, moisture accumulates, breeding foul-smelling mildew and allowing dry rot to attack interior woodwork. Worse, unless fresh air is channeled through the engine compartment, explosive gas fumes will settle in the bilge.

To ensure continuous interior airing, ducts and vents should be at key locations, as on the motor sailer at right. On the cabin top, two Dorade-type cowl vents, designed to admit the breeze while blocking out spray, circulate air through the main cabin. One, face to the wind, serves as an intake; the other, angled aft, acts as an outlet, as do louvers on the companionway door—a third, of mushroom style, draws stale air from the head.

Because of the danger of gas fumes accumulating in the bilge, the Coast Guard requires that engine compartments of boats with inboard power be ventilated. The system here, activated by a blower, is recommended; its intake and exhaust cowls should be kept clean to allow free air flow—as should the cabin-top vents.

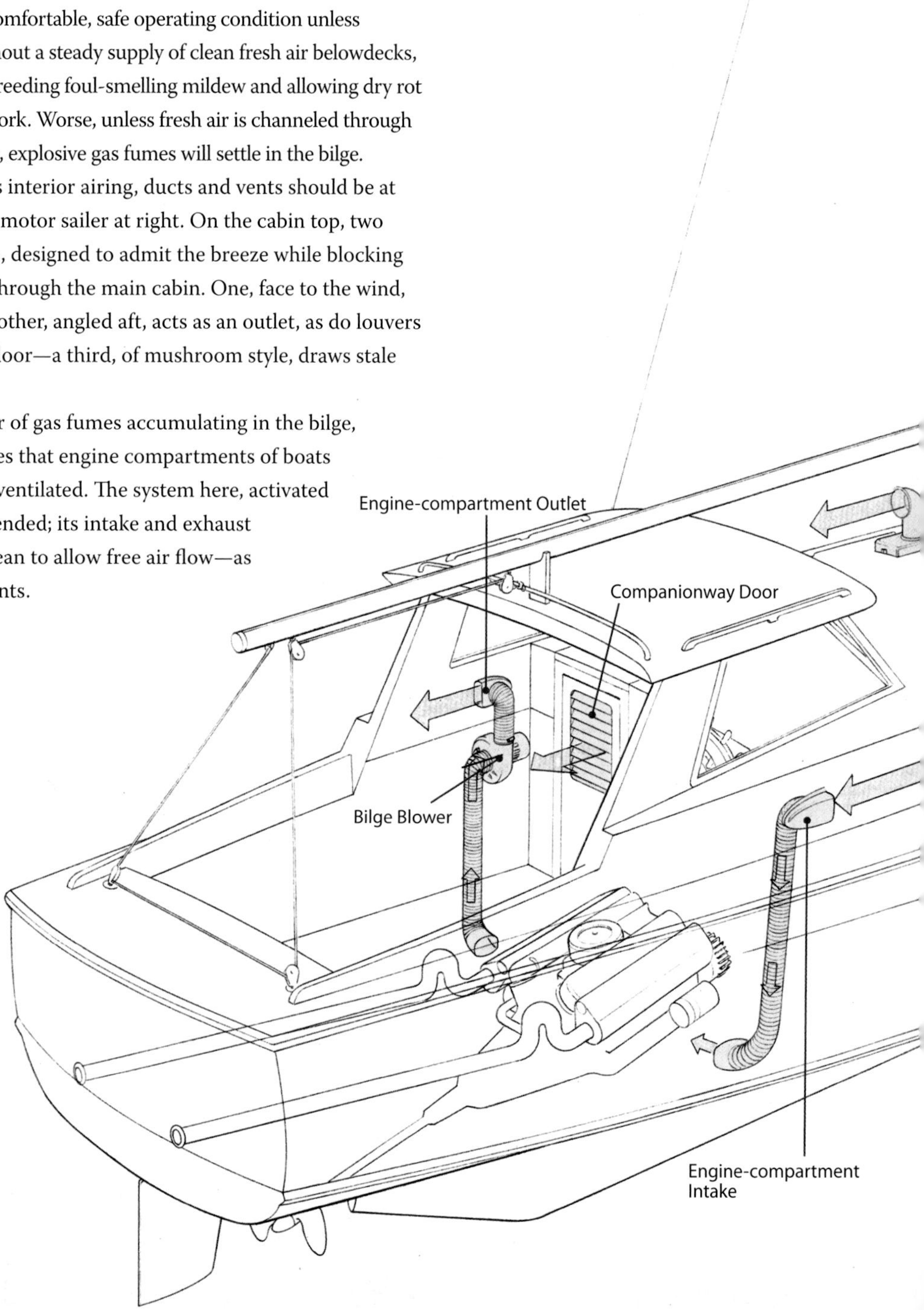

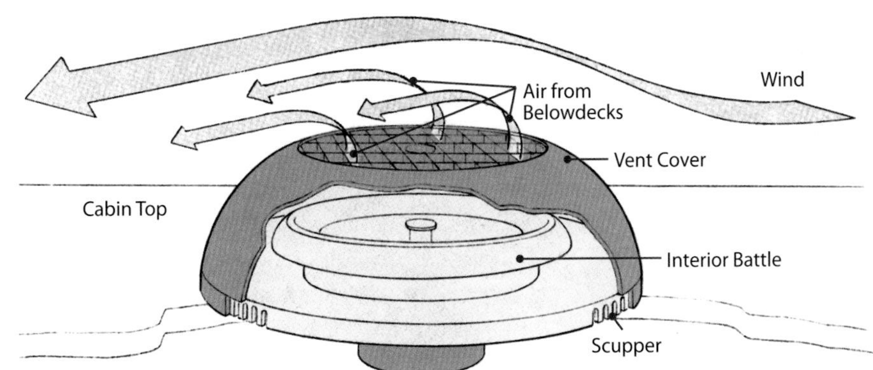

A mushroom vent draws air from belowdecks by means of aerodynamically generated suction. As the breeze blows across the opening in the vent cover, a partial vacuum occurs, pulling air up through the opening. At the same time, an interior baffle prevents spray from filtering into the cabin—allowing it instead to trickle out of a set of scuppers.

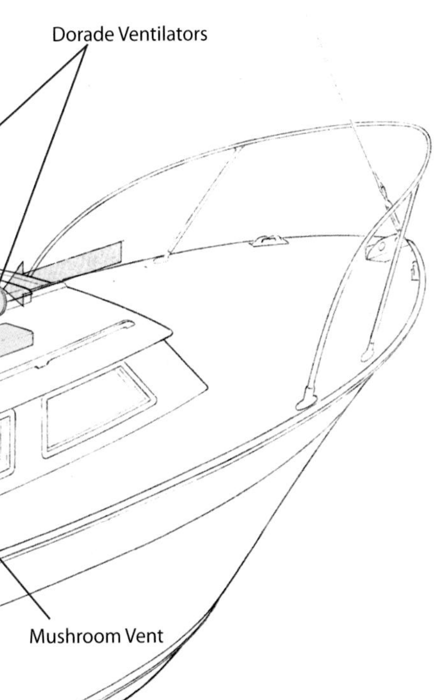

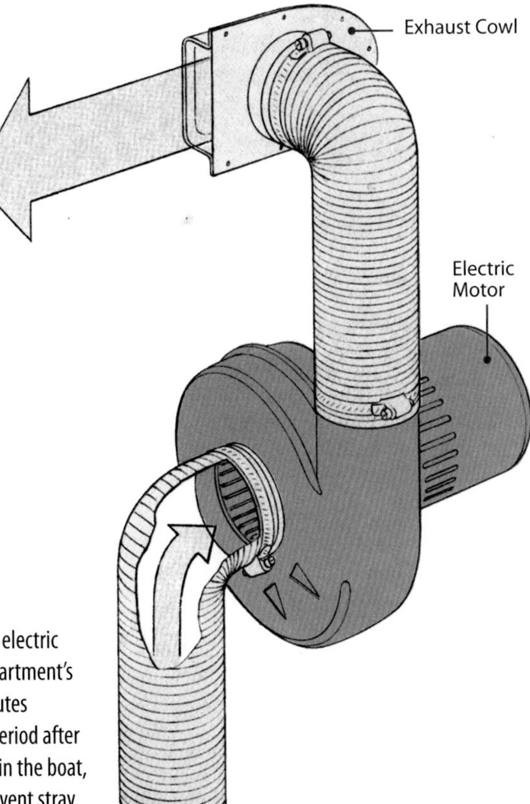

To rid the bilge of dangerous gasoline fumes, an electric bilge blower—placed close to the engine compartment's exhaust vent—should be operated for five minutes before starting up the engine and for a similar period after refueling. A blower should be mounted high up in the boat, as far above the bilge as possible, in order to prevent stray sparks from its wiring from igniting the fumes.

CHAPTER 5:
Fittings

Most of the action on pleasure boats takes place either on deck or aloft. Here the helm is manned, and the sails are hoisted and trimmed; fish are fought and gaffed; lines are cast off to begin a cruise and readied to make a mooring when the voyage is over. In fact, the success or failure of any voyage is, in many ways, a measure of the proper functioning of the fittings that enable the work above decks to be carried out. A jammed winch or block can suddenly transform a smart boat handling maneuver into an embarrassing, expensive bungle.

Intelligent care for the equipment on and above a vessel's deck is founded on an understanding of the stresses it must bear. The shrouds and stays that support a mast, for example, must be stout enough to withstand not only the steady pull of working sails but also the violent wrenching of an accidental jibe, or of a collapsed spinnaker suddenly refilled with wind. Blocks that reverse a line's direction—such as those that bring a spinnaker's sheet and guy forward from the stern to winches in the cockpit—must be designed to handle at least twice the maximum load likely to be put on the line. Grab rails, life lines and railings on both sailboats and powerboats must be mounted firmly enough to take far more than the weight of a single crew member, since there may be two or more deckhands hanging on or thrown against them when the vessel heels suddenly under the force of wind or wave, or the wake of a passing powerboat moving under full throttle.

Lines and sails are more vulnerable than hardware. A jib that is pressed hard on a bare spreader end may rub through in a matter of hours, and even the rounded edge of a railing can gradually sever a mooring line that has jumped its chock. Preventing chafe is thus a critical part of abovedecks maintenance. Sharp spots in the rigging must be padded either by wrapping them with tape or by installing fittings called boots. Fairleads and chocks should be checked for roughness, and even minor burrs should be filed smooth to prevent them from chewing away at lines. Chafing gear on dock and mooring lines should be periodically renewed.

Casual water from rain and spray also takes its toll. Hardware on deck and aloft should be regularly scrutinized for signs of corrosion. Owners of powerboats must take special precautions to shield their cockpits with canvas covers to keep rain water from collecting after each trip.

There are times, however, when the best way to cope with a troublesome deck fitting is to replace it with another. And it is good maintenance not to wait for a problem to arise: knowledgeable owners of new stock boats often begin outfitting their vessels by studying older versions of the same craft to see what other skippers have found necessary to replace.

The skipper of a cruising yawl cleans a deck-winch drum before lubricating the fitting. In the background, his neighbor checks out a mizzen-sheet block on the stern rail of his ketch.

Inventory on Deck

An alert skipper, working alone and in spare moments, can keep abreast of all the maintenance requirements for the most common and fundamental deck fittings, shown in blue on the 38-foot vessel at right. This particular craft is an auxiliary sailboat, whose rigging makes the task of topside upkeep more complex than would be the case aboard a powerboat. But the principles—and many of the specific tasks—of maintenance are the same for both sail and power.

The first and perhaps most constant job in deck maintenance is to be sure all screws are tight. Any screws that chronically come loose should be replaced with larger ones. Use lock washers to secure nuts that tend to loosen, or else drill holes through their bolts to accommodate cotter pins that will prevent the nuts from backing off.

Lubricate moving parts on such fittings as winches, blocks, turnbuckles, and cam cleats; also put a drop of oil on the locking pins of snatch blocks, track slides, and the pins on spinnaker poles. While being sure that these parts are kept free to move, beware of too much mobility in certain other cases. For example, a winch that turns more freely than usual may have a broken internal component that will cause it to fail under tension; disassemble it for inspection.

Sometimes loose fastenings will throw off the alignment of genoa tracks and mainsheet traveler tracks, causing their slides to stick. In such instances, resecure the tracks, and then file away any burrs. Using fine-grained emery paper, remove rust from such gear as chocks or fair-leads that carry line, since the roughness from surface oxidization of a metal can cause severe chafing.

Cover all such pinned fittings with protective tape or plastic. In a freshening breeze, even a single exposed cotter pin can start a tear in a spinnaker or genoa that may run across the entire sail.

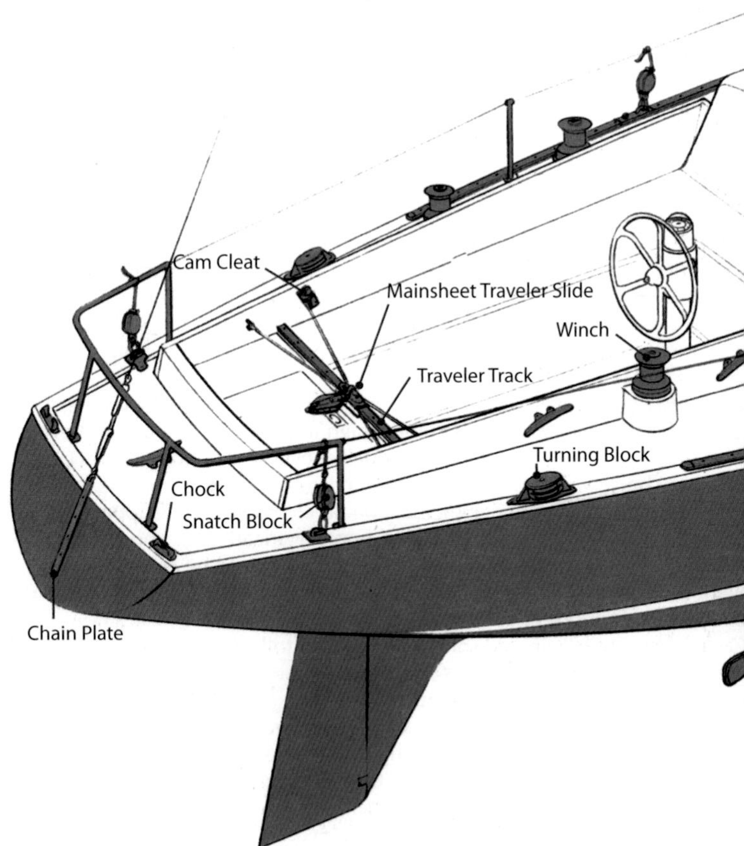

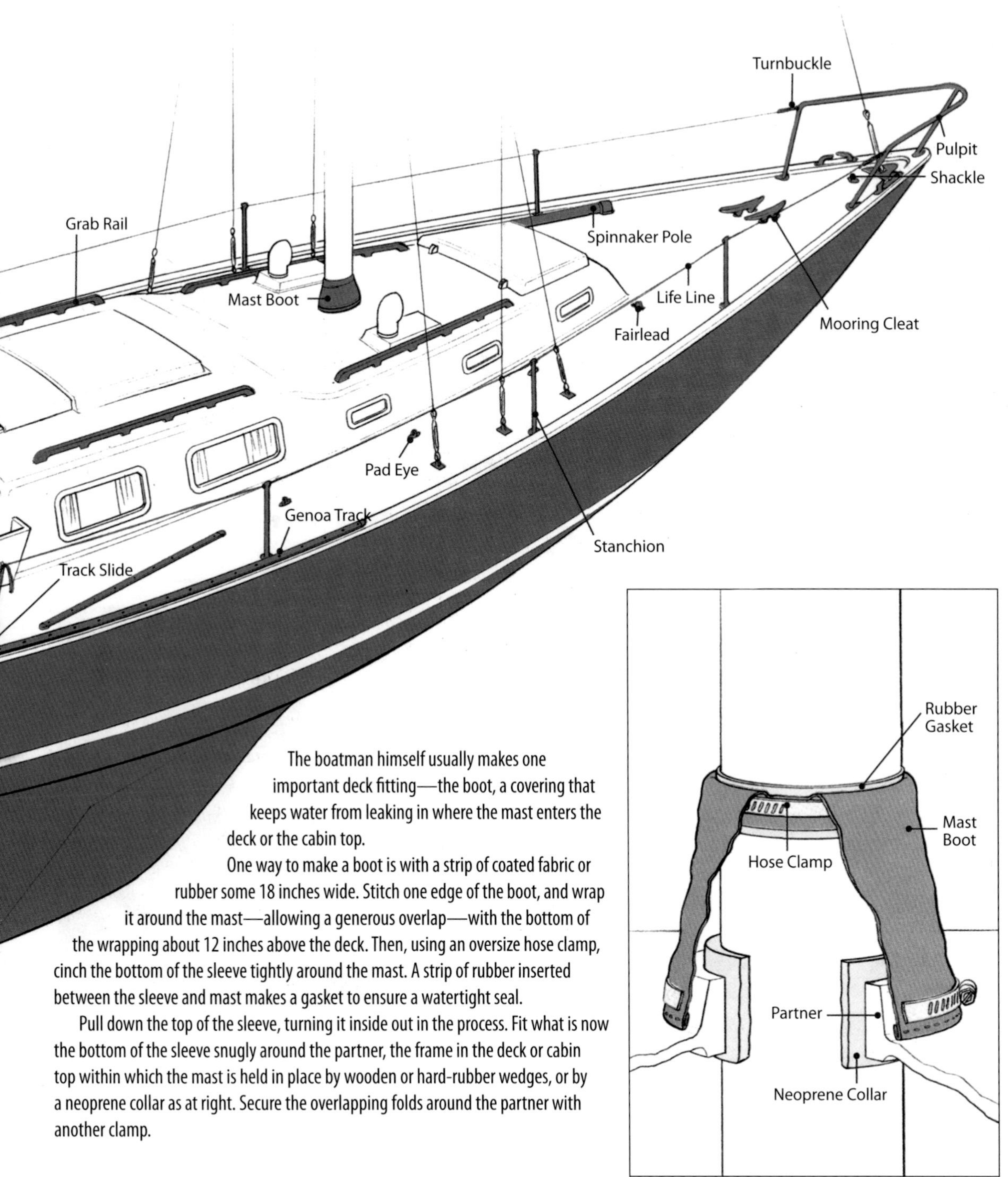

The boatman himself usually makes one important deck fitting—the boot, a covering that keeps water from leaking in where the mast enters the deck or the cabin top.

One way to make a boot is with a strip of coated fabric or rubber some 18 inches wide. Stitch one edge of the boot, and wrap it around the mast—allowing a generous overlap—with the bottom of the wrapping about 12 inches above the deck. Then, using an oversize hose clamp, cinch the bottom of the sleeve tightly around the mast. A strip of rubber inserted between the sleeve and mast makes a gasket to ensure a watertight seal.

Pull down the top of the sleeve, turning it inside out in the process. Fit what is now the bottom of the sleeve snugly around the partner, the frame in the deck or cabin top within which the mast is held in place by wooden or hard-rubber wedges, or by a neoprene collar as at right. Secure the overlapping folds around the partner with another clamp.

Tired Hardware

A life line sagging from a stanchion that has been bent in a dockside accident is not only unsightly but unsafe. The bent stanchion can be straightened by a professional, but this may create metal fatigue that can cause the fitting to snap—better to replace the stanchion. First detach the life line from the nearest turnbuckle and pull it through the eye of the stanchion. Then install a new stanchion, following the technique described on page 130. Finally, rethread the life line and twist the turnbuckle to draw it taut.

The corroded nut securing the pin in the hinge of this tabernacle—a special type that permits swinging the mast down for passage under low bridges—could fail any moment, allowing the pin to drop out and the mast butt to skid from its mounting. Remove the nut; wire-brush the pin, and lubricate it. Then put on a new nut of the same metal as the pin, to prevent galvanic corrosion.

This spinnaker-block pad eye has cracked under the tremendous stress placed upon it by the pull of the sail in a stiff breeze. Replace it, mounting the new fitting by the procedure shown on the following pages.

Cracks in the sheave in a wooden block sometimes occur when water seeps into the grain of the wood, as it alternately becomes soaked and then dries out after long exposure to the sun. Such a sheave will soon fall apart under the pressure of the line running through it. There is only one solution to the problem: the entire block must be replaced with one that is of comparable size.

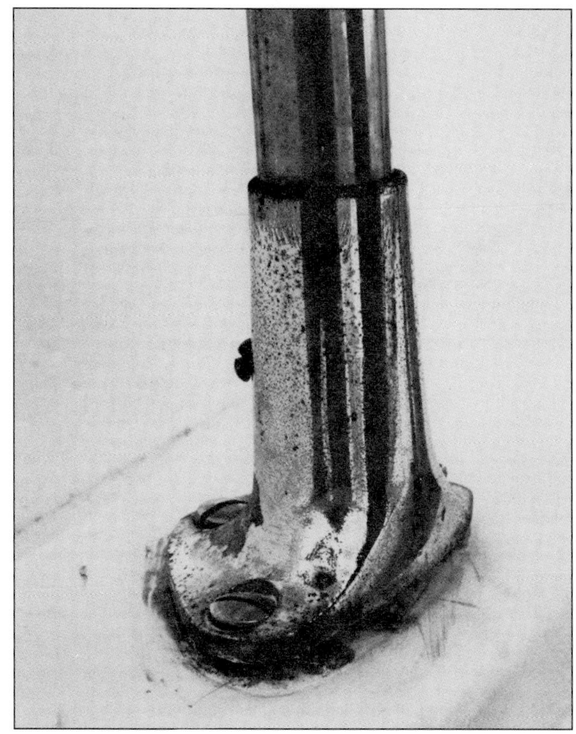

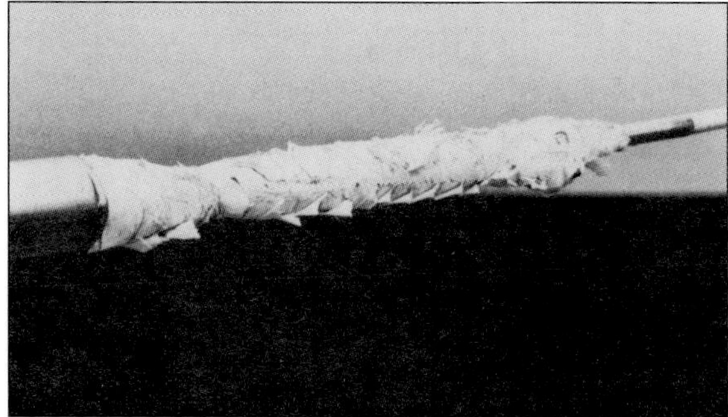

Antichafing tape that is wrapped around turnbuckles and other fittings may eventually itself become chafed or raveled, as here, through long usage. Moisture then seeps in under the layers of wrapping, where it becomes trapped and quickly corrodes the fittings. Remove the tape, inspect for corrosion, and rewrap with fresh tape.

Loosened bolts in the base of a pulpit stanchion endanger the entire pulpit. And dry, cracked bedding compound permits rot-generating seepage. Remove the bolts and clean out the old bedding compound. Apply fresh compound; retighten the bolts, and replace any badly rusted ones with new bolts of the same metal as the stanchion.

Keeping Things Tight

The way a deck fitting is secured depends upon the degree of strain it must be able to withstand. For example, fairleads can be lightly mounted with screws, since they only guide lines from one point to another, and are almost never subjected to a heavy load. But mooring cleats or lifeline stanchions, which must take heavy strains, should always be through-bolted and backed by a doubler—a flat piece of material, usually wood, that is installed under the deck and distributes the stress of the securing nuts and washers.

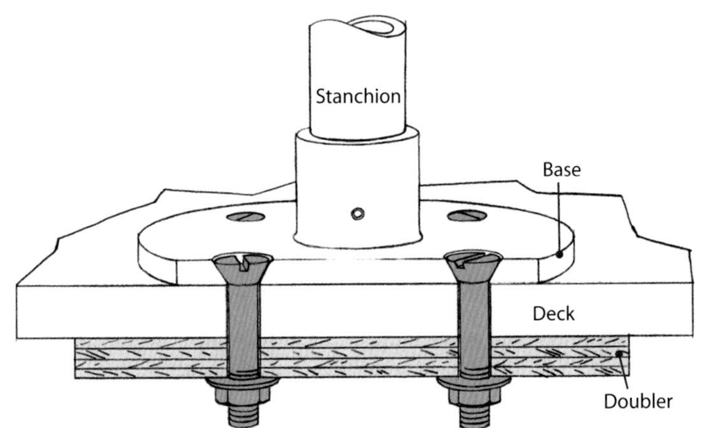

A life-line stanchion is secured by bolts that pass through its base fitting above the deck and through a plywood doubler below the deck. Rubber or neoprene washers on the bolts help to prevent water from leaking through the deck, and bedding compound will provide an additional watertight seal.

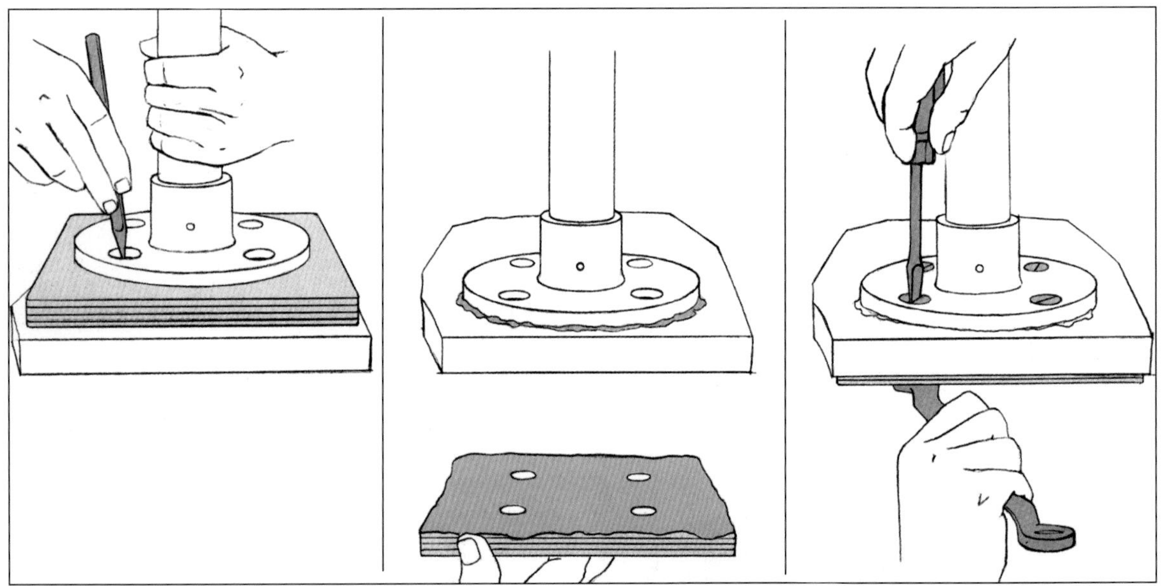

To remount a high-stress fitting like a stanchion, first slip the doubler beneath the base of the stanchion on the deck; mark the positions for the bolt holes on the doubler *(above, left)*, and then drill them out. Next, spread a liberal coating of bedding compound on both the bottom of the base and the top of the doubler *(middle)*, then have a partner belowdecks press the doubler in place, with its own bolt holes lined up with the others. Finally, use a screwdriver to keep the bolts from turning while the partner below tightens the nuts *(right)*.

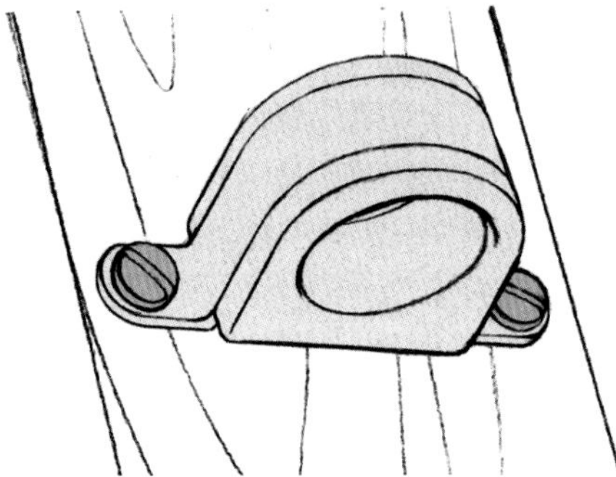

When a fairlead corrodes and requires replacement, always smear some bedding compound over the bottom of the new fitting before mounting; this prevents water from seeping beneath the fitting. Use ordinary wood screws for a wooden deck, sheet-metal screws if the deck is of metal or fiberglass (the latter variety has threads that extend all the way to the screwhead). If the old mounting holes have enlarged, use screws of slightly greater length and diameter.

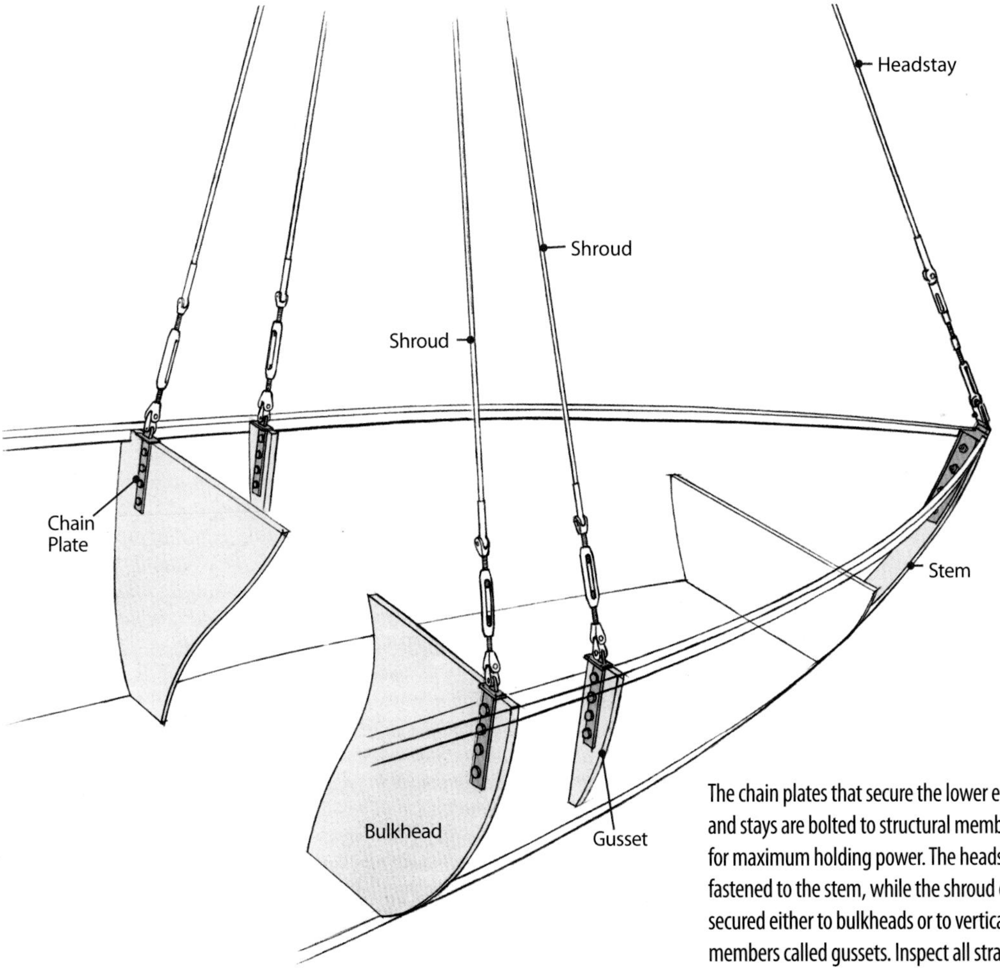

Headstay
Shroud
Shroud
Chain Plate
Stem
Bulkhead
Gusset

The chain plates that secure the lower ends of shrouds and stays are bolted to structural members of the boat for maximum holding power. The headstay chain plate is fastened to the stem, while the shroud chain plates are secured either to bulkheads or to vertical strengthening members called gussets. Inspect all straps regularly; tighten loose bolts. Any more serious failing means that the boat should go directly to a yard to be replaced by a professional.

How to Service a Winch

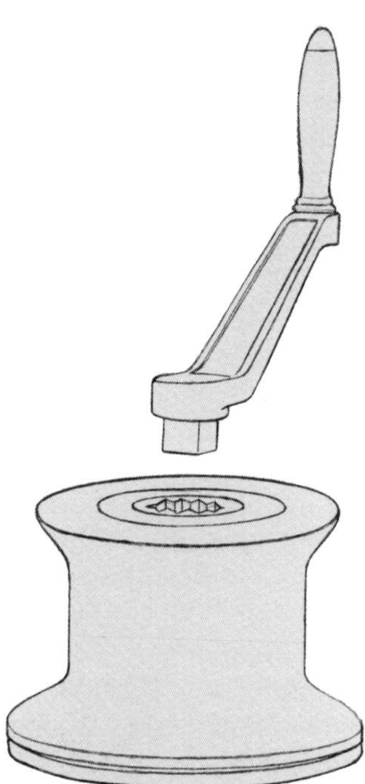

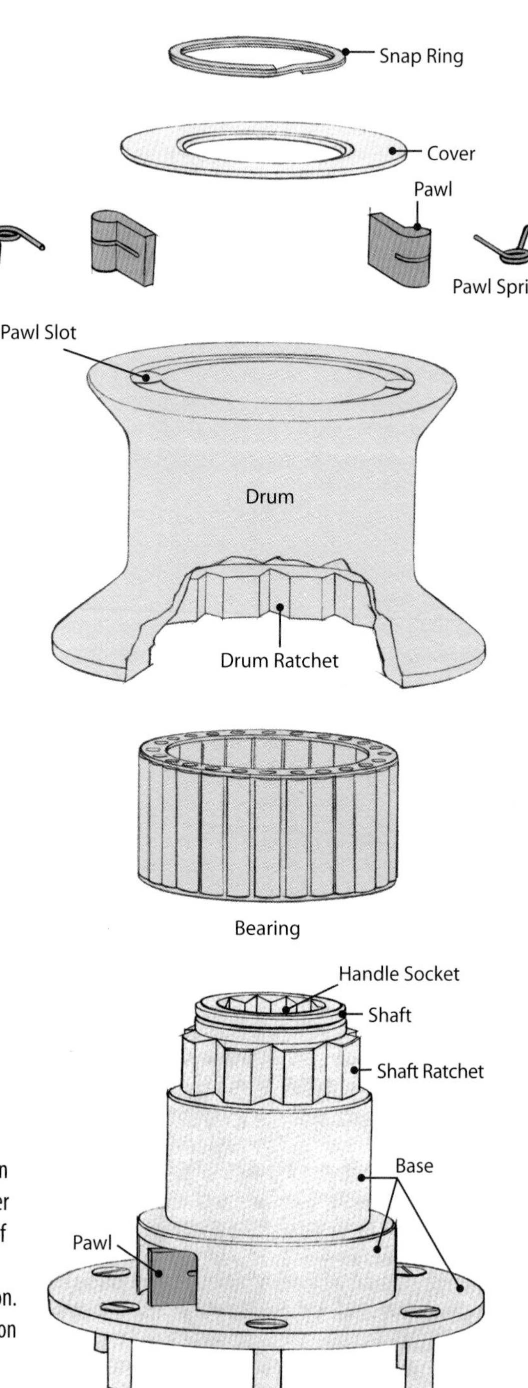

A deck-mounted winch, like other heavy-duty fittings, must be through-bolted to a doubler. On the model here, the mounting bolts—along with the other vital parts *(right)*—are concealed underneath the winch's drum and can be tightened only by disassembling the fitting. Periodic disassembly serves another maintenance purpose: because airborne pollutants and spray will inevitably penetrate a winch, clogging its internal mechanism or scouring out lubricants that keep it turning freely, the innards must be cleaned and relubricated every four months or so, as described on the opposite page.

Most of the working parts of this drum winch, shown in an exploded view, can be reached by prying off the snap ring *(top right)*, and then lifting off the cover and drum. During disassembly, carefully note the alignment of the two sets of pawls; these small, comma-shaped pieces of metal and the springs that hold them *(blue tint)* must be reinstalled exactly as before if the winch is to function. The upper pawls engage the ratchet on the shaft and transmit its rotary motion to the drum when the winch is cranked. The lower set engages the ratchet on the drum and prevents any backward slippage.

After disassembling the winch, put a few drops of a petroleum solvent onto a paper towel and wipe off the base *(right)*, the shaft and the inside of the drum. Use another paper towel and more solvent to clean the upper pawls and their springs; then lubricate these parts with light machine oil.

With a solvent-soaked paper towel, clean all old lubricant and accumulated dirt from the winch's bearing *(below)*. Then, holding the clean bearing in one hand, load two fingers with a generous dollop of new grease, and smear it liberally onto the bearing. However, do not apply so much grease that it drips from the bearing; a surfeit will clog the winch when it is reassembled.

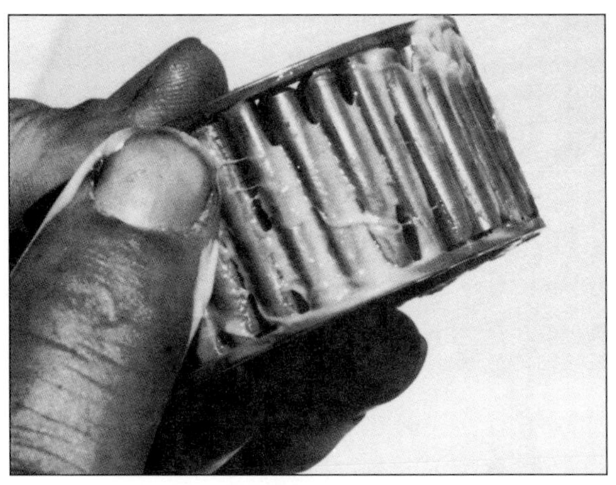

Before reassembly, lubricate the winch's lower set of pawls by squirting light machine oil into their openings in the winch's base *(above)*. Once a year, unbolt the base from its mounting and lift out these lower pawls and their springs for a thorough cleaning with solvent. When rebolting be sure that the nuts are snugged down tightly and evenly.

To reassemble the winch, place the pawls and springs back in their slots in the drum, slip the bearing over the base and place the drum over it. The protruding lower pawls will prevent the drum from seating properly at first. Press one of the pawls into its opening with a screwdriver *(left)*, then edge the drum over the pawl. Perform the same operation on the opposite pawl, and slip the drum on. Then replace the cover and the snap ring.

Buttoning Up a Boat

Perhaps the major problem of deck maintenance aboard a powerboat is making the vessel secure against rain and spray. This casual water can trickle below via the craft's large open cockpit, or around the edges of windows, doorways, or hatches, which tend to be bigger and thus more vulnerable than those on a sailboat.

First of all, the cockpit should have a firm-fastening cover—canvas and vinyl are the most popular—snapped in place whenever the vessel is left for any length of time at a dock or at anchor. (Small sailboats also benefit from being covered up when not in use.)

The cruiser shown here has two covers, one for the cockpit and another, a so-called navy top, for the bridge; they are stretched over a collapsible framework of metal tubing and fastened to the boat—and to each other—with metal snaps. If small rips or holes appear in the cloth, the boatman can mend them temporarily with waterproof tape. Or he can apply a permanent patch *(pages 142–143)*.

All openings to the belowdecks area must have waterproof seals, indicated at right by blue tints. The most convenient and effective seals are vinyl or neoprene tubing, and the adhesive-backed plastic foam available at marine-supply stores. Any of these will work on doors and hatches. Windows will sometimes leak around the frames or, more often, between the frame and glass. If the leak is minor, it can usually be stopped with a surface application of plastic sealant or bedding compound. But if the seepage persists, the window may have to be removed, frame and all, and then reinstalled with fresh bedding compound—a job that is best left to a professional.

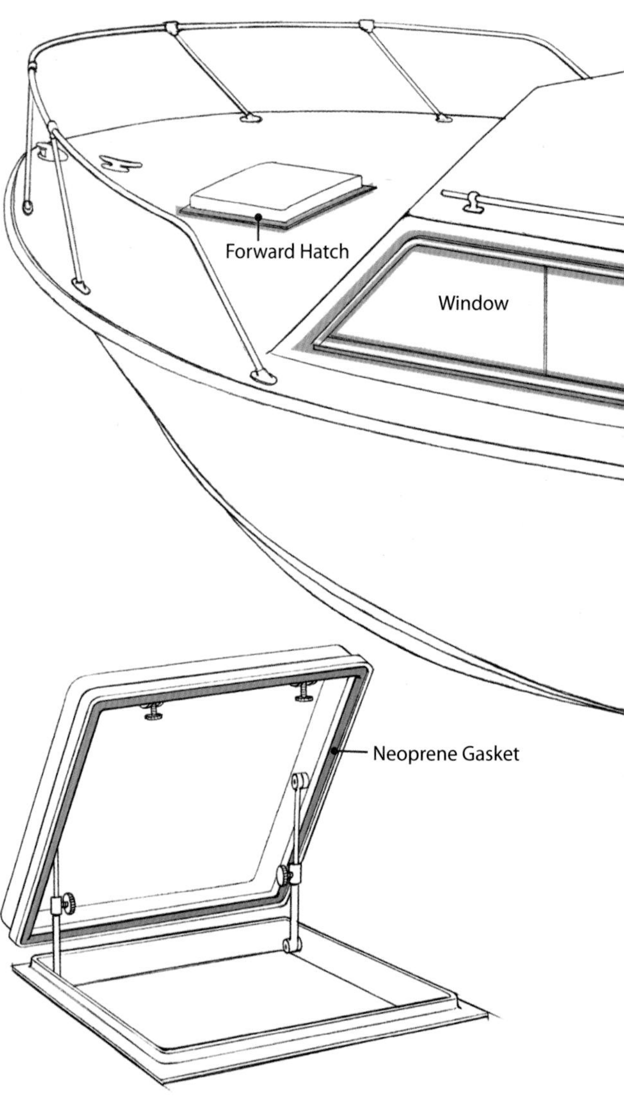

To weatherproof a hatch like the oneabove, install a gasket of neoprene tubing or adhesive-backed foam in the groove running around the inside of the hatch cover. To fashion a gasket for a flush-fitting engine-compartment hatch (on the cockpit deck in the large drawing above), attach the tape either to the underside of the cover or to the top of the ledge on which the cover rests.

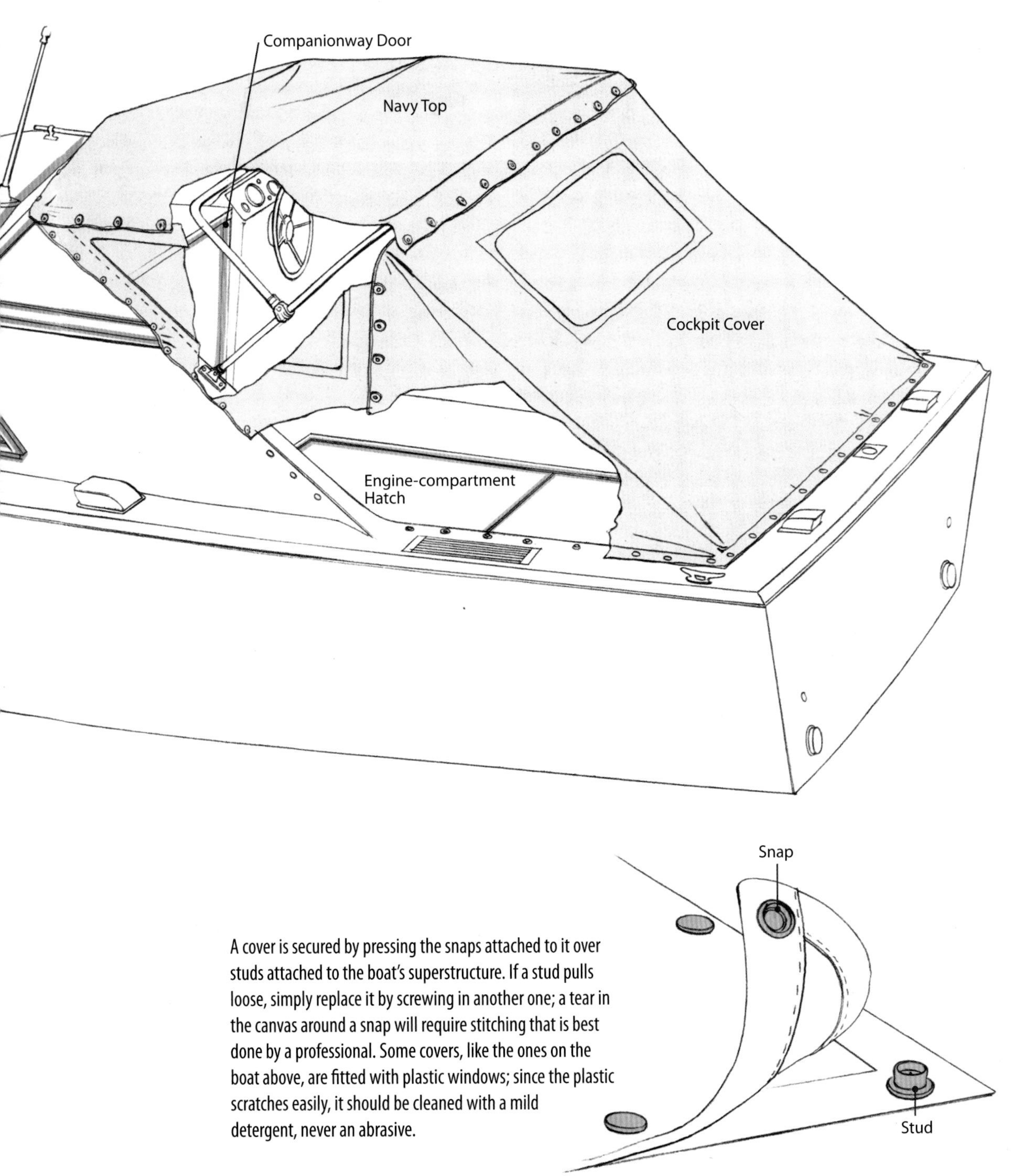

A cover is secured by pressing the snaps attached to it over studs attached to the boat's superstructure. If a stud pulls loose, simply replace it by screwing in another one; a tear in the canvas around a snap will require stitching that is best done by a professional. Some covers, like the ones on the boat above, are fitted with plastic windows; since the plastic scratches easily, it should be cleaned with a mild detergent, never an abrasive.

Upkeep Aloft

The complex network of lines, wires, and spars towering above a sailboat's deck requires constant, alert surveillance and frequent service. The parts of the standing rigging—the stays, shrouds, and their spreaders—that support the mast are easiest to inspect and repair when the mast is being removed for storage or being installed at launching time. But it is wise to make periodic inspections during the season by going aloft in a bosun's chair *(page 138–139)* and checking all key elements, working down from the masthead.

First, examine halyards and the topping lift for wear. If a boat is sailed in salt water, these lines should be rinsed with fresh water several times a season. The water must not be hot, for heat destroys the fibers of synthetic rope. (Treat the sheets, downhaul, and outhaul in the same way.)

Next, check the masthead sheaves and tangs; then inspect the standing rigging. In most boats the standing rigging is of stainless steel that will last up to five years without any real maintenance. However, some boats have standing rigging of galvanized wire, which is more susceptible to rust and corrosion, and tends to produce so-called fishhooks—protruding ends of broken strands *(opposite)*.

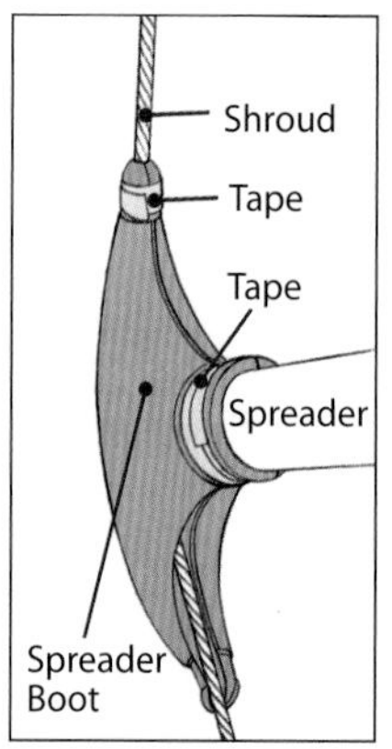

A rubber spreader boot like this one helps keep a sail from chafing or tearing as it rubs against the tip of the spreader when the boat is sailing close-hauled. Available at marine-supply stores, a boot is split down the middle so that it can be fitted around the spreader and the shroud; wrappings of waterproof tape hold it in place. Some boatmen use a cheaper, if less elegant, device—an old tennis ball slit on one side, jammed over the end of the spreader and then taped in place.

On galvanized wire, minor surface rust can be removed with a wire brush. Wherever rust is heavy, flex the wire; if a strand breaks, discard the wire. Also, replace any wire that is badly kinked or starting to unlay. Before stepping the mast, wash all standing rigging with fresh water and a mild detergent to remove dirt and grease. Buff away rust spots on metal rigging fittings such as blocks, tumbuckles, snap shackles, and the gooseneck; lubricate the moving parts regularly. On boom and mast cleats, file off burrs or sharp edges that could tear a line-or a hand. Tighten loose screws or bolts on fittings, and cover the ends of cotter pins *(left)*.

Keep mast and boom sail tracks well lubricated. An easy way to deal with the mast track is to lubricate it generously above the topmost slide of the lowered sail. Then hoist the sail, letting the slides carry the lubricant up the rest of the track.

If a boat's mast and boom are of wood, check often for cracks. Minor defects can be repaired with comparative ease. Wood spars also must be given a yearly coat or two of varnish. Aluminum spars need little care beyond a few washings with detergent and a coating of wax each season to inhibit corrosion. But an aluminum spar with even a small crack demands immediate welding or replacement.

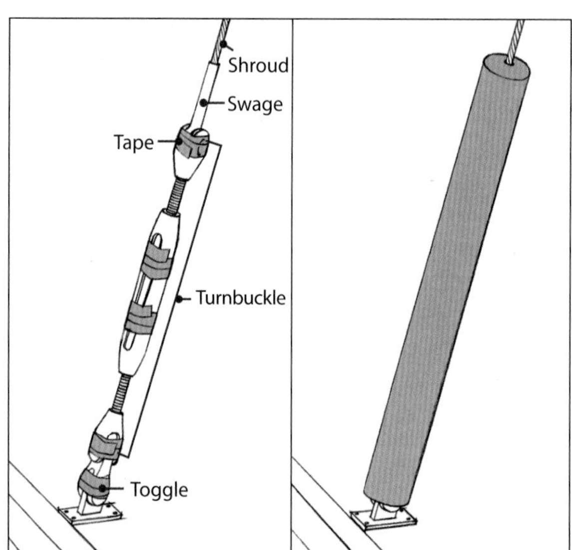

Sails and hands must be protected from the sharp ends of cotter pins that keep turnbuckle and toggle pins from backing out. Many boatmen wrap waterproof tape around these fittings wherever cotter pins are in use. Another method is to slip a plastic tube over a shroud or stay before the rigging is set up, then slide the tube down over the fittings *(above)*. A cap atop the tube keeps water out.

Spars and Rigging

Fishhooks—the nautical term for strands of wire rigging that have broken and curled outward—are a sign of wear, and a menace. They can rip sails and leave painful cuts in bare hands. A fishhook in galvanized wire can be snipped off with cutters and taped over. If a rash of them appears, it means the wire itself is deteriorating. Replace it.

Splitting of the wood at the end of a spar constructed of long, glued pieces like this boom should be given prompt attention; otherwise, the seam will widen. To repair the flaw, remove all adjacent fittings, pry open the seam with a thin-bladed chisel and force marine glue into the opening with a putty knife. Pull out the chisel and hold the seam closed with C-clamps for at least 24 hours.

A Boost up the Mast

A bosun's chair is an essential piece of gear aboard any cruising sailboat. Attached to the main halyard, it provides a reasonably safe and convenient means of going up the mast, either for urgent repairs or for periodic inspection and maintenance chores.

A bosun's chair of modern design, like the one shown at right and opposite, is both safer and handier to work from than the traditional type *(below)*. The newer one consists of a canvas sling with sewn-in wood seat, pockets and loops for spare parts and tools, and a safety belt.

When going aloft, however, the belt alone should not be depended on for safety. The person to go up the mast should be the lightest member of the crew, while the two huskiest crewmen do the actual hoisting—one cranking the winch, the other tailing. While going up, the person on the chair should always keep firm hand contact with some part of the mast or rigging. And an additional safety line should always be carried to secure aloft.

Except in extreme emergency, work aloft should be performed only on a calm day; otherwise, the roll of the boat may bang the crew member painfully against the shrouds, stays, or the mast itself.

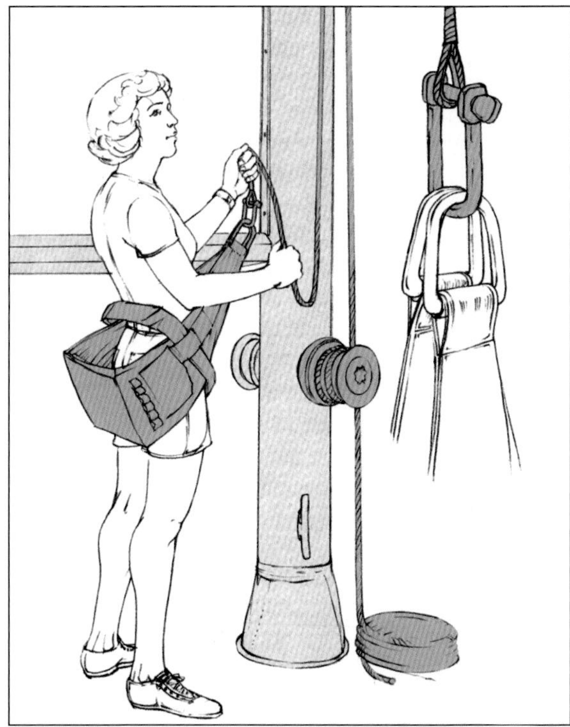

Preparing to go aloft, a crew member checks the shackle connecting the bosun's chair to the halyard to be certain the clevis pin is locked. The chair's safety belt has already been tightened around her waist. Just before starting up, she will fasten about 8 or 10 feet of line to the rings at the top of the chair. Once aloft, she secures this line to nearby rigging to prevent a fall in the event that the halyard parts.

The Traditional Design

The old-fashioned bosun's chair—still in common use—consists of a wood slab with loops of line crisscrossed beneath it. The loops hold a climber if the board should split. The upper segments of the loops, known as the bridle, are lashed together, making an eye for a shackle.

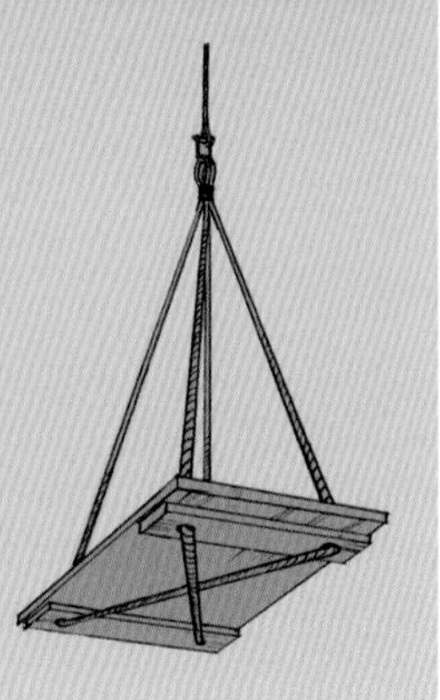

As one crewman cranks the winch and the other keeps a steady strain on the end of the halyard, the climber is slowly hoisted up the mast (1). When she reaches the work area, she ties the life line to the spreader and hooks one leg over it to steady herself (2). On deck, a crewman secures the halyard around its cleat. When the work has been completed, the climber will cast off the safety line and swing back to the mast. On deck, one crewman will then ease off on the halyard slowly, while his partner guides the line to keep its turns aligned on the winch.

Repairs on Sails

Next to the boat itself, sails are often a mariner's most expensive equipment, and they deserve scrupulous care. However, a sail's life is not necessarily shortened if it is punctured or ripped slightly on a sharp point such as an untaped spreader tip or cotter pin, or if it is popped open by a puff of wind at a spot weakened by chafing. Proper repairs can remedy all but very extensive damage.

When a sail rips, immediately lower it, before wind pressure can enlarge the hole. Then, holding the edges of the rip close together and taking care not to pucker the cloth, make a temporary repair. This is most easily done with the commercial rip-stop tapes and adhesive patches available at marine-supply stores. If the rip occurs at a point of great stress, such as the clew, the sail should be repaired with a simple stitch called a sailmaker's darn.

In a well-equipped loft, California sailmaker Grant McCormick mends a ripped jib. Like all skilled hands, he concentrates on keeping each stitch as tight as the last, so that wind pressure will put an even strain on his darn.

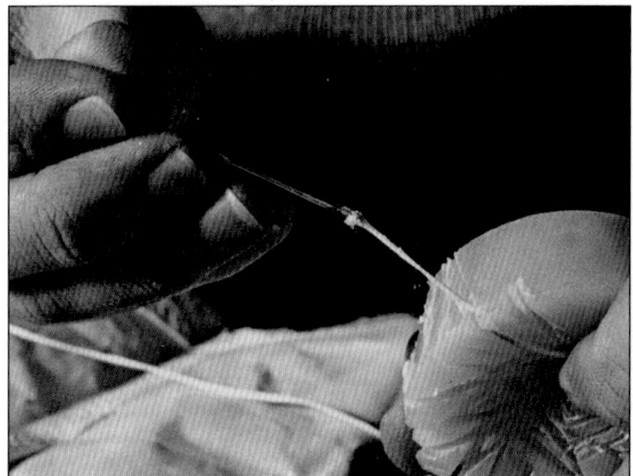

Before starting a mending stitch on a sail, pull the thread through a cake of beeswax; this consolidates the fibers of the thread and makes it stronger and less likely to snag.

Next slip a sailmaker's palm over your darning hand, and seat the needle butt in the palm's metal socket. This permits a strong push to force the needle through the tough sailcloth.

The Simple Sailmaker's Darn

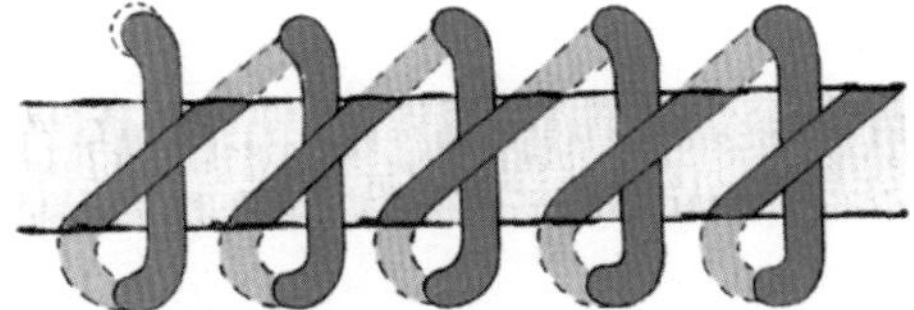

The sailmaker's darn is diagramed here from the point of view of a right-handed stitcher with the sailcloth lying upon his lap. The thread should be knotted at one end and brought up through the cloth, directly across the rip, down through the cloth, then diagonally up and over the first stitch to begin the sequence again. Five or six stitches per inch will provide maximum strength.

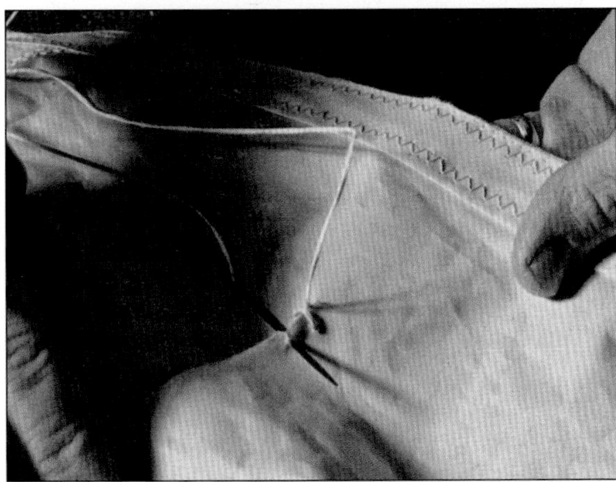

With the cloth in your lap, start at the left end of a rip; push the needle, with its waxed thread, up through the cloth at the far side of the tear about a quartet inch from the edge.

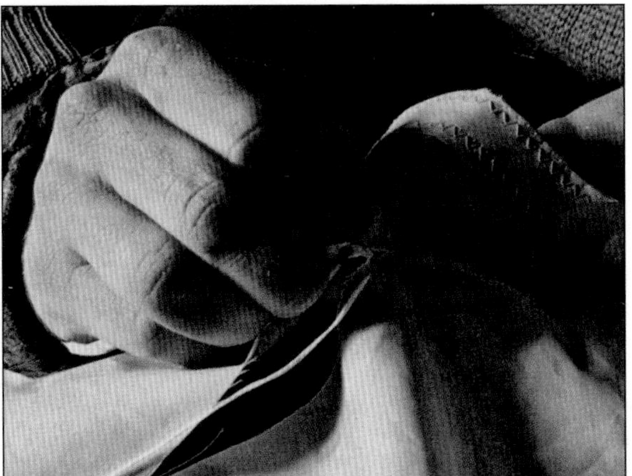

Next, in one motion, press the needle down through the cloth at the near edge, and then up through the tear. This creates a straight stitch that will pull the tear's edges together.

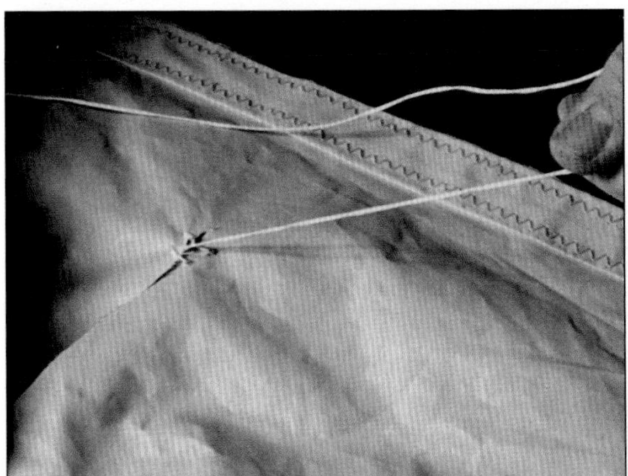

After bringing the needle up between the edges of the tear, tighten the thread. Then cross the thread over the stitch just made, dip down and repeat the stitching cycle.

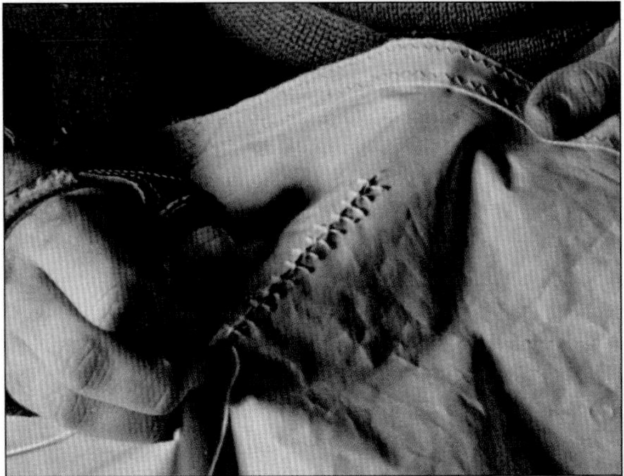

To finish off the mend, make two or three stitches close together. The sail can now be put back into service; however, a patch *(page 142)* would provide a stronger mend.

Sewing a Sturdy Patch

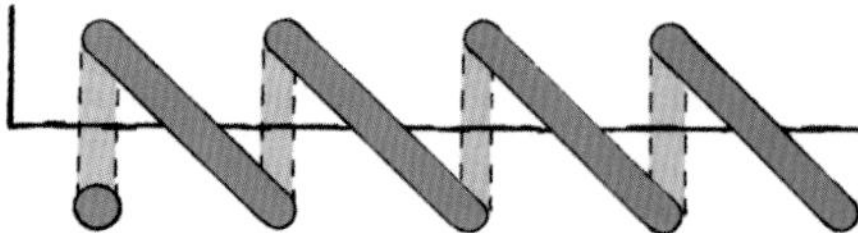

A patch should be affixed to a sail by the overhand stitch diagramed above, as seen from the stitcher's viewpoint. First, knot the end of well-waxed thread. Starting outside the edge of the patch, thrust the needle down through the sail, then up again through both the sail and the patch, leaving a stitch on the underside of the work that is perpendicular to the edge of the patch. Next, take a longer, diagonal stitch on top of the seam. Then repeat the short, straight underside stitch—and so on, all around the patch. As with the sailmaker's darn, five to six stitches per inch are recommended for best results.

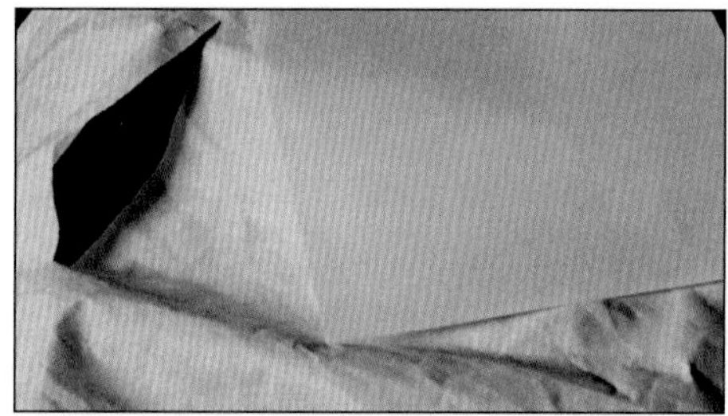

Cloth for patching should match the sail in both fiber and weight. The patch should be rectangular, with at least one and a half inches to spare at each end of the tear. The edges of the patch can be kept from fraying either by turning them under or, in the case of synthetics, by cutting the patch to size with a so-called hot knife—an electric tool that melts the edges. When positioning the patch, align its weave with that of the sail; otherwise the stress on the patch will be uneven, producing creases in the sail and ultimately weakening the fabric.

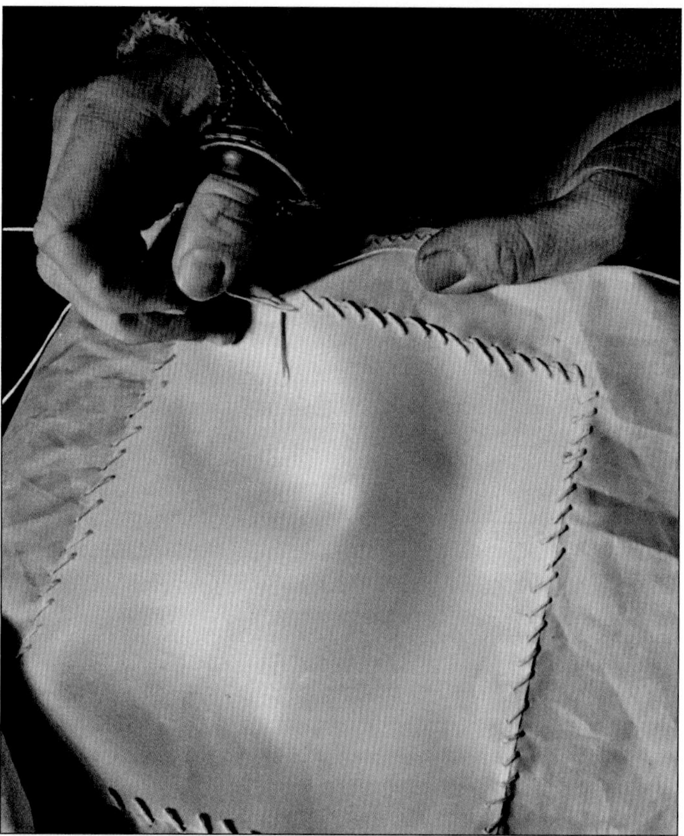

Tack the patch in position over the tear with several pieces of adhesive tape. Then sew down the patch using an overhand stitch all around its edges. Tighten each stitch just as much as the one before so that tension on the sail will be evenly distributed. And be sure to hold the patch as flat as possible against the sail as the work proceeds.

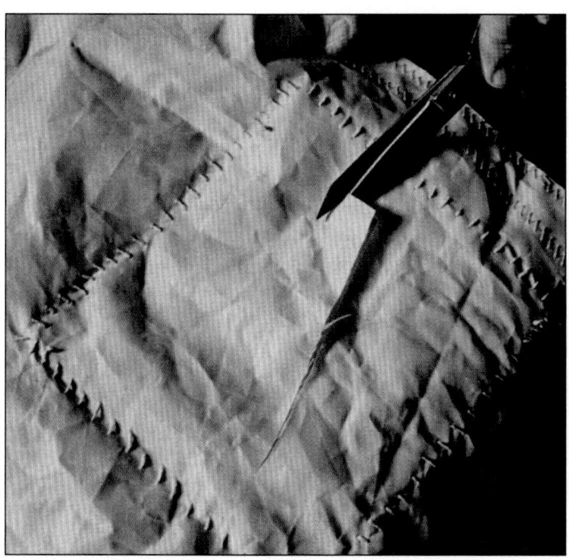

After sewing all around the patch, turn over the sail and cut out a rectangle around the diagonal tear, leaving one and a half inches of fabric inside the seamline for a hem.

At each corner of the rectangle, make a diagonal cut, called a miter, about three quarters of an inch long. This allows the raw edges to be folded under to form hems.

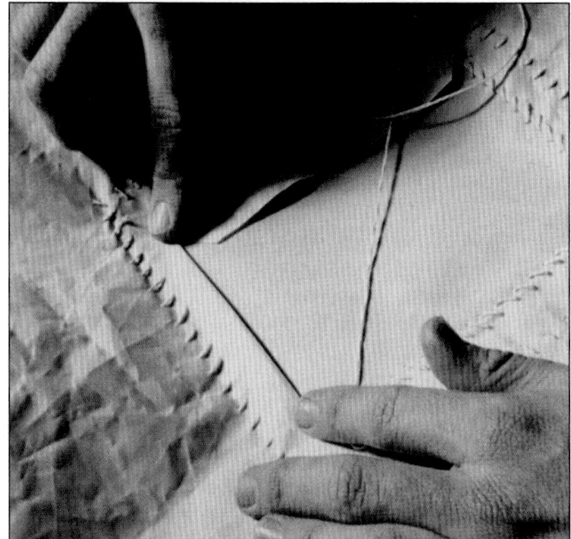

Neatly fold under one edge of the cutout and sew it to the patch along the fold line, using the overhand stitch and continuing to work on the opposite side of the sail.

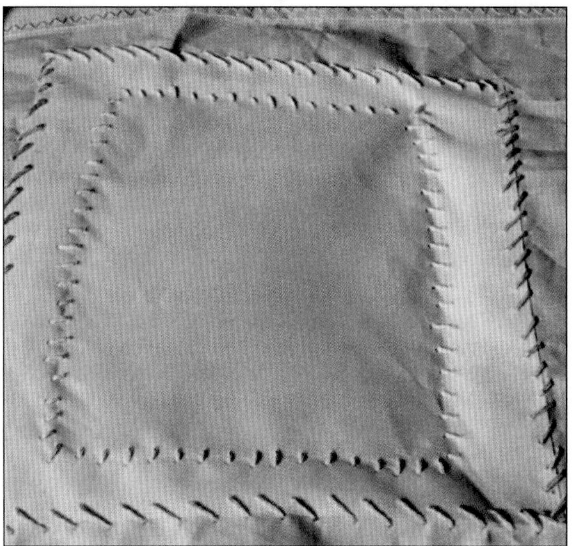

Fold under each successive edge and keep sewing in even stitches all around the patch. To finish the work, anchor the thread by making two or three stitches close together.

Stowing Sails

Proper washing, drying, and storage will help to enhance a sail's appearance and to prolong its life by offsetting the harmful—and unavoidable—effects of its basic operating conditions: stress, sunshine, spray, wind, and sometimes heat.

Any sail that has been exposed to salt spray should be rinsed with fresh water; dried salt left on the cloth will absorb moisture, inviting mildew that can stain even synthetics like nylon and Dacron. Scrub a stained sail with a mild soap, using a sponge or a soft-bristled brush. Then rinse it thoroughly. Traces of soap in the sail could increase the fabric's sensitivity to the ultraviolet rays in sunlight that tend to break down nylon and Dacron fibers.

Avoid hoisting or hanging a sail to dry in strong winds; constant flapping weakens the fibers. Wrinkling has the same effect, so always carefully furl or fold a sail, and store it out of the sun in a bag or beneath a cover on a spar. Bags fend off ultraviolet rays but not heat; a bagged sail left to bake in a car trunk, for instance, will rapidly deteriorate.

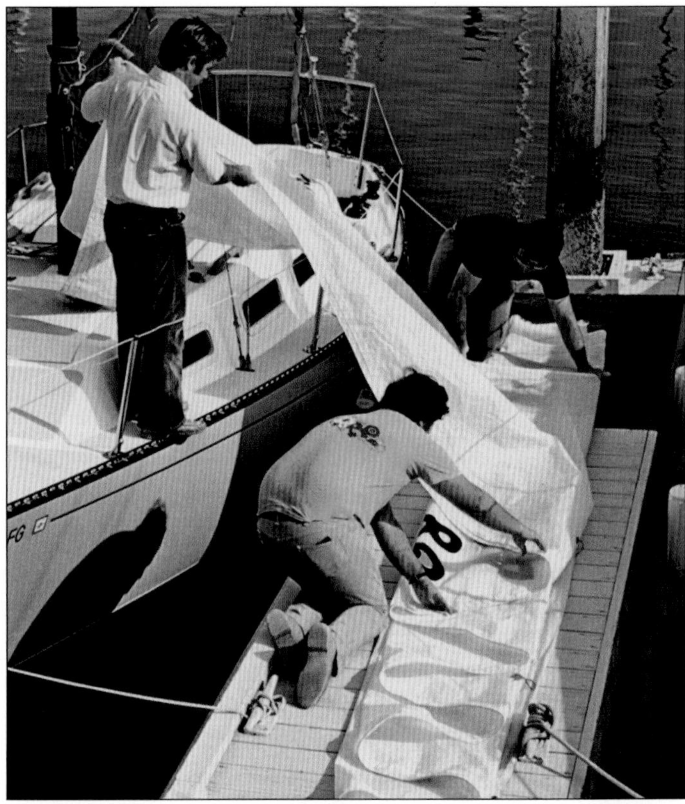

A sail being readied for bagging should be laid out on a flat surface like a dock *(above)* or lawn, and folded in smooth, accordion pleats from the fool up to the head. Roll the folded sail from the tack to the clew—the corner that is farthest aft when the sail is raised—then slide it carefully into the bag.

Though sails are best stored in bags, especially for long intervals, for shorter periods they can be conveniently and safely stored right on their spars. After a sail has been lowered and bound to a spar, it should be swathed in a sturdy cover, Use a cover that is sufficiently roomy to allow good ventilation but still snug enough to shield the sail from dirt, moisture, and sunlight.

One easy way to rinse a sail that has been exposed to salt water is to lay it on a lawn, and as the boatman above is doing, sluice it on both sides with a garden hose. The sail can be either left on the ground to dry or spread over a few cardboard boxes to increase air circulation around it and thus hasten drying. At the end of the season, the sail should be laundered, bagged, and stored in a cool, dry place.

CHAPTER 6: Winterizing

In the northern two thirds of the United States, winter forces most pleasure craft into temporary retirement. And even in warm climates, a vessel must occasionally be taken out of service for cleaning, painting, and repairs. Thus, every boatman should learn how to store his boat for extended periods. The process usually involves four steps: hauling, or taking the boat out of the water; laying up, i.e., removing almost everything removable from the boat and providing protection for the rest; supporting the boat's hull while it is on land; and sheltering it from the elements.

For some boats an obvious place to store it is in the water. Ingenious devices developed since World War II will keep the water ice-free in boat slips of harbors that normally freeze in winter *(page 155)*. Storage afloat is particularly recommended for wood boats, since their planks tend to shrink when out of the water, sometimes causing fastenings to loosen or caulking to fall from the seams.

While wet storage is fast increasing in popularity, most boats are still stored on land. Owners of small, easily transported craft usually keep them at home, but any boat that cannot be trailered will probably reside in a boatyard, either indoors or out. Outdoor storage is cheaper and offers a boatman a pleasanter environment for spring refitting. Moreover, the outdoors is healthier for wood boats, because moisture in the air limits the shrinking of planks. Indoor storage, on the other hand, is kinder to steel hulls, which can rust, and to fiberglass boats as well. The outer gel coat of fiberglass tends to fade in sunlight.

A skipper seeking yard storage for the first time or in a new location will do well to inquire among experienced boatmen about the reputations of yards in the area. He should also determine what kind of fire, theft, and damage coverage his and the yard's insurance policies provide. And because boatyards often have a glut of business in the fall and spring, he should set firm dates for hauling and relaunching his boat. His insurance policy may be a factor in fixing these dates; many policies cover operations afloat only during the regular boating season, and the boat should be on land whenever such coverage is not in effect.

Before making a final commitment to a yard, the boatman should find out which phases of laying up he can or must do himself and which the yard can do better—or will insist on doing. Most yards, for instance, list bottom cleaning among their services, but not all provide indoor storage for spars. Since protection against the weather is vital for wooden spars and desirable for aluminum ones, a boatman may have to find storage for himself. Finally, no matter how or where an owner stores his boat, he should visit it regularly or, if he cannot go himself, should ask a reliable friend to inspect it.

Securely cradled and snugly covered against wind and weather, boats stored in a snow-covered Falmouth, Massachusetts, yard await the arrival of springtime.

Laying Up

The storage of a boat begins with a series of laying-up chores split between the vessel's owner and professional yardmen. The division of labor is less likely to be determined by the difficulty of the tasks than by the owner's budget or by boatyard policy, since an average boatman can manage all but a major job like unstepping a sizable mast *(right).* Most work should be done at dockside, where it is easier to perform than later when the boat has been hauled and set on its cradle.

The first phase of the job consists of removing perishables, items that might tempt thieves, or those that suffer from heat, cold, or damp. Obvious removables include books, dishes, food, clothing, bedding, tools, fenders, life preservers, dinghies, oars, boathooks, lines, sails, and outboard motors. Somewhat less obvious are tanks of cooking gas—a potential fire hazard if the lines to the stove develop a leak—and light bulbs, which should be removed to keep them from corroding permanently into their sockets. Detachable electronic gear and compasses should be stored in a warm, dry place ashore after submitting them to any necessary professional attention.

The second phase of laying up is to protect the boat's permanent fixtures. Wash with fresh water and lubricate all fittings that have moving parts. Oil all hinges, and apply a film of petroleum jelly to any exposed hardware likely to corrode. Find out the yard's policy on fuel tanks: some yards require that tanks be topped off to prevent condensation; others, wary of the fire hazard, want the tanks totally drained. Drain or pump out old, acidic engine oil and replace it with fresh oil. In cold climates, pump antifreeze into the engine's cooling system to avert burst piping. Remove batteries, store them in a warm, dry place, and keep them from going dead with "trickle charges" of steady low-voltage current. Most yards will do the latter; but it can be handled at home by purchasing a small charger that can be attached to the battery and plugged into a wall socket.

After finishing the inevitably dirty work on the engine, clean the deck and the boat's interior thoroughly. To cut down on spring maintenance, paint or varnish badly weathered areas. When the boat has been hauled, scrub or hose any marine growths off the bottom. After it has been cradled, or blocked and shored, drain and clean the bilges, and give the hull's outer surface a protective coating—wax for fiberglass, paint or a mixture of linseed oil and turpentine for wood.

As a first step toward extended dry-land storage of a 40-foot sloop, yardmen prepare to remove the mast with a power hoist. After detaching shrouds and stays, they lift the spar—held by a sling just below the lower spreaders—and swing it to the dock. The rigging will be checked before the mast is stowed on horizontal supports.

Preparing an engine for storage begins with a compression check—a job usually done by a professional. Inserting a pressure gauge in place of each spark plug in turn, he turns over the engine with a remote-control switch. Any cylinder that registers lower pressure than the rest may have a burnt valve or a broken piston ring that must be replaced.

To protect an engine's cooling system for cold-weather storage, a yardman first disconnects the raw-water hose from the engine's seacock. Then he puts the hose's free end in a pail of antifreeze *(above)* and runs the engine until the pink liquid flows from the exhaust—indicating that the water jacket of the engine is filled with antifreeze.

A final step in preparing an engine for storage in any climate is to coat the cylinders with oil to prevent corrosion, which could permanently damage the motor. Here the yardman squirts about four tablespoons of 30-weight oil into each cylinder. He will then crank the engine over by hand several times before he replaces the spark plugs.

In order to winterize the head, first open the intake and the discharge seacocks. Then unfasten the hose from the intake seacock and connect it to a container of antifreeze that is not alcohol-based (the alcohol in engine antifreeze would damage plastic hoses used elsewhere in the plumbing system). Work the head's pump until a gallon of antifreeze has circulated. Finally, reconnect the hose and close the discharge seacock.

The same kind of nonalcoholic antifreeze used for the head should be circulated through the sink plumbing; the antifreeze is noncorrosive and nontoxic, leaving no harmful residue when the plumbing system again supplies water for cooking and drinking. Drain the fresh-water tank, then attach the antifreeze jug to the hose to the sink, and pump the handle of the sink faucet until antifreeze flows from the faucet.

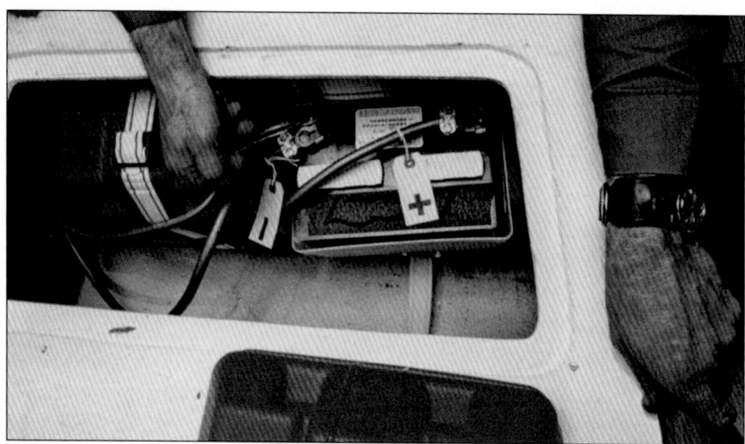

Before removing the engine battery for storage ashore, tag the positive and negative cables to avoid reconnection problems. Coat the cable clamp and the terminals with petroleum jelly to prevent corrosion.

Hauled out on a modern boatyard's powerful traveling lift, a sloop receives an immediate hosing to remove slime and other marine growths from the bottom before they can dry and harden. The lift will then set the boat into its cradle, to be raised aboard a massive wagon by hydraulic jacks and rolled into the shed for storage.

Supports and Covers

A boat stored on land must be kept level and stable, and it must be adequately supported in the right places. These strictures can be met in a variety of ways. Small boats are often stored on their trailers. Many larger boats are stored, year after year, in the wooden or steel shipping cradles in which they arrived when new, or in similar ones built to order by a boatyard. Finally, some owners still use the traditional method of resting the keel on wooden blocks and propping the hull upright with heavy timbers.

If possible, the boat should be blocked or cradled high enough so that the boatman can work comfortably beneath it. The side supports, or poppets, should be placed at bulkheads or at other strong points in the hull. A powerboat will probably need additional support beneath the engine, and sailboats may require even more props for their long overhanging bows and sterns.

Any boat stored outdoors also needs a waterproof cover that is resistant to fire, rot, and mildew. It must protect the boat against the elements while permitting maximum ventilation inside the hull: condensation in a boat can warp or rot wood, rust metal, damage electronic gear, and foster mildew on fabrics. Even covers of so-called breathing fabrics like canvas, through which some air can pass, also need bow and stern vents and should be held above the deck by a framework. Before lacing on the cover, the boatman should open all doors, hatches, ports, lids, and drawers to let air circulate freely.

The trailer of the powerboat above serves as a convenient cradle. The trailer itself should be jacked up and supported on concrete blocks placed beneath the frame and tongue to ease the strain on wheels and springs. The assemblage must rest on firm, level ground; any tilting could distort the trailer frame and possibly damage the hull.

The sailboat and the powerboat shown at left are well supported in their wooden shipping cradles, which conform precisely to the shapes of the hull. Padding—old carpeting or the like—serves to protect the hulls wherever they touch the cradles; such padding should be renewed as it wears out.

A sailboat hull with its keel resting on wooden blocks is held in position by heavy timber shoring. Additional blocks and timbers keep the lower ends of the shores from sinking unevenly into the ground. A plywood strip placed between two of the shores helps to distribute the weight of the boat.

The frame attached to the boat above to support its storage cover is pitched steeply enough on both sides to shed rain or snow easily. The height of its peak also allows the owner to move about the deck during visits for inspection or maintenance. This frame is made of aluminum tubing and scrap lumber, with padding around the joints to keep the cover from ripping. Easy to disassemble, it can be made use of season after season.

Small- and medium-sized powerboats like this inboard can be draped with canvas over the cabin and back across a cockpit ridgepole—a piece of light lumber that is supported every few feet by A-frame joists.

To keep out the weather, lace in a boat's cover snugly and pull it down close to the waterline; allow some slack for shrinkage of canvas when wet.

Antidote for Ice

Often the best place to store a boat during winter is in its natural cradle, the water—provided there is no ice around the hull. Happily, even in cold climates, this proviso can be met by the simple trick of bringing relatively warm water up from the bottom to keep ice from forming on the surface. One way to do this is to suspend beneath the boat a small electric-powered propeller *(right)*, available at large marine-supply outlets. Another method, which is mainly used at boatyards, is to pump air from a dockside compressor through a special perforated hose lying on the bottom; bubbles rising from the hose serve as the lifting force for the warmer water.

The boat's plumbing must be protected with antifreeze or, if the owner plans to use his vessel during the winter, by an onboard electric heater that is operated around the clock.

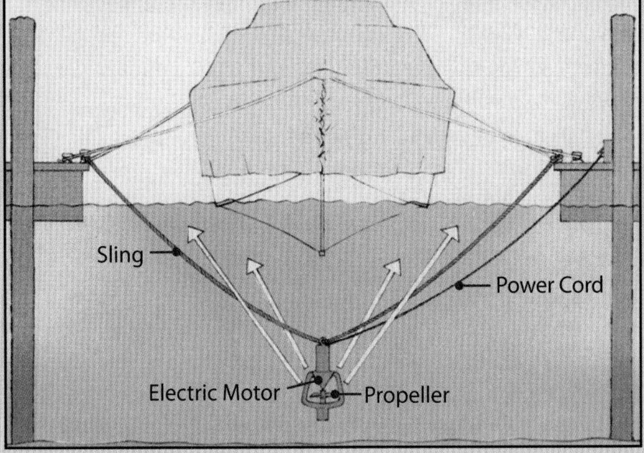

Glossary

Aft Toward the stern.
Amidships In or near the middle of a boat, either along the longitudinal axis or from side to side.
Athwartships Across the boat.
Belay To secure a line, usually to a cleat.
Binnacle Housing of the compass.
Bleeding A process for removing air from the fuel system of a diesel engine.
Block A wood or metal shell, enclosing one or more sheaves, through which lines are led.
Boom A projecting spar used to hold down and extend the foot of a sail.
Boom vang A single line—usually wire—or a block and tackle commonly used to hold down the boom while reaching or running.
Bow The forward part of the boat. (The word prow, cherished by poets, describes a ship's ornamented stem and is otherwise avoided by seamen.)
Bulkhead Any wall in a boat.
Cabin trunk A structure built up above the deck and providing headroom below.
Cam cleat A quick-release cleat having two side-by-side, spring-loaded cams with teeth. A line leading between the cams is held in the teeth but can be released by a quick upward pull on the line.
Centerboard A plate of wood or metal, hinged on a pin and lowered into the water through a watertight housing, or trunk. A centerboard resists the tendency of a sailboat to slide sideways when sailing.
Chafing gear A covering put around a short section of line to reduce wear, or on the rigging to protect the sails.
Chain plate A narrow metal plate attached to the hull as a fastening point for shrouds and stays.
Chock A metal fitting, usually mounted on or in a boat's rail, to guide hawsers or lines for mooring or towing.
Cleat A wood or metal fitting with two projecting horns, Fastened to some part of the boat, to which a line is belayed.
Clevis pin A small cylindrically shaped pin used to close shackles or outhaul fittings, or to fasten a turnbuckle to a chain plate.
Coaming A raised framing around deck openings, such as hatches or cockpits, to keep water out.
Counter The underside of the overhanging part of the stern above the waterline.
Cringle A circular eye, often formed by a metal ring or grommet set in the corners or on the edges of a sail and used for fastening the sail to spars or running rigging.
Cuddy A small enclosed space or cabin in a small boat.
Dorade ventilator A deck box with cowl and internal arrangement that allows air but not water to enter the cabin.
Downhaul A length of wire or line that pulls down the tack of the sail or the foremost end of the boom to tighten the luff.
Fairlead A metal, plastic or wooden eye—usually attached to a deck—that guides a line in a desired direction.
Feeler-gauge A thin metal strip of a specified thickness or a round metal wire of a specified diameter used to check clearances between parts.
Forestay A supporting stay leading from the mast forward, aft of the headstay.
Forward In or toward the bow.
Furl To roll, fold, or wrap close to—or around—something, as in furling a sail or flag.
Genoa A large headsail set on the headstay and overlapping the mainsail.
Gooseneck The fitting, connecting mast and boom, that allows the boom to swing laterally and vertically.
Gudgeon A socket into which a pin called a pintle is fitted to attach the rudder to the boat.
Halyard A line used either to hoist or lower a sail.
Headstay Foremost stay supporting the mast. The jib is set on the headstay.
Heel fitting The lowermost attachment of the rudder to the keel.
Inboard Toward a boat's centerline. Also, a common contraction for a boat with an inboard engine.
Jib A triangular sail set on the headstay.
Mainsheet The line used to pull in and let out the mainsail.
Marlinespike A pointed metal tool used in splicing.
Mast groove A slit running the length of the mast to receive the boltrope along the luff of the sail.
Mast step Socket in which the heel, or bottom, of a mast is stepped.
Masthead cover A cap that fits over the mast to keep rain water out of the tube and holds headstays and backstays.
Outboard Out from the hull, or toward the outside, away from the centerline. Also, a contraction for outboard motor.
Outhaul A fitting on the boom to which the sail's clew is attached, and by means of which the fool of the sail is stretched out along the boom.
Pad eye A plate—secured to the deck—having a circular or U-shaped extension used to hold blocks.
Partner A reinforcing frame, made from planks or fiberglass, rising a little above the deck around a through-deck mast.

Pay To coat with a waterproof compound.
Pedestal A vertical, freestanding column that supports a boat's wheel and houses the steering chains or the upper portion of the cables.
Pintle A pin that fits into a gudgeon to attach the rudder to the boat.
Primer bulb A rubber bulb in an outboard's gas line; when squeezed and released, the bulb sucks gas out of the lank and into the line.
Pulpit A strong railing mounted at the bow or stern of ocean-racing sailboats to prevent crew members from going overboard. Also, a railed platform extending forward from the bow of a sport fisherman, used as a vantage point for sighting, spearing or gaffing fish.
Purchase A tackle, usually permanently rigged, used most often for mainsheets.
Quarter Either side of a boat's stern; to sail with the wind on the quarter.
Quarter block A pulley on either side of a boat's stern.
Reeve To pass the end of a line through a hole or opening, as through a block or a fairlead.
Reach rod A metal rod used for engine control linkages.
Rudderstock The shaft on which the rudder pivots, and the shaft that connects the rudder to the steering system. Also called rudderpost.
Scupper A hole or opening in a rail, hatch or ventilator, to allow water to drain off.
Shackle A U-shaped metal fitting with a cross pin or clevis pin that fits across the opening of the U as a closure. A snap shackle has a spring-loaded closing pin.
Sheave The grooved wheel in a block, or in a masthead filling or elsewhere, over which a rope runs. (Pronounced shiv.)
Sheet A line used to trim a sail.
Shrouds Ropes or wires led from the mast to chain plates at deck level on either side of the mast, which hold the mast from falling or bending sideways.
Snatch block A block hinged on one side and latched on the other so that it can be opened to receive the bight of a line and then closed to hold the line securely.
Spar General term for any wood or metal pole—mast, boom, yard, gaff, or sprit—used to carry and give shape to sails.
Spinnaker A full-bellied, lightweight sail set forward of the mast on a spinnaker pole and carried when a sailboat is reaching or running.
Spinnaker pole A long, light, portable spar used to extend the foot of a spinnaker.
Spokeshave A carpenter's plane with handle grips on either side, generally used in shaping curved surfaces of hull planks.
Spreaders Pairs of horizontal struts attached to each side of the mast and used to hold the shrouds away from the mast, thus giving them a wider purchase.
Stanchion An upright metal pole, bolted to the deck, which supports the life lines that encircle the deck.
Stay A rope or wire running forward or aft from the mast to support it. The headstay is the foremost stay on which the jib is set; a forestay is aft of the headstay and carries a staysail; the backstay offsets the pull of the headstay.
Stem The forwardmost part of the bow.
Stern The rear, or after, part of the boat.
Strake A row of planking or plating running the length of a hull. The sheer strake is the hull's topmost plank; the garboard strake is next to the keel.
Stuffing box A fitting around a moving part, such as the propeller or rudder shaft, that is located where the moving part goes through the hull. A stuffing box contains waxed packing, compressed by a packing gland, to seal the through-hull passage from water.
Swage A cylindrical metal shank that is cold-rolled onto the end of a wire as a terminal.
Tabernacle An abovedecks mast step, sometimes built with a heavy pivotal bolt that allows the mast to be lowered.
Tang A metal fitting on a mast to which the top of a shroud or stay is attached.
Tautener A metal fitting used to take up steering-cable slack.
Thimble A grooved round or teardrop-shaped metal or plastic fitting spliced into an eye of rope or wire to prevent chafe and distortion of the eye.
Toggle A small fitting—shaped like a shackle—at the bottom of a turnbuckle that fastens it to a chain plate.
Topping lift A halyard attached to the spinnaker pole that is raised or lowered to keep the spinnaker properly trimmed; a line from the masthead to the end of the main boom to support the boom.
Topside On deck.
Transom The aftermost part of the stern, usually bearing the boat's name.
Traveler A bar or track secured to a sailboat's deck athwartships so that the sheet of a sail, attached to it by block or similar means, can slide back and forth as the boat tacks or jibes.
Turnbuckle An adjustable fastening for attaching the standing rigging to the chain plates, and for adjusting the tension on the standing rigging.
Turning block A block fixed on deck and used to alter the direction of a line by as much as 180°. A small turning block is often called a cheek block.

Index

c=chart
i=illustration
p=photo
t=table

Discover these other great books from Fox Chapel Publishing

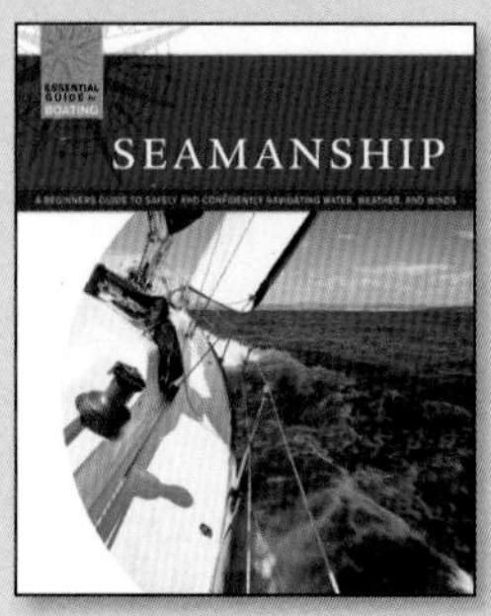

Seamanship

A Beginner's Guide to Safely and Confidently Navigate Water, Weather, and Winds.

By Skills Institute Press

A how-to manual to get you started. Seamanship provides in-depth coverage of boat handling and navigation, reading the weather and water, and dealing with and preventing extreme situations such as capsized boats.

ISBN: 978-1-56523-554-0
$19.95 • 160 Pages

Boating Disasters

How to Avoid, and Survive, the Most Horrendous Disasters on the Water

By Skills Institute Press

ISBN: 978-1-56523-590-8

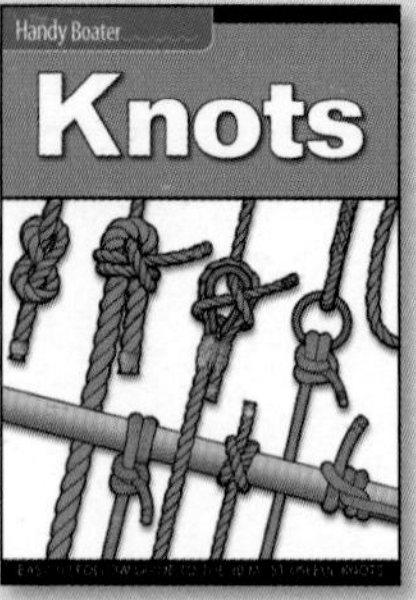

Knots

Easy-to-Follow Guide to the 30 Most Useful Knots

By Skills Institute Press

ISBN: 978-1-56523-589-2

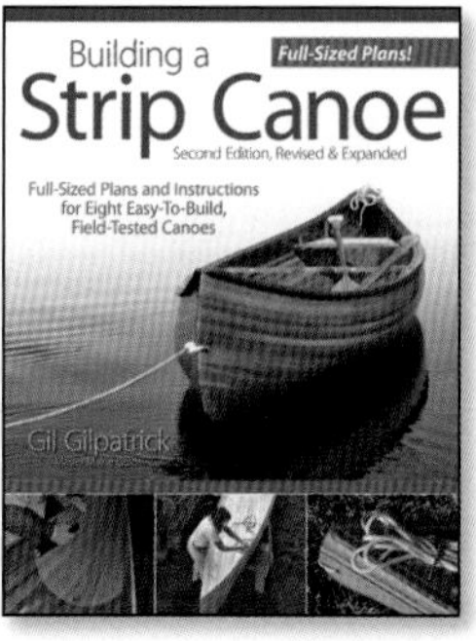

Building a Strip Canoe, 2nd Edition

Full-Sized Plans and Instructions for Eight Easy-To-Build, Field-Tested Canoes

By Gil Gilpatrick

Paddle along with an expert outdoorsman and canoe builder as he shares his experience in guiding both novice and accomplished woodworkers in building a canoe with easy step-by-step instructions.

ISBN: 978-1-56523-483-3
$24.95 • 112 Pages

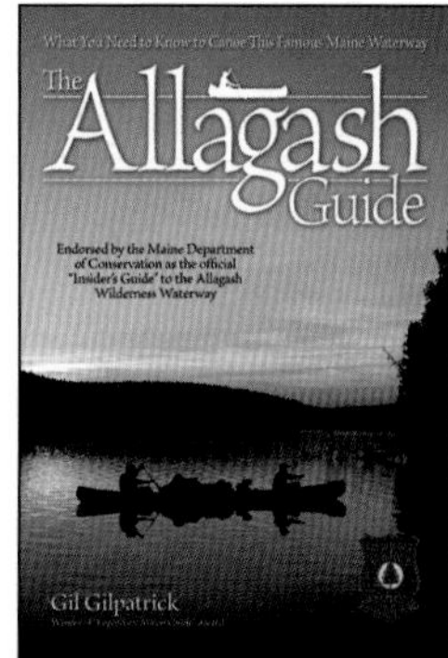

The Allagash Guide

What You Need to Know to Canoe this Famous Maine Waterway

By Gil Gilpatrick

A book so extensively detailed about canoeing the Allagash River in Maine, by expert outdoorsman Gil Gilpatrick, it's like having him along for the trip.

ISBN: 978-1-56523-488-8
$11.95 • 104 Pages

Allagash

A Journey Through Time on Maine's Legendary Wilderness Waterway

By Gil Gilpatrick

Take a journey down the awe-inspiring Allagash River with Gil Gilpatrick as he skillfully weaves historic facts and speculative fiction into fascinating stories about this legendary waterway.

ISBN: 978-1-56523-487-1
$19.95 • 232 pages

Look For These Books at Your Local Bookstore

To order direct, call **800-457-9112** or visit *www.FoxChapelPublishing.com*

By mail, please send check or money order + $4.00 per book for S&H to:

Fox Chapel Publishing, 1970 Broad Street, East Petersburg, PA 17520